FROM CHANAKYA TO MODI

Praise for the Book

'Aparna Pande has written an insightful account of India's world view – both its long-term continuities and its steady evolution – explaining clearly how Indians use metrics that differ from those applied by other cultures and nations when they consider their place in the world. *From Chanakya to Modi* is required reading for anyone who wishes to understand this re-emerging power and its likely impact on Asia and the world.'

– Shivshankar Menon, *former foreign secretary and national security advisor*

'*From Chanakya to Modi* is a magnificently readable survey of Indian foreign policy. Aparna Pande has interrogated the ideational, material and institutional underpinnings of India's efforts to cope with its external environment. In the process she illuminates anew how India has attempted, since its independence, to protect its interests while staying true to its ideals. This book is a wonderful primer that will help a broad readership make sense of the persistent tensions in Indian foreign policy.'

– Ashley J. Tellis, *Tata chair for strategic affairs, Carnegie Endowment for International Peace*

'Aparna Pande's retracing of how India projects itself to the world is both panoramic and granular. India is compelled to view the world not just as a modern nation-state, but also with the pride and burden of 5,000 years of history, she says. This, coupled with a colonial-era bureaucratic structure, prevents India from breaking out of the status quo in the manner that an emerging economy must.'

– Shekhar Gupta, *senior journalist and author*

'Dr Aparna Pande's *From Chanakya to Modi: The Evolution of India's Foreign Policy* is that rare book. It is written by someone outside government, unencumbered by policy fatigue or being too close to the powers that be.'

– Neena Gopal in the *Deccan Chronicle*

'Pande's book is not a simple narrative, but a deep analysis which looks at foreign policy through the prism of India's heritage, as well as the ideas and individuals who shaped it, the principles and interests that they pursued and the institutions and strategic culture they have created.'

– Manoj Joshi in the *Outlook*

'*From Chanakya to Modi: The Evolution of India's Foreign Policy* not only explains the continuity and the constancy of certain concepts but also their growth, evolution and adaptation to an ever-changing world.'

– Seema Sirohi in The Wire

'Pande's book is an excellent primer on how India has engaged with the world and will continue to do so – through realism with imperial hues, tempered by its civilizational responsibilities and grace. As such, it will be widely read by those who want to understand the neural roots of contemporary India's strategic intent.'

– Abhijnan Rej in the *Swarajya* magazine

'Aparna Pande's sleek offer in less than 200 pages, *From Chanakya to Modi: The Evolution of India's Foreign Policy*, is an overview of an Indian view of the world over two millennia, in which the emphasis is on continuity. Not that she is unmindful or dismissive of the changes that are taking place in India's strategic posture under Modi, but her focus is on the underlying principles that guide them all — from Chanakya to Modi, as the ambitious title suggests.'

– Varghese K. George in *The Hindu*

'Aparna Pande's *From Chanakya to Modi* leads one to a deeper understanding of Indian foreign policy with civilizational roots, traversing through two imperial administrations of foreign origin.'

– South Asia Journal

'In a valuable schema, Pande identifies four broad influences, whose interplay has defined India's regional and international trajectory... She believes that India can't realize her potential for greatness with institutions that were designed for the maintenance of the colonial enterprise.'

– C. Raja Mohan in *The Indian Express*

FROM CHANAKYA TO MODI

EVOLUTION OF INDIA'S FOREIGN POLICY

APARNA PANDE

HarperCollins *Publishers* India

First published in hardback in India in 2017 by
HarperCollins *Publishers* India

HarperCollins Publishers India, Cyber City, Building 10-A, Gurugram,
Haryana-122002, India
www.harpercollins.co.in

First published in paperback in India in 2020 by
HarperCollins *Publishers* India

2 4 6 8 10 9 7 5 3 1

P-ISBN: 978-93-5357-907-4
E-ISBN: 978-93-5264-539-8

Typeset in 11/14 Sabon MT
By Saanvi Graphics Noida

Printed and bound at
MicroPrints India, New Delhi

MIX
Paper
FSC FSC® C218906

This product is made of FSC®-certified and other controlled material.

HarperCollins Publishers, Macken House, 39/40 Mayor Street
Upper, Dublin 1, D01 C9W8, Ireland

To my brother and sister-in-law, Chaitanya Pande and Mona Kwatra Pande

Contents

Introduction

IN 2015, A Delhi-based motor accidents tribunal adjudicated that animal-driven, slow-moving vehicles (or bullock carts) often caused serious accidents. Instead of banning these vehicles from the road, the court simply asked for them to be regulated.[1] The story serves as a metaphor for India's tendency to add the new to the old, instead of replacing it. A century after the first motor car appeared on the streets of India, bullock carts, animals (cows, buffaloes and dogs) and humans still share the same streets with motor vehicles. In most countries, horse-driven carriages disappeared within a few years of the arrival of motor cars. As recently as the 1980s, one of India's leading technical schools, the Indian Institute of Management, even had a project to build a better bullock cart that would carry heavier loads but with less wear and tear for the bullocks.[2]

India's desire to combine the traditional with the modern permeates also the realm of its relations with the rest of the world. Addressing the United Nations General Assembly (UNGA) for the first time as prime minister in September 2014, Narendra Damodardas Modi, championed the adoption of an International Yoga Day,[3] a proposal that was adopted by the UNGA on 11 December 2014.[4] During Modi's maiden address before the United States Congress on 8 June 2016, he chose to mention yoga as one of the cultural connections that bind the United States and India. 'Our people to people links are strong and there is close cultural connect between our societies,' he said, adding, 'SIRI [the intelligent personal assistant on iPhones] tells us that India's ancient heritage of Yoga has over 30 million practitioners in the US.'[5]

On 21 June 2016, Modi joined 30,000 fellow citizens in a mass session of yoga in the heart of New Delhi.[6] Interestingly, Modi's supporters cited the global prevalence of yoga and the ease with which the United Nations adopted an international day for yoga as a sign of India's arrival on the world stage as a major global power. Conventional definitions of what it means to be a great power would differ with this view. Increasing number of people practising the ancient regimen of yoga has little to do with the current influence of the Indian state around the world. Similarly, being a champion of anti-colonialism, a leading voice amongst the post-colonial developing countries, having been one of the founders of the Non-Aligned Movement (NAM), or even a prominent voice in multilateral institutions like the United Nations may give India global recognition and pride but it is hardly a substitute for hard power.

Many Indians believe their country has economic power, military strength and an important geostrategic location. To them, that alone should be enough for global power status coupled with India's 5000-year-old civilization. However, in a recent book provocatively titled *Why India Is Not A Great Power? (Yet)*, leading Indian strategist Bharat Karnad asserts that India does not fulfil the requirements of global power status, at least at the present moment. Karnad maintains that to be a great power a country needs 'a driving vision', a sense of 'national destiny', defining of 'national interests', and 'willingness to use coercion and force in support of national interests' along with 'imaginative' use of both hard and soft power.[7] India is several steps short of that position.

That Indians believe that the popularity of yoga is evidence of India's importance in the world explains how India views itself from a very different perspective than other nations. Indian leaders often suggest that the more India participates in multilateral organizations, adopts principled stands on global issues, champions global peace and disarmament and speaks out against military alliances, the higher the pedestal it occupies on the world stage. The reality of the world – and the role India plays in it – is more complex. This book is an effort to examine how India's world view has evolved over the years and what institutions, ideas and attitudes have shaped it.

1

India and the World

AN APOCRYPHAL STORY suggests that on his first day in office, every prime minister of modern India reads a letter on India's foreign policy ostensibly written by the country's first prime minister, Jawaharlal Nehru. The letter starts with the words, 'Dear successor, many generations have passed since this letter was written but this letter is as valid for you today as it was for me and your other predecessors.' It goes on to list India's interests and concerns and outlines the parameters within which an Indian leader can formulate his country's foreign policy. The story about the imaginary letter demonstrates the abiding grip of history and tradition on the way India sees and interacts with the world.

With some variation, India's external relations have shown remarkable continuity and consistency since Independence in 1947, notwithstanding changes in leaders and ruling political parties. India is not alone in such constancy. Most countries base their foreign policy on a template shaped by their national experience and view of self. In India's case, its foreign policy paradigm borrows from its civilizational heritage as much as from modern ideas about national interest. Even when a policy idea appears new, it actually echoes one of several recurrent themes.

In his book *Special Providence* (2001) leading American thinker Walter Russell Mead identified four approaches that have shaped American foreign policy since US independence in 1776. US relations with the world, Mead argues, can be understood in light of defining ideas advanced by significant individuals at various times in US history. Thus, according to Mead, the Hamiltonian school of foreign policy, named after first secretary of the treasury, Alexander Hamilton, 'sees the first task of the American government as promoting the health of American enterprise at home and abroad'. The Wilsonian ideal, enunciated by President Woodrow Wilson, 'believes that the United States has both a moral and a practical duty to spread its values through the world'. The Jeffersonian view, put forward by President Thomas Jefferson, 'has seen the preservation of American democracy in a dangerous world as the most pressing and vital interest of the American people'. The Jacksonian approach, crafted by President Andrew Jackson, 'represents a deeply embedded, widely spread populist and popular culture of honor, independence, courage and military pride among the American people'.[1] Makers of US foreign policy have tended to follow one or a combination of these schools of thought through most of US history though some have tried to embrace the European approach, which Mead terms 'continental realism', based on maintaining a balance of power to protect America's global interests.

A similar analysis of India's global outlook would help identify the context and underlying principles of India's foreign policy. Several scholars have attempted to explain India's world view though, unlike Mead in relation to the United States, they have not offered neat categories of Indian policy approaches. For example, in *India: A Wounded Civilization* (1976) Nobel laureate and Trinidadian of Indian descent, Sir Vidiadhar Surajprasad (V.S.) Naipaul, argues that India's problems are not external or caused because of periodic invasions or conquest. He sees India as plagued with the crisis of what he refers to as a 'wounded old civilization' that while 'aware of its inadequacies' is 'without the intellectual means to move ahead'.[2] Naipaul's broad-stroke analysis, when applied to Indian foreign policy, would suggest a desire for international respect without having the resources to exercise global power and a refusal to accept that reality.

Another perspective is offered by Sunil Khilnani, who, in *The Idea of India* (1997), argues that contemporary India has been shaped by a 'wager' of India's educated urban elite on modern ideas and modern agencies. 'It was a wager on an idea: the idea of India,' Khilnani argues. India's 'nationalist elite itself had no single, clear definition of this idea and one of the remarkable facts about the nationalist movement that brought India to independence was its capacity to entertain diverse, often contending visions of India ... Indian nationalism before independence was plural even at the top, a dhoti with endless folds. ... It contains people from markedly different backgrounds yet whose trajectories were often parallel.'[3] According to this standpoint, nationalism subsumed India's diversity and its advocates hoped to build a modern India inspired by the past but connected to the present and looking towards the future.

In *Emerging Power: India* (2001) Stephen Cohen classifies Indian strategic thought as divided between those he styles Nehruvian (which includes the Gandhian view), militant Nehruvian and finally Realists and Revivalists.[4] Similarly, in his book *India's Foreign Policy: Retrospect and Prospect* (2010) political scientist Sumit Ganguly argues that personal, national and systemic factors framed Nehru's views and were responsible every time any of Nehru's successors changed or adapted his policies.[5] This view casts Nehru and his ideas as the major point of reference in modern India's world view.

Indians take pride in the fact that India is a 5000-year-old civilization even if its modern incarnation as a democratic state is only seventy years old. Modern India's founding fathers, Nehru being the most significant among them, sought to craft policies that would incorporate both India's historical legacy as well as its future geopolitical ambitions. The Indian desire to pursue modernity as well as exercise influence in the contemporary world is inextricably linked with a world view shaped by India's rich history and a decision-making process heavily influenced by tradition. India's interaction with other nations is dominated by an Indian world view that pays special attention to India's civilizational heritage as well as its colonial past. The Indian sense of self and of the world, as well as the architecture of Indian institutions, has been profoundly affected by the experiences of the colonial and post-Independence era.

At the core of India's foreign policy lies a desire for autonomy in decision making resulting from the impact of British colonial rule when that autonomy did not exist. While every nation prefers freedom in foreign policy decisions and actions, India emphasizes sovereignty in every policy it makes and every action it takes. This explains the country's unwillingness to sign up as a formal ally of the world's major powers. A strong moral overtone is also visible in India's foreign policy, which can be linked both to its history as well as the extremely moralistic national struggle under India's founding father, Mohandas Karamchand ('Mahatma') Gandhi (1869–1948). There is a strong belief not only that India is destined for great power status but also that India is an example for the world, especially the developing countries.

The vast legacy of India's founding fathers is the direct result of its long independence movement. India's first prime minister, Jawaharlal Nehru (1889–1964), played a crucial role in the independence struggle and served as foreign minister in addition to being prime minister for seventeen years. He laid down the principles of Indian foreign and security policy in his writings, speeches and policy decisions. For thirty-five years or so after his death, Nehru's successors preferred to continue with the Nehruvian framework, making only cosmetic changes whenever required.

In the realm of institutions, the legacy of the British Raj seems paramount. India is a strong federation with a Westminster style parliamentary form of government where the permanent bureaucracy plays a dominant role in both the making and execution of policies. The role of individuals, especially the prime minister, is reflected in decision making even where bureaucratic structures, such as cabinet committees, are ostensibly in charge.

The British institutions of governance were modelled on the feudal system of satraps that existed under India's earlier empires, especially the Mughals (1556–1857). In that system, the emperor was the *mai-baap* (literally, mother-father but figuratively 'the font of authority') or ultimate protector and benefactor. As the king sat in the capital, he was remote from the average person. The local landlord or priest, often supported by a mansabdar (imperial bureaucrat under the Mughals) enjoying the king's patronage, represented authority in India's small towns and villages. The British, starting with the East India Company, took this culture of government through patrons/benefactors down to the grass roots. Under the British, the district magistrate was both judge and collector of taxes.

Independent India inherited the British arrangement, under which every aspect of life – from schooling to health care, from law and order to infrastructure development and business – required patronage, approval or permission from a government official. India's founding fathers, including Nehru, had a paternalistic outlook and were also suspicious of market forces. While the British used their expansive bureaucracy solely for colonial advantage, Nehru and his successors concentrated powers in the hands of the bureaucracy and the state because of the belief that they knew best how to protect India's unwashed and unlettered millions.

In the field of foreign relations, this paternalism resulted in diplomacy conducted mostly outside the realm of public discussion with foreign visits put on display to show the respect and prestige of India. India's foreign service thus became an elite within the elite of the country's permanent bureaucracy.

In addition to the personalities and institutions, external relations of any country are also defined by its sense of self and its view of its place in the world. The overarching idea that shaped Indian foreign policy right after Independence was the notion of India's geostrategic as well as civilizational primacy. India occupies the largest area of the South Asian subcontinent. Surrounded by the Himalayan mountain ranges to the north and the Indian Ocean to the south, Indians believe geography has dictated that the subcontinent is one entity.

For every Indian government security has meant ensuring that the subcontinent remains stable and peaceful. India's outlook on its immediate neighbours is heavily influenced by the Indian view that these countries are an integral part of Indian civilization. While the concept of a geographic 'sphere of influence' for a major power is widely understood, Indian philosophers and empires have, over time, also delineated a 'civilizational sphere of influence'[6] for India.

Located at the intersection of the trade routes between South Asia, Central Asia and the Middle East, ancient Indian kingdoms and empires maintained cultural and economic relations with Mesopotamia, Greece, China and Rome. With the exception of the Chola dynasty (300 BC–AD 1300), which built an overseas empire, Indian armies did not seek conquest of lands outside the subcontinent. Ancient Hindu treatises on statecraft and religion recommended isolation from other civilizations. Kings could conquer territory from neighbouring kings within India but annexing other cultures or peoples was deemed unethical.

Ancient Indian philosophers and strategists fall both in the realist as well as the idealist camps. The foremost strategist and writer on Indian realism was Kautilya, also known as India's Machiavelli. His masterpiece the *Arthashastra* (literally 'Science of Political Economy') was actually a treatise on statecraft and management of kingdoms. For some analysts, the *Arthashastra* has framed modern India's foreign policy though others count it as only one of several influences. Idealist literature from ancient times reflects the moralist influence of Buddhism and Jainism. It is reflected most prominently, in the modern era, in the views of Mahatma Gandhi, the most well known face of the Indian national struggle and the father of the modern Indian nation.

Although ancient Indian strategists and Indian empires were aware of the world around them, it was under the British Raj that India found itself connected strategically to a neighbourhood beyond the subcontinent, spreading from the Gulf to South-East Asia. India's policy towards its geographic neighbours today is heavily influenced by the Raj's view that the interests of the Raj dictated the interests of the nearby states, not vice versa. This is the root of India's oft-expressed desire to keep outside powers from gaining influence in South Asia, often referred to by some as the Indian Monroe doctrine. The treaties that India signed with her immediate neighbours after Independence also bore the British legacy. India's 1949 treaty with Bhutan was identical in almost all respects to the one Bhutan signed with the British in 1910. In 1950, when India and Afghanistan signed a treaty, the tribes on both sides of the Durand Line asked if India 'would continue British Raj policy of subsidy and arms' but India declined the offer.[7]

Belief in the greatness of Indian civilization lies at the core of contemporary Indian nationalism. As early as 1922 an Indian editor argued in an article published by the *New York Times*: 'India, with a population comprising one-fifth of the human race, cannot eternally remain the "adjunct" of a little island [Britain] 7000 miles away from her shores'.[8]

Under Gandhi's leadership, the Indian national movement embraced moral ideals, which in turn have led to the emergence of a sense of Indian exceptionalism – that India is unique, special and an example for the rest of the world. The very first resolution passed by the Constituent Assembly of India on 13 December 1946 stated: 'This ancient land attains its rightful and honoured place in the world and makes its full and willing contribution to the promotion of world peace and the welfare of mankind.'[9] An anonymous article in the July 1949 issue of *Foreign Affairs* described India as 'an infant state' that was 'no newcomer to history, no offshoot or colony newly risen to nationhood'.[10]

In the decades immediately after Independence, this desire to be seen as a global leader, albeit a moral one, often amplified the preaching overtones of Indian foreign policy. India's championing of anti-colonialism and anti-racism and its campaign against apartheid in South Africa were part of this policy. So was India's demand for reforms not only in the United Nations Security Council but also in the international economic order, including the International Monetary Fund and the World Bank. India saw the world's major powers, especially the industrialized capitalist nations, as unwilling to cater to the interests of previously colonized poorer countries. India's leading role in the creation of the Non-Aligned Movement (NAM), the Group of 77 (G-77) and BRICS (Brazil, Russia, India, China, South Africa) represents its effort to create international institutions that are not run by western European powers or the United States of America.

Lacking resources to participate in the cold war and fearing that participation would tear the fragile nation apart, India's leaders sought to stay away from military alliances and adopted what they insisted was a non-aligned path. Non-alignment was different from neutrality as it did not imply a refusal to take positions in global conflicts. It was simply a refusal to join any bloc, giving India the option of seeking assistance from both the US and the Soviet Union while being able to speak against either on specific issues. India saw non-alignment as a way of keeping the cold war out of South Asia and of protecting itself against the perils of being drawn into clashes it sought to avoid. This would ensure a peaceful and stable environment for building the country, especially its economic and military capabilities.

Championing non-alignment helped India build ties with countries in Asia and Africa emerging from colonial rule, before whom India projected herself as a potential model and leader of former fellow colonies. Lacking in economic and military capability, India adopted the high moral ground in the hope of playing a greater role in world affairs and to punch above its weight.

India benefited from non-alignment but things did not always pan out as expected. While India remained non-aligned, Pakistan joined the Western camp. The cold war was never far from India's borders: communist China (initially aligned with the Soviet Union) shared India's frontier; Iran and Pakistan joined the US-led Central Treaty Organization (CENTO) and provided listening posts to the Central Intelligence Agency (CIA); the Soviets looked upon

Afghanistan as a crucial neighbour even before sending in their forces there in 1979. American and Soviet navies both operated in the Indian Ocean, occasionally seeking the right to visit Indian ports.

While India was able to obtain some military and economic aid from both cold war blocs, it was never able to achieve the absolute autonomy in decision making it sought. It had to turn to the US after the war with China in 1962 and to the Soviet Union during the Bangladesh crisis of 1971. Domestic, regional and international circumstances circumscribed India's options, a lesson in the limits of a poor, developing country being able to act as a global leader based on the size of its population or historical and moral claims.

During two centuries of British rule, Indians had no control over economic, foreign or military policies. Even during the two world wars, when thousands of Indian soldiers fought as part of the British army around the world, Indians served as cannon fodder rather than as decision makers. That experience has led to an Indian reluctance to send its troops abroad under multinational command. United Nations peacekeeping missions have been an exception to this rule. Peacekeeping under the aegis of the United Nations has a moral dimension and fulfils India's desire to play a global role in addition to demonstrating India's credentials in helping less fortunate countries. India refused to send troops for the wars in Korea (1950–53) or Vietnam (1955–75) or for the Gulf War in 1991.

Many people were surprised when during the US-led war in Iraq in 2003, the Indian parliament and cabinet actually debated an American request for the participation of Indian troops. India did not join the war in the end but that India debated such an issue was for many a first and showed the changes in how Indians, and others, view India's global role.[11]

India's reluctance to send troops outside its borders does not, however, extend to its immediate neighbourhood. India sent troops to Sri Lanka in 1987–90 to enforce a ceasefire between the government and Tamil rebel guerillas, and to Maldives in 1988 against a coup attempt. India has also fought four wars with Pakistan, including the 1971 war that resulted in the creation of Bangladesh. In the Indian view, the immediate neighbourhood is still part of the subcontinent and so is India's arena for maintaining security.

In the economic realm, India has desired self-sufficiency and autarky since Independence. Some of India's founding leaders hoped to create self-sufficient villages as envisaged in Gandhi's slogan of 'Ram Rajya' (literally 'Ram's Rule', meaning an ideal state). On the other hand, Nehru, a Fabian socialist, believed that the commanding heights of the economy should remain in the hands of the state. Most leaders of the Indian National Congress, which led India to independence and ruled at the Centre uninterrupted until 1977, shared a mistrust of the intentions and desires of the corporate sector.

India emerged with a mixed economy, with dominant public sector enterprises eclipsing the private sector until economic reforms in 1991. Economic reforms during the 1990s boosted India's private sector but even now public sector enterprises remain significant. India's pursuit of autarky has sometimes conflicted with its desire for efficiency in military capability. India maintains a vast array of state and public sector enterprises in defence manufacturing but is also one of the world's top importers of defence equipment.

If Gandhi is the father of modern Indian identity, Jawaharlal Nehru is indisputably the man who shaped India's foreign policy after Independence. The ideals and ambitions of India's first prime minister and foreign minister are referred to as 'Nehruvianism' and have left an indelible mark on India's world view, shaped under Nehru's stewardship from 1947 to 1964.

Nehru's personality was the product of paradoxes. He was an aristocrat by birth but his political views were those of a thorough democrat. He was born an Indian but was an internationalist in outlook. He opened eyes in a Hindu home but grew up to be a diehard secularist bordering on atheism.

Nehru's views were framed both by his British education as well as by the nationalist struggle. Unlike his contemporaries he had travelled the world and so viewed the world and India's role in it from an international lens. As a lover of history he could see that while India was weak today, one day it would be a powerful country. As an internationalist and an idealist, he championed multilateralism and strong international institutions. As a realist, while he sought peace he understood the importance of economic and military power.

Nehru was profoundly influenced by his mentor, Gandhi, and like him sought to change India and the world. After Gandhi's assassination within a year of Independence, Nehru saw himself as the father of his people and attempted to lay down the structure for modern India. He was fondly referred to as Chacha (Uncle) Nehru, a description he liked and tried to live up to by attempting to do many things and being many people at the same time. He wanted India to be economically self-sufficient, to raise its people from poverty and to emerge as a developed nation.

Nehru recognized India's diversity both as an opportunity and a threat. He feared fissiparous tendencies, primarily religious, and sought to keep India territorially unified and independent. He was a secularist who believed India would survive only if it embraced secularism and pluralism. Nehru believed wholeheartedly that a diverse and complex nation like India could best be kept together through voluntary union of ethnicities, religions, and racial and linguistic groups. For him, democracy was the way forward for India, and Nehru saw his role as that of educating both India's elite and masses on the merits of democracy.

Nehru also did not want India to become absorbed with itself to the point of becoming isolated from the world. Among his concerns was the prospect of a third world war resulting from contending military alliances, armed with nuclear weapons. He hoped to prevent a future war by preaching to the world's powers to move away from warmongering. Granville Austin has called Nehru 'an impatient democrat' and 'national nanny' and while both titles suit

Nehru, the title 'international nanny' would be equally apt.[12] Nehru saw himself as a guide, a mentor not only to his own people but also to the rest of the world.

Nehru saw himself as a guide for India's new leadership and bureaucracy, many of whom had less global exposure than him. During the seventeen years that he was prime minister, he wrote letters every fortnight to the chief ministers of each of India's states. In each letter, he described in detail not only his key domestic policy decisions but also explained the context of those decisions. The letters also provided details about every foreign visit by the prime minister, visits by foreign dignitaries to India and included details of what was discussed.

Through these letters, Nehru hoped to educate his chief ministers about domestic as well as world affairs. Thus, his letters explained developments like the merger between Egypt and Syria resulting in the creation of the United Arab Republic or Indonesia's domestic troubles of March 1958.[13] 'We in India cannot cut ourselves off from this world situation and have to play our part in it whenever occasion demands it,'[14] he wrote in another. In his view, India had 'built up some kind of a reputation the world over and we are respected even by those who do not agree with us'.[15]

For him, the fortnightly letters were part of his effort to build the new state, offering and seeking advice with the second tier of Indian leaders. The tradition began and ended with Nehru as his successors had neither the interest nor the patience to act as teachers for other politicians. His interest in the minutest of details is reflected in one of the letters he wrote to his chief ministers in which he talks about the need to change the height of the broom used to sweep floors to improve both its efficiency as well as to ensure that the person using it did not face any health problems.[16]

Critics read into Nehru's letters, speeches and writings a reflection of his personal loneliness and his desire to find company and solace in the people of India who were under his care.[17] But Nehru sought to lead India into the world beyond the subcontinent through his books, letters and speeches. He was perhaps more concerned about India's historical tendency to insulate itself from the world beyond than to ease personal loneliness by connecting to Indians at the grass roots. His letters and speeches reflect his anguish at international conflict, his fervent desire that others see the world and India as he did and to promote changes he knew would help the world. They voice his helplessness when things did not turn out as he had hoped they would, alongside his irritation and frustration, as well as his dream for the future.

Nehru is the only Indian prime minister to date who discussed foreign policy issues in speeches across the country. He explained, sometimes to an audience of illiterate peasants, why India had signed a treaty or refused to sign one or why non-alignment was the best course for India. India's literacy rate at the time was abysmally low, standing at around 12 per cent in 1947.[18] When asked why he discussed foreign policy in remote villages, Nehru responded by arguing that the masses would understand complex decisions only if they were explained to them.

Nehru sought to lead by personal example, sometimes even at the cost of concentrating too much work in his office. As prime minister he often replied personally to diplomatic cables from various Indian missions rather than wait for his officials to do so. During his seventeen years in power, Nehru made it a point to attend every session of parliament held while he was in Delhi, to emphasize the importance of parliamentary responsibility. He answered almost every question directed at the government, whether related to foreign policy or economics. As one of Nehru's foreign secretaries noted, 'The heaviest burden during the Parliament session was his practice of briefing himself in the minutest detail on every question that was to be answered, not only the questions relating to the Ministry of External Affairs but on all the questions of all the ministries in the government.'[19] This centralization was not always appreciated by cabinet ministers or civil servants, who saw it as a recipe for slowing down the wheels of government.

Nonetheless, Nehru's policies helped India achieve a certain stature on the global stage. Nehru's successors retained the policies and institutions he crafted, making only cosmetic changes to the Nehruvian framework. Nehru forged broad consensus on various aspects of India's foreign policy, and succeeding governments seemed reluctant to carve new paths in external engagement. The first major change in Indian foreign policy, away from Nehruvianism, occurred only after the end of the cold war and the collapse of the Soviet Union.

From the 1990s onward, India started building closer ties with Western powers, especially the United States. Economics has now become a major factor in Indian foreign policy though India's 'Look East' policy also invokes historical and cultural ties with East and South-East Asia. Still, Indians do not want to appear to have abandoned non-alignment, which remains part of India's foreign policy rhetoric.

It is almost as if new beliefs are being explained as an extension of the old religion. For example, in 2012, a group of leading Indian analysts published a policy brief titled 'Non-Alignment 2.0: A Foreign and Strategic Policy for India in the 20th Century', outlining the need for India to maintain its strategic autonomy, remain an example to the world and build its economy. The report insisted on describing India's new post-cold-war paradigm as a continuum of non-alignment during the cold war. No wonder then that India's emerging commonality of strategic interests with the United States coincides with its leaders still religiously attending annual sessions of the virtually defunct Non-Aligned Movement.

If major strands in India's contemporary foreign policy are to be classified along the lines of Walter Russell Mead's classification of schools in US foreign policy thinking, at least four trends can be readily identified: Imperial, Messianic Idealism, Realism and Isolationism.

The 'Imperial' school of thought draws primarily from the most recent pre-Independence experience of decision making known to

India, the period of the British Raj. For this outlook, India is the centre and Delhi knows best. India's post-Independence policy towards its immediate South Asian neighbours exemplifies this policy best. Delhi, whether under the British or after, has always believed that India's Central government is best suited to make security decisions. Just like British officers during the Raj, the advocates of an imperial foreign policy for independent India insist that its South Asian neighbours should agree and accept that India's security needs are theirs as well. Even the idealist Nehru reflected a Curzonian mindset[20] when it came to the subcontinent and India's adjacent states. His daughter, Indira Gandhi, proclaimed what came to be called the Indira doctrine, similar to the American Monroe doctrine, reserving primacy for India in making security decisions for its neighbourhood.

'Messianic Idealism,' reflecting the mantra of global peace, justice and prosperity has served as the strong moral component of India's foreign policy, inspired by the moral legacy of ancient Indian thought reiterated during the national struggle under Mahatma Gandhi. Proponents of this perspective believe that India is an example for the world and that India has the duty to proclaim that example for other nations. This element of Indian exceptionalism often forms part of India's view of itself and of the world. Every Indian leader, whether Gandhi or Vivekananda, whether Nehru or Modi, has demanded that the rest of the world accord India stature commensurate with its civilizational contribution.

It is a function of India's messianic idealism that Indians, whether the lay public or their leaders, have always believed in India's heritage as a great civilization and have anticipated the future as a great power. It is almost as if all India has to do is to wait for the world to accept its greatness. India has often claimed the moral high ground in international relations and believed that it has the right to preach to other nations about what policies to adopt. During the cold war, India used multilateral venues, like the annual United Nations gatherings and the NAM and G-77 groupings for philosophical elocutions on right and wrong that others saw as sermonizing.

At the same time, Indians have had no qualms in anchoring external relations in 'Realism'. From ancient times, realist and idealist philosophies have coexisted in India and the post-Independence era is no exception. Indians reflect a cultural ability to entertain seemingly contradictory thoughts parallel to each other. Belief in moral principles did not turn Indian leaders into pacifists. Notwithstanding messianic idealism, New Delhi has always recognized the importance of hard power. Indian foreign policy has woven into its thread the ideas of ancient Indian thinker Kautilya (also known as Chanakya), who is sometimes referred to as India's Machiavelli. Kautilya argued that a state should be willing to use any of the following four means to achieve its goals: *Saam, Daan, Dand* and *Bhed* (persuade, gift, punish and divide).

For all its messianic idealism the Indian state has a Hobbesian view of the world where India can depend only on itself. This explains the strong desire for strategic autonomy, the push for economic autarky and the pursuit of military self-sufficiency. Indian leaders from Nehru onwards have recognized the importance of all elements of national power, including military power. The emphasis on economic growth in recent years is also tied to the realization that India's great power ambitions would not be realized without having the means to pay for a strong military, among other things.

While desirous of playing a global role, India has also been reluctant to be drawn into global issues or ideologies. There is a strong streak of 'Isolationism' in India's global outlook. It is one of India's many paradoxes that it wants to be seen as a great power and is still often reluctant to do what is required of most great powers. Ironically, the British were the first power/empire in India that had an outward world view. Until the advent of the Raj, with the exception of the ancient south Indian Chola dynasty, no other Indian empire had sought to extend itself beyond the Indian subcontinent. Indian philosophers too asserted that would-be emperors or sovereigns must build an empire within the subcontinent and not outside. Thus, to many Indians, external entanglements hark back to the imperial outlook of the Raj instead of representing a genuinely swadeshi (home-made) world view.

Modern India has consistently been reluctant to involve itself in international conflicts and blocs though Nehru's non-alignment ideology was a way of being involved in the world without external commitments that would bind India to specific choices. India was trying to get the best of both worlds. Even now, India wants to be a permanent member of the UN Security Council without building the power potential possessed by other permanent members. For Indians influenced by isolationism, keeping India territorially intact, building a strong economy, eradicating poverty and creating a just society have often been more important than playing an active role in global conflicts or choosing between ideologies and blocs. While India wants to be considered a global power, not just a regional one, there are limits to which India will exercise its hard power.

India remains reluctant to send its troops abroad except for UN-mandated peacekeeping missions. The only wars India has fought have been within the subcontinent demonstrating that for India the subcontinent is still an extension of its civilizational homeland while the rest of the world remains too distant. This was true under Nehru and is true under Modi today, notwithstanding Modi's apparent desire to align India more closely with the United States and to create a grouping of Pacific powers aimed at containing China.

Of all India's prime ministers, Nehru best incorporated different strands of thought in defining India's global outlook. For that reason, Indian foreign policy has sometimes been referred to as *Nehruvian* – a combination of Messianic Idealism with some parts of Imperial, Realist, and Isolationist elements.

2

A Rich Heritage

INDIA IS AN ancient land unified by geography and tradition. Most Indian languages use the same word for yesterday and tomorrow, reflecting belief in life as an eternal cycle. Sceptics see this as the reason for contemporary India's failure in keeping pace with the times. 'No people whose word for "yesterday" is the same as their word for "tomorrow" can be said to have a firm grip on the time,' author Salman Rushdie observed acerbically in his novel, *Midnight's Children*.[1] Others argue that India's rich heritage keeps it going even if it is not up to par with the world's currently developed nations. As politician and author Shashi Tharoor put it, 'India is not, as people keep calling it, an underdeveloped country, but rather, in the context of its history and cultural heritage, a highly developed one in an advanced state of decay.'[2]

Five thousand years of continuous civilization nurtured in the vast space between the Himalayas to the north, the Indian Ocean in the south and the Hindu Kush and Arakan mountains in the west and east has bred a sense of Indian exceptionalism. Others might judge the modern Indian state by its economic indicators, its low ranking on the human development index, or its apparent political and social chaos. For Indians, however, the Indian subcontinent represents one civilization and one indivisible historic entity, whose past achievements are a source of immense pride and even cause for a sense of superiority. Inspired by the concept of the eternal cycle of life, Indians remain confident that their tomorrow will be as good as their yesterday, if not better, and the Indian republic reflects the glory of past dynasties and empires. India's interaction with the rest of the world has almost always been informed by this civilizational sense of India's self.

Indians take pride in the ability of their culture to subsume others' lifestyles, including those of invaders and conquerors. There is a timelessness to what constitutes being Indian. Outsiders come to India and end up staying, adopting Indian culture while Indian culture adapts to external influences. The history of the empires in India, some indigenous and others initiated by foreigners, is telling. Even when the ruling dynasty comprised non-Indians, the empire in India retained a uniquely Indian quality. Thus, the Mughals may have been Turkic but their empire was very much Indian and British rule in India did not escape an Indian stamp. This simple historic fact has led to a firm belief in the absorptive capacity of Indian culture and civilization. In Indian thinking, India is too big to be taken over by others; instead, others end up being Indianized.

Among India's occupiers, the British were perhaps the least willing to go completely native. They maintained a separateness that the Aryans, Scytho-Parthians, Greeks, Mongols, Turks and Afghans did not. Even then, instead of diminishing India's sense of self, British colonial rule only helped create a framework of institutions that enabled India to grow beyond its self-imposed isolation. The Indian independence struggle gave Indians a platform to restore India's glorious past while building an independent future.

Before the advent of Western colonial powers, Indian empires asserted a civilizational sphere of influence from the Persian Gulf to South-East Asia. Geography also played a significant role in emphasizing and defining the importance of India's land and sea borders. Indian empires often incorporated neighbouring territories in order to create buffer states to ensure security. Modern India has inherited both the belief in a civilizational sphere of influence and in the idea that geographic neighbours are critical to a state's security against invasion, irredentism and disintegration. For the makers of India's foreign policy, the Indian subcontinent is one entity, the states neighbouring India are important for India's security and India's immediate area of interest extends from the Middle East to South-East Asia.

India's inheritance in the sphere of philosophy and thought has added to the world view shaped by geography and security compulsions. Writing in the 1960s, American scholar on South Asia Norman Palmer noted, 'Almost every aspect of foreign as well as of domestic policy in India seems to be rooted in tradition and to have philosophical underpinnings.'[3] The invoking of tradition varies depending on the personality of contemporary India's current leader. For example, Nehru cited history frequently in his speeches whereas some of his successors did not. Modi's deference to tradition comes in the form of leading mass yoga sessions on International Yoga Day more than in historic references in speeches. There is, however, a continuous trend of turning to India's heritage both to generate national pride and to explain contemporary policies.

India's five millennia as a civilizational entity has always involved engagement with the outside world. Right from the earliest times, Indian kingdoms and empires maintained ties with other countries and regions. There is evidence of diplomatic relations between ancient Indian kingdoms and those in China, Rome, Greece, Egypt and Mesopotamia. The Hindu and Buddhist religions that arose in India expanded beyond the subcontinent, providing evidence of India's links beyond its shores and mountains. Some South-East Asian empires were even led by dynasties which practised Hinduism and Buddhism – such as the Sri Vijaya Empire in present-day Cambodia, Thailand and Indonesia (Java) during the seventh century.

The makers of modern India have often sought inspiration from their country's long history. Most Indians believe that India and Indians have a rich inheritance, including philosophies and ideas, and contemporary India can only grow under the shadow of its past. This general principle, of the present being guided by the past and the future only reflecting it, also applies to the realm of foreign policy.

For example, Kotha Satchidananda Murty, an Indian philosopher and professor, compares and contrasts Indian philosophical streams with those of the West. Writing in the 1960s, Murty asserts there were two philosophical streams in Indian foreign policy, one realist and the other idealist or moralist. Murty traces Indian realism to ancient treatises like the *Arthasastra*s, *Dharmasastra*s and *Nitisastra*s and refers to this as the 'positivistic Kautilyan theory'.[4] A key element of Indian realism was that this theory was applicable only for 'states within India' and did not apply beyond the subcontinent.

For Murty, the idealistic and moralistic stream in Indian politics comes from Buddhism and Jainism. Murty refers to this as the 'autochthonous and moralistic Ashokan theory' and according to him, these views were intended to have 'universal application' in contrast with locally applicable Indian realism.[5] Ashoka (269–232 BC) was the greatest emperor of the Mauryan dynasty who embraced Buddhism and attempted to govern according to his new religion's humanitarian tenets.

Murty divides ancient Indian realists into two groups: the '*Arthasastrins*' and the '*Dharmasastrins*.' Those he refers to as the Arthasastrians, or the followers of Kautilya, were akin to 'Machiavelli's "foxes"' who 'recommend artifice, infiltration, subversion, propaganda and economic pressure in preference to war which was always risky and expensive'.[6] Opposed to them were the Dharmasastrins, or those who follow Manu, who are 'Machiavelli's "lions"' who 'advocated heroic war for just ends, win or die'.[7]

Murty divides ancient Indian idealists into two schools as well: the Buddhists and the Jain–Hindu pacifists. The former 'thought the entire world could be converted to dharma [cosmic order] by peaceful means', while the latter 'advocated ahimsa or non-violence but did not rule out the use of force'.[8] Thus, India's ancient diplomatic tradition was a mix of isolationism and involvement, not very different from non-alignment in modern times. For that reason, Nehru often described non-alignment as 'a positive concept with an implicit philosophy behind it' and insisted that 'its roots go back to the time of Asoka and earlier'.[9]

American political scientist Quincy Wright thought that Indian philosophers provided a better framework for understanding international relations than Western ones. Unlike the West, which has been influenced by the Platonic insistence on universality, ancient Indian philosophy and political thought did not assume a universality of ideas. Hence, it is not surprising that Indian governments 'have seldom been consistent in the application of whatever principles they may profess'.[10] Echoing Quincy Wright's views, Giri Deshingkar points out, 'One prominent characteristic of the Hindu reading of reality is that the good is always mixed with or accompanied by the evil.'[11]

This ties into Nalini Kant Jha's assertion that ancient Indian philosophers did not equate 'public with private morality' and understood that 'a statesman acting on behalf of the state has to take into account the interests and wishes of his people while deciding on his action'.[12] Nehru frankly admitted this in his speeches over the years, and some of his actions, such as the police action in Goa, reflected this view. Unlike his approach to the French Indian colonies of Pondicherry, Karikal, Yanam, Mahe and Chandernagore, now called Chandannagar, where he waited for the colonial power to hand over territory to India after a referendum, he chose to annex Goa by force against the objections of the colonial power, Portugal.

For Nehru, such inconsistency was a necessary function of statecraft. France was willing to return its Indian possessions to an independent India whereas Portugal was not. The annexation of Goa reflected India's concern that Portugal would delay giving up its sovereignty interminably. Waiting and negotiating were better options in case of a liberal France while force was the only course in dealing with an intransigent Portugal. Nehru had already stated in a speech on 8 March 1948 in the Constituent Assembly: 'I can quite conceive of our siding with even an imperial power. I do not mind saying that in a certain set of circumstances that may be the lesser of the two evils.'[13]

Any study of the influence of ancient Indian thought and practice on modern India must start with Kautilya. Also known as Chanakya, Kautilya (c. 370–283 BC), was a philosopher who served as adviser to Chandragupta Maurya, the founder of the Mauryan Empire, the first of India's dynasties to hold sway over large parts of the subcontinent. A lot has been written on the influence of Kautilya on India's strategic thinking. His magnum opus, the *Arthashastra* (the craft of politics and economics) espouses his famous 'mandala' theory – the idea that the king or state (*vijigishu*) seeking extended influence by becoming universal monarch (*chakravartin*) must view himself as being at the heart of a series of concentric circles (mandalas). The *Arthashastra* is spread over fifteen books, totalling 150 chapters and covers all subjects from political philosophy and theory to public administration, diplomacy, foreign policy and intelligence gathering.

Like Machiavelli's *Prince*, Kautilya's treatise addresses a king who is desirous of effectively managing an empire. The book lays out the world as Kautilya sees it, pointing out challenges and opportunities for the king. Like classical realists – Thucydides, Machiavelli and Hobbes – Kautilya too saw the world as anarchic and as one where every state had to depend solely on itself. In order to survive in this anarchic world, the king needed to distinguish between friends and enemies as well as potential allies and potential foes.

In Kautilya's concentric circles, your immediate neighbour is your natural enemy as he covets your territory and resources and is positioned to take them if he is more powerful than you. The neighbour's neighbour, however, is your natural friend because he can covet your neighbour's territory but cannot invade you until he becomes your neighbour. This identification of friends and potential rivals proceeds outward in mandalas or circles. Every state in the mandala system faces the same predicament: they all face a series of concentric circles of enemies and friends.

While Kautilya's influence on the Indian approach to the world is undeniable, scholars differ on the depth of his impact on modern Indian strategic thought. According to analysts such as Bangladeshi political scientist Rashed uz Zaman and German international relations scholar Michael Liebig, Kautilyan thought is at the root of Indian strategic thinking and India's policies can only be understood if we understand Kautilya. Others disagree, arguing that Indians admire Kautilya for writing a treatise on statecraft twenty-three centuries ago but do not always consult him before making policy. The admiration manifests itself in symbolic gestures like naming the diplomatic enclave in New Delhi as Chanakyapuri (literally 'Chanakya's city') after Kautilya. But according to these scholars, Kautilyan thought is not the principal inspiration for people such as Nehru, who shaped Indian foreign policy in the formative years after Independence.

According to Rashed, Kautilyan influence is evident when one contrasts the 'rhetoric' of Indian policies and 'their actual implementation'.[14] Rashed asserts that Indian leaders like Nehru used a 'façade' to present their policy in moralistic terms when in reality India was building its military potential[15] – something Kautilya would have advised. Rashed further argues that even after the end of the cold war India still follows Kautilya in being 'wary of depending on one group of allies'.[16] Despite close relations with Western countries, India still maintains ties with Russia, old friends in the developing world from the Non-Aligned Movement and is an active participant in the BRICS organization. The layered alliances and the mistrust of all allies reflects an embrace of the mandala theory.

Like Rashed, Liebig too argues that non-alignment is simply Kautilyan realism adapted to the modern world. Liebig asserts that not only did Nehru read the *Arthashastra* but also mentioned it in numerous writings and even wrote an article under the pseudonym

'Chanakya.'[17] Liebig sees Kautilyan influence in everyday Indian life. To him the naming of the diplomatic enclave as Chanakyapuri and of a street in Delhi called Kautilya Marg (Kautilya Road) represent this influence. Liebig sees great significance in television serials about Chanakya or about the Mauryas. He observes that Chanakya's portrait hangs prominently on the walls in departments of political science at various Indian universities.

Some of these arguments, however, seem facile. Television serials on, say, Henry VIII and his wives in Britain reflect entertainment value and interest in the life of the monarch, not his philosophical influence on current British foreign policy. Moreover, political science departments in European universities might display portraits of Machiavelli, Thucydides or Morgenthau even when their professors and students embrace views critical of these realists. Not only does New Delhi have a Kautilya Marg, it also names its streets after other historic figures and foreign dignitaries. Even the Mughal emperor, Aurangzeb, who is seldom admired by Hindus or tolerant Indian Muslims, till recently, had a street named after him. The main road in almost every Indian city is named after Mahatma Gandhi but that does not lead to Liebig to conclude that Gandhi's views on non-violence form the core of India's foreign policy.

Modern India's founding generation was divided between realists and idealists and both helped shape India's world view in varying degrees. Kautilyan realism inspired Nehru's colleagues, Sardar Vallabhbhai Patel and Netaji Subhas Chandra Bose, both of whom are viewed as classic Indian realists in their views as well as policies. In his book *Makers of India's Foreign Policy* (2004), former Indian foreign secretary J.N. Dixit asserts that for Patel and Bose the main aim of foreign policy was to safeguard India's national interests 'by whatever means available and whatever equations necessary' and, if necessary or warranted, they did not rule out use of force.[18]

On the other hand, Mohandas Karamchand Gandhi (Mahatma Gandhi to most people) represented the moralistic legacy in politics, represented in Ashokan and Buddhist values. Gandhi referred to his movement for independence from British rule as Satyagraha (literally 'truth force') and for many he 'defined and continues to define the normative and moral terms of reference of India's foreign policy'.[19] Gandhi's contribution to the moral dimension of India's foreign policy lay in the championing of principles that were later adopted by independent India's officials. Gandhi espoused the ideals of tolerance, insisted that good ends can only be attained by good means and emphasized peace and non-violence in all circumstances. His views provided the framework for the doctrines of *Panchasheel* (five principles of peaceful coexistence) and non-alignment that became the bedrock of Nehruvian foreign policy.[20]

Nalini Kant Jha, an Indian international relations scholar, argues that the Buddhist doctrine of 'the middle path' influenced India's foreign and economic policies in the modern era. In economic policy India chose a mixed economy instead of either full-fledged socialism or free-market capitalism. Jha asserts that India preferred to stay in the middle during the cold war because it shared values with both blocs. With the Western countries India shared ideals like democracy, individual liberty, human rights, rule of law, secularism and pluralism as well as the need for a scientific temper. At the same time, India appreciated the anti-colonialism and Asia-centrism of the Soviet Union even as it was 'repelled by the Soviet submerging of the individual in the name of the State'.[21]

India's preference for the middle path had emerged even before independence from Britain. In his first official pronouncement on foreign policy on 7 September 1946, Nehru, as interim prime minister and external affairs minister, stated: 'We propose as far as possible to keep away from the power politics of groups aligned against one another. ... We send our greetings to the people of the US, to whom destiny has given a major role in international affairs ... To that other great nation of the world, the Soviet Union, which also carries a vast responsibility for shaping world events, we send greetings.'[22] This, in effect, was a succinct statement of non-alignment even before that term had been coined.

In a recent book, Priya Chacko furthers the argument that moral influences lay at the core of India's post-Independence foreign policy. According to Chacko, for Nehru foreign policy was a tool to help construct India's identity as a post-colonial state. However, there was an underlying contradiction at the core of this policy: modernity was perceived both as responsible for India's past colonization as well as the cure for India's backwardness. Chacko maintains that this ambivalence is the reason for the strong moral dimension of Indian foreign policy. The only way out of this ambivalence was by asserting India's 'civilizational exceptionalism – the idea that India is equipped with unique moral qualities'. India as a 'moral power' would change the existing global norms and ways of conducting international relations and move the world from violence towards peace.[23]

The idea that India could lead the world, albeit in a different way than traditional global or regional hegemons, has periodically surfaced in Indian political thought only to be questioned or criticized by Indian leaders. At the 2006 *Hindustan Times* Leadership Summit, Nehru's granddaughter-in-law, Sonia Gandhi, spoke on the idea of India as 'The Next Global Superpower' in her capacity as leader of the Congress party, which ruled India at the time. She said that being a superpower 'evokes images of hegemony, of aggression, of power politics, of military might, of division and conflict,' insisting that these images did not reflect India's aspirations.

Sonia Gandhi argued that for centuries 'India exercised a profound influence on the course of world history and it did so without exercising any covert power'. Citing Mahatma Gandhi, Sonia asserted that Indians were able to take on the superpower of the day 'through the mere force of his values and ideas'. She ended her speech by stating: 'We Indians have always known our place in the world even when the world was treating us lightly. ... Why should we think of ourselves as a "Global Superpower"? Why not instead work towards becoming a global force for Peace, Progress and Prosperity?'[24] The 2012 policy document *Non-Alignment 2.0* too argued that India was an example to be followed by the world,[25] implying that India could be a moral leader without necessarily having the wherewithal associated with being a great power.

Pursuit of the middle path is not the only legacy of antiquity in contemporary Indian thinking about international relations. Anti-imperialism, which became a key ingredient of India's foreign policy as a legacy of colonial rule and the Indian national movement, is also traced by scholars such as Murty to ancient Indian writings. Murty points out that no ancient Indian writer, whether realist or idealist, 'advocated or contemplated the extension of Indian culture outside of India by force'.[26] In a sense, India's ancient philosophers were isolationists and 'there was a kind of Monroe doctrine towards states outside India' forbidding aggressive wars on states or cultures outside of the Indian subcontinent.[27]

This ties in with Jha's view that even though ancient Indian monarchs sought to become chakravartin (supreme ruler dispensing justice and maintaining peace), the boundaries of his rule were limited to the geographically and culturally defined region of the subcontinent.[28] Indians did not like exercising power beyond their shores and could not philosophically accept others occupying their land or ruling over them. When Nehru said, 'India's foreign policy is grounded in the ancient tradition and culture of this country',[29] he also suggested that India's opposition to Western imperialism could be traced back to the ancient Indian world view.

The Chola Empire (300 BC–AD 1279) was a notable exception to India's eschewing overseas entanglements. It was the only Indian empire that sought not only trade ties with other civilizations but a political presence beyond India's geographical boundaries. The Cholas' willing militarism and activist external policy enabled this South Indian dynasty to last from the third century BC to the thirteenth century AD. Initially the Cholas only extended their political and cultural influence into present-day Sri Lanka. In doing so they followed the path of other south Indian dynasties like the Pandyas (sixth century BC to twelfth century AD) and the Pallavas (third to ninth century AD), who saw the island just south of India's coast as a natural extension of India rather than as imperial expansion. During the eleventh century AD, however, the Cholas invaded the Sri Vijaya Empire in present-day Indonesia, breaking from the tradition of isolationism and acting as an activist great power in south-East Asia.

Historians disagree on the reasons for Chola expansion into South-East Asia and the extent of their subsequent political influence in that region. For some, the reason was the simple desire to control trade routes while others discern aspirations for political control similar to those of imperialist nations. According to some historians, the Chola invasion was simply a one-off military raid as they did not have the capacity to control a region so far away from their heartland; their naval prowess was insufficient for long-term overseas colonization. Others assert that the Cholas left a viceroy in Java, creating longer-lasting political influence.[30] Disagreement among historians about the circumstances notwithstanding, the fact of an Indian empire extending its political influence outside of the subcontinent demonstrated the willingness of some Indian rulers – and their advisers – to expand India's sphere of influence as early as the eleventh century.

Just as ancient Indian philosophy casts its shadow on the orientation of Indian foreign policy, another long-lasting legacy of the medieval era is the religious and cultural pluralism that came with the rise of Muslim sultanates and the establishment of the Mughal Empire. The sultans of medieval India, as well as the Mughal emperors, were Muslims from outside India who made the subcontinent their home. They came to India from Persia and Central Asia, bringing with them the threat of further invasions from rival Muslim dynasties.

Under the Mughals, India became cognizant of the need to secure ties with the predominantly Muslim west and north-west – a policy consideration that remains paramount even today. In strategic terms, the Mughals knew that in order to safeguard their empire from rival rulers in Persia and Central Asia they needed control of the key forts of Kabul and Kandahar (present-day Afghanistan). A weak or friendly Central Asian ruler would be beneficial as it meant that the Mughals needed to spend fewer resources on safeguarding their empire's border. The British continued with the policy of building buffer zones along India's northern frontiers and modern India acquired that outlook.

The Mughals also had emotional reasons for seeking to extend their influence into Central Asia. The founder of the empire, Babur, was a Central Asian prince from the principality of Fergana (present day Uzbekistan, Tajikistan and Kyrgyzstan) who lost his throne to rivals and entered north India hoping to build his resources in order to recapture his original kingdom. Babur was never able to regain his Central Asian crown and his son Humayun and great-grandson Shah Jahan tried unsuccessfully to fulfil their ancestor's dream. Other Mughal emperors, like Akbar, Jahangir and Aurangzeb gave up the dream of recapturing Babur's principality and focused primarily on consolidating the empire in India. The subcontinent became ethnically and religiously more diverse under Mughal rule, laying the basis for a culturally pluralist India.

An affinity for the regions west and north-west of India, a frontier policy based on the concept of buffer regions and the use of Persian as the official language were not the only legacy of the Mughals affecting external relations. The British also inherited from the Mughals an institutional legacy of a personality-driven administration. Under the Mughals, while an imperial council or council of nobles (Diwan-i-Humayun) existed, the emperor was the decision maker.[31] The Mughals bequeathed lack of institutions and personalization of power to India's subsequent rulers. The British replaced Persian with English, tried to create a professional governing elite and laid some foundations of institutional governance. But they were unable to shake off the culture of personalized governance honed by seven centuries of sultanate, including Mughal rule. The ruler was more important than rules in Muslim-ruled India and the penchant for Indian officials to see themselves as the focus of the state has endured.

However, it can be argued that the modern Indian nation and India's contemporary sense of self were shaped primarily during the era of British colonial rule and not earlier. The British brought with them printing and modern means of communications, such as railways and the telegraph. They created schools, colleges and universities and a system of formal education that did not exist before on such scale. Indians in various regions could now travel to other parts of the subcontinent with greater ease, share ideas, organize and even react as colonial subjects with an ease they had previously not known. Although resentful of colonial rule, modern-day India owes much to British rule, both in the realm of ideas as well as institutions.

The British Indian Empire – or the Raj – left an entire infrastructure of institutions and personnel, which were inherited by the Indian state. In addition, Indian leaders and strategists inherited the world view of the Raj that went beyond looking only at the immediate periphery of South Asia and instead sought India's influence from the Gulf to South-East Asia and even beyond. The role for the Indian Empire envisaged by London left an indelible mark on New Delhi's post-Independence strategic thinking.

For the British, India was the heart of their global empire, the jewel in the British queen or king's crown. It provided both economic and military wherewithal as well as manpower for sustaining the empire in Africa, East Asia, the Pacific islands and the Caribbean. As historian Lawrence James points out, for over a hundred years, the Indian Empire had 'underpinned' Britain's global power status by providing it with 'markets, prestige and muscle'.[32]

India was both a low-cost producer as well as a market for British products. The British Indian army was critical to maintaining British presence around the globe. In order to sustain Pax Britannica across the world, London believed it needed to maintain control of India. It sought to do this by defending its imperial policy both as a civilizing mission as well as one that kept the subcontinent from breaking apart due to communal or ethnic differences.

To understand the views of those who saw the Indian core of the empire as part of Britain's global civilizing mission one need only to turn to Philip Mason, author of the two-volume *The Men Who Ruled India*. For Mason, a former British Indian civil servant, people like him were akin to Plato's ideal philosopher-kings: the guardians who had been brought up and educated so that they would be the ideal rulers. As Mason asserted, India needed British guardianship just as a child needs parents.[33]

Mason's books, originally written under the pseudonym Philip Woodruff while he still served in government, justified the notion of the 'White Man's Burden'.[34] They also made the argument that India would fall apart if the British were not governing the region. That, for people like Mason, the British should have continued to govern India is evident from the post-Partition epigram in his book: 'To the Peoples of India and Pakistan whose tranquility was our care, whose division is our failure and whose continuance in the family of nations to which we belong is our Memorial.'[35] Indian civil servants trained by the British carried some of these paternalist beliefs into their conduct long after the British left the subcontinent.

The humane justification for the empire notwithstanding, a majority of British civil and military officials saw India's importance in its location and its strategic importance for British security. Without India, Britain would only be a small European island nation with a population insufficiently large to defend and manage an empire extending across the world. The Indian Empire helped ensure British paramountcy from the Gulf to the Pacific. The Indian army was Curzon's cannon fodder to be used from Africa (Natal, Somaliland, Uganda, Rhodesia, Sudan and Egypt) to the Middle East (Aden) and Asia (Mauritius, Singapore, Hong Kong and Tibet).[36] Indian 'coolies', clerks and small traders were needed to exploit the resources in tropical climates where large numbers of British were unavailable, unwilling or unable to live. India enabled Britain to make up for its size, population and lack of natural resources.

Control of the seas was critical to Britain's colonial endeavour. British leaders as far back as Curzon were influenced by the ideas of Alfred Thayer Mahan, American naval strategist and historian, who emphasized the importance of sea power. Thus, in the eyes of the British, their security in India would be 'materially affected by an adverse change in political control of the [Persian/Arabian] Gulf'. Secure British presence in India was also needed to ensure the 'safety of the great sea route, commercial and military, to India and the Further East'.[37] For Curzon and his successors, the entire sea route from Britain to India had to be construed as Britain's sphere of influence. During times of British hostility with Russia, any country or power in the Persian Gulf allowing Russia the use of its port was to be regarded by Britain 'as a deliberate insult, as a wanton rupture of the status quo and as an international provocation to war'.[38]

Indian strategist and historian, K.M. Panikkar argued that it was only after the incorporation of India that the British could exercise influence over Asia because they now had 'a vast storehouse of power and resources and with a great army and an efficient administrative machinery'.[39] Policies adopted towards Persia, Afghanistan, Tibet, China, Burma and the Arab Middle East were influenced by security considerations based on the geopolitical advantages of a base in India.

Advocates of empire in Britain recognized India's importance to their global project. For example, Sir Winston Spencer Churchill's obsession with India reflected the realization that without India, the British Empire would not survive and Britain would no longer be a global player. Churchill may have combined his realism with a professed humanitarian impulse. His father, Lord Randolph Henry Spencer Churchill, served as Secretary of State for India (1885–86), during which time he asserted, 'Our rule in India is, as it were, a sheet of oil spread out over, and keeping free from storms, a vast and profound ocean of humanity.'

As early as 1931, the younger Churchill wrote that the 'finest achievement of our history' was the 'rescue of India from ages of barbarism, tyranny and internecine war, and its slow but ceaseless forward march to civilization'.[40] For Churchill, a withdrawal of British rule would either lead to 'Hindu despotism' or 'renewal of those ferocious internal wars'.[41] The 'loss of India', Churchill argued, would be 'final and fatal' for Britain and would 'reduce us to the scale of a minor power'.[42] Thus, for Churchill, India was the 'most truly bright and precious jewel in the crown of the King' whose loss 'would mark and consummate the downfall of the British Empire'.[43]

When it came to the question of India's independence, Churchill insisted that after two centuries the British had rights and interests that they needed to defend.[44] 'India,' he claimed in a conversation with a leading Indian businessman, 'is a burden to us. We have to maintain an army and for the sake of India we have to maintain Singapore and Near East strength.'[45] British rule over India, in Churchill's view, was a favour to India and Britain was having to incur the additional responsibility of colonizing other countries and regions to facilitate India's defence. To Churchill, calls for India's independence interfered not only with Britain's global role but also with the contribution Britain was making towards India itself.

Most British Indian civil and military officials held views similar to Churchill's on India. In a conversation with Churchill during World War II, General Claude Auchinleck, stated: 'India is vital to our existence. We could still hold India without the Middle East, but we cannot hold the Middle East without India.'[46] Auchinleck was commander of British forces in the western desert at the time and later became commander-in-chief of the Indian Army and supreme commander of all British Forces in India and Pakistan.

This view that India and its army were critical to British global policy led to frequent disagreements between the government in London and the administration in Delhi. The former sought an army, which could be deployed globally while the latter preferred to use the force to curb domestic unrest and maintain its borders. Both the 1938 and 1939 Committees of Imperial Defence argued that India was 'the most suitable area east of the Mediterranean in which to station reserves for the Middle and Far East'.[47]

The 1939 Committee tried to meet prominent Indian politicians to obtain their views on military expenditure and role of the military. The Indian National Congress rebuffed the meeting request whereas the Muslim League met with the committee. The committee's report thus stated, 'If a Hindu majority came to power, it would drastically change military policy since defence strategy and expenditure would leave British hands for the first time.'[48] This view that the 'Hindu' Congress would be worse for British interests than the 'Muslim' League influenced British views of the Indian independence struggle and how British officials viewed the future.

Belief in India as the springboard for security of regions to its west and east had resulted in a British project, beginning in the eighteenth century, to create closer ties between the Persian Gulf and India. From 1763, civilian and military officers of the East India Company helped control and administer the Gulf for the British. From 1824 onwards these officers reported to the political resident in the region, who was always an officer from the British Indian services. Hence, India was 'the base' for the British both in times of peace and war and 'stability' in the Middle East 'rested' on British rule over an undivided India.[49]

The reasoning that India was necessary for Britain, and the Far and Near East were important for India's security, permeated the thinking of British officials at almost all levels. It also affected the foreign policies of both India and Pakistan after Independence. In his book *Wells of Power: The Oilfields of South Western Asia: A Regional and Global Study*, British Indian civil servant Sir Olaf Caroe echoed Curzon and Churchill. He argued, in the context of the cold war pitching the West against communist Russia, that control of India (and Pakistan, after Partition) was critical to control of the Gulf region. Caroe also argued that the stability of the Middle East depended on British control of an undivided India, and with its break-up Pakistan would have to take over this role.[50]

On the other hand, India's founding fathers had a different vision for India's engagement with the rest of the world. For Nehru, India, as one of two main Asian civilizations, would symbolize the rise of Asia. A few months before Independence, in March 1947, he championed the Asian Relations Conference that was held in Delhi and was attended by delegates from many parts of Asia, even from countries that were still under colonial rule. Nehru believed that India had been forced to participate in imperial adventures against its will and that independent India would not send its troops out of the country. Indian reluctance to send its troops, except under UN mandate, is a legacy of this colonial past in addition to being influenced by its ancient isolationist history.

Some Indians, like Panikkar, saw Independence as an opportunity for India's rise and embraced the views of British strategists about India's centrality in influencing the Near and Far East. Panikkar saw benefits for India in associating closely with Britain and maintaining, as a sovereign country, the policies of regional primacy that had been devised for the British Empire. He described a Triune Commonwealth: 'a reconstituted Indian empire, on the basis of the freedom of India, Pakistan and Burma'.[51] In a 1919 pamphlet *Indian Nationalism*, Panikkar and an unnamed British colleague had called for the need to 'knit India to England and England to India in a free partnership'.[52]

Decades later Panikkar explained his view thus: 'The old Indian empire as a common defence area had much in its favour. It included Aden, as an outpost, kept the Persian Gulf and the Oman coast within the orbit of Indian policy, neutralized Tibet and held strongly to the Eastern frontier of Burma.' For Panikkar, the 'surrender' of Aden to the colonial office was 'the first short-sighted step' that led to the breakup of this scheme. Other drastic steps were the transfer of the Persian Gulf to the foreign office, the separation of Burma in 1935, the weakening of Indian policy towards Tibet and British Indian influence in Kashgar. 'What seems to be required in the light of the experience of the present [Second World] war is the reconstitution of the old Indian empire on a different basis.'[53]

Panikkar spoke of a 'fourth British empire' which would be 'a world commonwealth in a true sense and one which will be justly entitled to claim the moral leadership of the world'.[54] Panikkar believed that since, in 1947, a newly independent India was too weak to defend herself and needed to build her military and economic strength and obtain modern technology, and the best way to do so was through cooperation with Britain.[55]

In his 1943 book *The Future of South-East Asia*, Panikkar had already argued that in history India had been the 'only' power able to control South-East Asia or what he called 'Further India'.[56] Panikkar saw India as the security provider as well as the key economic power for the region because of its 'geographical position, size, resources, manpower and industrial potential'.[57] He even cited President Quezon of the Philippines who declared: 'Without a free India, no nation in South East Asia can be free.'[58] That Panikkar was not alone in this view is seen in the 1946 book titled *India's Foreign Policy* written by Iqbal Singh, which argued for defence-based regional groupings both for the Middle-East and South-East Asia, with India at the core of both.[59]

In a 1948 pamphlet titled *Regionalism and Security*, published by the Indian Council of World Affairs, Panikkar argued for the creation of a regional organization comprising several countries: India, Pakistan, Ceylon, Burma, Malaya, Iran, Iraq, Afghanistan, Thailand, French Indo-China, Indonesia, Australia and Britain. VT Krishnamachari, in his chapter for Panikkar's book, argued for the creation of a defence council of all these countries and even spoke of military and naval bases in Socotra, Mauritius, India, Ceylon (Sri Lanka) and Singapore.[60] For both Krishnamachari and Panikkar the dominant country in the grouping would be India.[61]

Several other Indian strategists too saw Independence as the opportunity for India to break out of its isolation and play a role on the world stage. One of them, P.N. Kirpal, wrote in 1945, 'Three great highways connect her [India] with the rest of the world. From Calcutta towards the South and South-East, the sea routes reach Australia and New Zealand, the islands and countries of South-East Pacific and the great powers of China and Japan in the Far East. From Bombay and Karachi here are old and easy sea routes to the Middle East, Africa and Europe. From Delhi to the passes of the North-West our railway system reaches the most ancient of the world's highways of commerce and culture, the land route from India to Europe.'[62] According to K.N.V. Sastri, India was to become not only a first-rate military power but also a country that achieves 'moral greatness and spiritual height'.[63]

These views of several early Indian strategic thinkers and policy planners reflected the British outlook about India's neighbourhood, national interest and sphere of influence, albeit with an Indian twist. According to British strategists the British Indian Empire was at its core, a 'kernel' comprising the British Indian provinces and princely states. The next layer were states like Bhutan and Nepal over whom the Raj exercised control of their defence and security policies. A further layer was that of a ring of buffer states or territories like Afghanistan, Tibet and Persia – and even Xinjiang – that the British hoped would remain neutral in any conflict. In this world view, India's area of interest stretched from the Gulf on the one hand to Indo-China on the other.[64]

To those trying to weave in ancient Indian philosophy with British strategic thought, there was a Kautilyan quality to the foreign policy of India under British colonial rule. As Caroe explained: 'A large idea lay behind all consideration of the defence of British India, an idea of a great circle of security, continental and oceanic, radiating from the then India, surrounded by buffer states on the landward frontiers, the seas securely held by the Royal Navy and overall in latter days the mantle of airpower. It dated from a period when maintenance of the security of India was a ruling principle of every British government and it was developed as part of the world order enforced during the century of the Pax Britannica.'[65] The British had, in some ways, operationalized Kautilya's mandalas even if British officers were unfamiliar with the *Arthashastra*.

Like British policymakers, modern Indian strategists have

consistently spoken of India's abiding strategic interest – economic and defence – in the Gulf and the Middle East. In 1944 Hriday Nath Kunzru, a member of the Indian National Congress, wrote that India's importance to the global community lay in her geostrategic location and large military and economic resources.[66] According to Panikkar, 'The Indian Ocean area together with Afghanistan, Sinkiang and Tibet as the outer northern ring constitute the real security of India. Geographically also this is one strategic unit, with India as its great air and land centre and as the base and arsenal of its naval power. From the central triangle of India the whole area can be controlled and defended.'[67]

It is under British colonial influence that India's neighbourhood is deemed to stretch from the Gulf and East Coast of Africa to South-East Asia. Indian strategists often seem to agree with Caroe's assertion that it is 'impossible' to visualize the Gulf unless that prism includes India which 'stands at the centre of the Ocean that bears its name'.[68] Modern India has always seen itself as a key player in the Middle East. Even before Independence, Nehru built close ties with his peers in Egypt and Turkey and reached out to Arab and Persian politicians and intellectuals.

Unlike the British era, independent India did not base its ties across the region through military prowess. Nehru did not like military alliances and preferred political, economic and cultural relations on a bilateral basis. Still, India's policy towards its immediate neighbourhood or periphery has been a continuation of the British policy where the interests of the Raj dictated the interests of the nearby states, not vice versa. This is the root of contemporary India's oft-expressed desire to keep outside powers from gaining influence in South Asia – a sort of Indian Monroe doctrine.

India's independence from British rule came after a protracted struggle led by the Indian elite that had been fostered over time during the colonial era. This national movement, comprising differing strands of thoughts and views, has deeply influenced contemporary India in all aspects, including foreign policy. Some leaders of the national movement sought to retain India's past while others sought to modernize India. The underlying belief of all, however, was that 'India with a more ancient civilization, longer religious and social traditions, and with its ancient literature and intellectual tradition, had much to contribute to the rest of the world'.[69] According to writers like Paul Power, the anti-colonial and anti-fascist stands of the Indian National Congress before Independence have been more influential in modern India's foreign policy than 'the amoral political advice of Kautilya's *Arthashastra* dating back from the fourth century'.[70]

The early leaders of India's national movement shaped not only the struggle for independence but also defined the contours of independent India's policies. The formation of the Indian National Congress (INC) in 1885 provided a permanent organizational structure for Indians to discuss and debate political issues, including their views on international development. Soon after formation, the Congress started making pronouncements on foreign affairs through resolutions, notwithstanding the fact that British India's international relations remained firmly in British hands. For the Congress, not only was India part of the British Empire, its sons and daughters were spread around the globe as businessmen, labourers and students. The British Indian army served in far-off places, justifying the Congress's interest in the treatment of Indians everywhere as well as in events that affected Indian lives.

Many of the positions adopted during the independence struggle have resonated in India's post-Independence world view. For example, Dadabhai Naoroji's epic work *Poverty and UnBritish Rule in India* (1901) and the writings of Romesh Chunder Dutt (1848–1909) on the British agricultural and revenue arrangements in India inspired the socialist economic policies of the Indian National Congress and post-Independence India. Naoroji's 1901 book was written as a critique of Britain's economic exploitation of India and was meant to advance the case for Indian independence.

The Congress was, in principle, against involvement of Indian troops in any imperialist war or adventure. Still, during World War I the Congress supported the Allied war effort with medical units and military volunteers. Mahatma Gandhi was amongst those who supported and pushed for this assistance. Gandhi and others hoped that if India supported the British, the latter would grant India Dominion status after the end of the war. They were, however, disappointed.

In 1919, the Congress planned to send a delegation led by veteran Congress leader, Bal Gangadhar Tilak, to the Peace Conference at Versailles, but the British government refused to provide passports to members of the delegation. Tilak then sent a letter to Georges Benjamin Clemenceau, French prime minister and president of the Peace Conference. In his letter Tilak wrote: 'India is self-contained, harbours no designs upon the integrity of other states and has no ambition outside. With her vast area, enormous resources and prodigious population she may well aspire to be a leading power in Asia. She could therefore be a powerful steward of the League of Nations for maintaining peace of the world'.[71] The wording of the letter could as well be part of a statement by officials of independent India after 1947.

In 1921 the Congress passed a resolution that repudiated the aggressive policies of the Raj and reassured foreign countries, especially India's neighbours, that upon attainment of self-government, India's foreign policy would be one of friendship towards all. In 1925, at the fortieth session of the Congress party in Kanpur, a resolution was passed for the need 'to look after the interests of Indians abroad and to carry on educative propaganda in the country regarding their position in the British Empire and foreign countries'.[72]

A resolution passed at the Madras session in 1927 declared: 'The people of India have no quarrels with their neighbours and desire to live at peace with them and assert their right to determine whether or not they will take part in any war. The Congress demands that these war preparations be put an end to and further declares that in the event of the British government embarking on any war-like adventure and endeavouring to exploit India in it for furtherance of their imperialist aims it will be the duty of the people of India to refuse to take any part in such a war or cooperate with them in any way whatsoever.'[73]

The 1928 Calcutta session resolution declared: '... that the Congress has taken a decision to develop contacts with other countries and peoples who also suffer under imperialism and desire to combat it.'[74] The Congress resolutions also put forth the concept of an Asia whose fate is tied together. This idea was put forth at the 1926 Gauhati session as well as at the 1928 Calcutta session that sought a conference on Asia in 1930.[75] This finally materialized in the form of the March 1947 Asian Relations Conference.

In 1936 Jawaharlal Nehru inaugurated the foreign department of the Congress and in 1940 a separate Indians Overseas Department was set up. The Congress also supported freedom struggles in other colonies and countries. It built ties with the Wafd party in Egypt, the Kuomintang in China and with parties in Indonesia and other countries of the Middle East and South-East Asia. Resolutions of the Indian National Congress repeatedly spoke out against imperialism.

As World War II approached, Congress resolutions opposed fascism and Nazism: criticizing Japan's aggression against Manchuria, Italy's taking over of Abyssinia and Germany's dismemberment of Czechoslovakia. Not only did the Congress pass resolutions but it also raised funds and sent aid for the Abyssinian and Spanish loyalist causes. As foreign secretary of the Congress party, Nehru visited Spain, Czechoslovakia, Russia and even Chungking in China.[76]

At the 1938 Haripura session of the Congress, a resolution was passed that the '... people of India desire to live in peace and friendship with their neighbours and with all other countries and for this purpose wish to remove all causes of conflict between them. Striving for their own freedom and independence as a nation, they wish to respect the freedom of others and to build up their strength on the basis of international cooperation and goodwill.' The resolution further stated:

> India can be no party to such an imperialist war and will not permit her manpower and resources to be exploited in the interests of British imperialism. Nor can India join any war without the express consent of her people. The Congress therefore entirely disapproves of war preparations being made in India and large-scale manoeuvres and air raid precautions by which it has been sought to spread an atmosphere of approaching war in India. In the event of an attempt being made to involve India in a war this will be resisted.[77]

A few months later, in September 1939, the Congress Working Committee issued a statement, declaring: 'If the war is to defend the status quo, imperialist possessions, colonies, vested interests and privilege then India can have nothing to do with it. If, however, the issue is democracy and a world order based on democracy then India is intensely interested in it.'[78] The Congress steadfastly opposed the British war effort and most Congress leaders spent the war years in prison or in exile.

The 1942 Quit India resolution of the Congress passed in Bombay championed the cause of a world federation, pointing out that

> ... the future peace, security and ordered progress of the world demand a world federation of free nations, as on no other basis can the problems of the modern world be solved. Such a world federation will ensure the freedom of its constituent nations, the prevention of exploitation by one nation over another, the protection of national minorities, the advancement of all backward areas and peoples and the pooling of the world's resources for the common good of all.[79]

Congress's non-cooperation with the British during the war years created space for the Muslim League's demand for partition of India; but it did have the effect of forcing the British to reconsider their belief in holding on to India indefinitely. By the time the war ended, Indian independence became inevitable. In 1945, though not yet an independent country, India was represented at the San Francisco Conference and signed the United Nations charter.

Thus, over the years, the political party that led India to independence had laid down the guiding principles for the conduct of India's international affairs. These included expression of a desire to cooperate with other countries, support for anti-imperial and anti-colonial struggles and championing peace around the world. The Congress also committed India to abiding by the Charter of the United Nations, promoting Asian solidarity and seeking the recognition of India as a non-militarist great power. Many of India's post-Independence initiatives, including non-alignment, the Panchasheel (five principles of coexistence) and the opposition to multilateral military alliances can be traced to the deliberations of the Indian National Congress during the independence struggle.

3

Ideas and Individuals

JUST AS HISTORY and geography shape foreign policy, some individuals and their ideas also have a profound impact on how a nation looks at the world outside. During India's long struggle for freedom from British colonial rule, several leaders including Mohandas Karamchand Gandhi, Subhas Chandra Bose, Vallabhbhai Patel and Chakravarti Rajagopalachari made pronouncements on international relations. It was the foreign policy views of Jawaharlal Nehru, however, that prevailed over all others. US Secretary of State Dean Acheson considered Nehru critical to India's global role, 'so important to all of us, that if he did not exist – as Voltaire said of God – he would have to be invented'.[1] Most of Nehru's successors held on to his tradition, with minor changes, as a guarantee of India's stability in dealing with the rest of the world.

Nehru was both politician and scholar. Observing him as prime minister, sociologist Edward Shils pointed out: 'Few men so intellectual by disposition, occupy positions in any countries.'[2] Born into an elite Hindu family, Jawaharlal Nehru had been schooled at prestigious British institutions known for training Britain's ruling class: Harrow Public School and Cambridge University. In his own words he returned to India 'perhaps more an Englishman than an Indian' and 'looked upon the world almost from an Englishman's standpoint'.[3] It was his intellectual curiosity that transformed him into an interpreter of India to the world.

Described as the 'founding architect'[4] of India's foreign policy, Nehru was deemed unique among his contemporaries for his keen interest in global affairs. Nehru was the principal Congress personality speaking on foreign policy beginning in 1922. Indian National Congress resolutions and statements on international affairs often reflected his views. After becoming prime minister, Nehru once remarked that he was attracted to premiership because he could then allocate to himself the external affairs portfolio.[5]

Nehru had travelled extensively well before his rise to pre-eminence within the independence movement. On some occasions, the Congress took advantage of his personal travel to seek representation at international forums. In 1927, Nehru represented the Congress at the League Against Imperialism in Palais D'Egmont at Brussels. Two years later, he positioned himself as an internationalist when, as president of the Congress, Nehru stated that India could not afford to ignore what was happening in the world around her. 'We have our problems, difficult and intricate, and we cannot run away from them and take shelter in the wider problems that affect the world but if we ignore the world, we do so at our peril,' he argued.[6]

During the 1930s because of his wife Kamala's convalescence – and later death – at a sanatorium in Lausanne, Switzerland, Nehru spent considerable time in Europe. This enabled him to build relationships in England, Spain, Czechoslovakia, Poland, Hungary and even the United States. Nehru later travelled to countries that were still under colonial rule. Trips to Indonesia (formerly Dutch East Indies), Morocco, Algeria (formerly French North Africa), and Egypt enabled Nehru to build close ties with individuals who later played key roles and came to power in their countries. He also visited Turkey, partly for sightseeing but also to study the Kemalist experiment in establishing secularism after the collapse of the Ottoman Empire.

Nehru met with Mustafa al Nahhas Pasha (1879–1965), leader of the Wafd party and later prime minister of Egypt, during a 1938 trip to Cairo.[7] A Wafd party delegation later attended the annual session of the Congress party in 1938–39. In 1939, Nehru visited China and established contacts with leaders of the Kuomintang government including Chiang Kai-shek.[8] The Indian National

Congress organized a boycott of Japanese goods in response to Japanese aggression against China and also sent a medical mission under Dr Kotnis in support of the Chinese resistance.

By the time Viceroy Lord Archibald Wavell formed India's interim government in September 1946 in anticipation of Independence, Nehru had sufficient international exposure to be assigned the portfolios of external affairs and Commonwealth relations. In his first radio broadcast in that capacity on 7 September 1946, Nehru stated that India would try 'as far as possible, to keep away from power politics of groups, aligned against one another'. Nehru envisioned the world as one torn apart by 'rivalries and hatreds and inner conflicts' and envisaged India's role as working towards 'a world commonwealth'.[9] In a speech given on the floor of the Constituent Assembly on 13 December 1946, Nehru laid out the broad contours of his foreign policy: 'This ancient land attains its rightful and honoured place in the world and makes its full and willing contribution to the promotion of world peace and the welfare of mankind. We approach the world in a friendly way. We want to make friends with all countries.'[10] For Nehru, these were not just words but deeply held beliefs.

Over the years, Nehru repeatedly asserted that his foreign policy was not something crafted by him alone. 'It is a policy inherent in the circumstances of India, inherent in the past thinking of India, inherent in the whole mental outlook of India, inherent in the condition of the Indian mind during the freedom struggle and inherent in the circumstances of the world today.'[11]

However, Satchidananda Murty argues convincingly that there was nothing inevitable about the way India's foreign policy evolved and the policy was 'shaped almost exclusively' by Nehru.[12] According to Murty India's geography and the legacy of history may have created a certain environment but Nehru's unique beliefs shaped India's foreign policy, using circumstances and history as justification.

Nehru's British education and his close ideological ties with British socialist intellectuals built during the 1930s and '40s served as major influences on his persona. His foreign policy outlook had a touch of Fabian socialism and liberal internationalism along with a deep belief that a strong state – not the market – is critical for the growth and development of a country like India. The spirit of freedom that Nehru imbibed in England and his close observation of British parliamentary democracy made him an 'uncompromising' opponent of all forms of totalitarian rule.[13] Hence, Nehru sympathized with the Allies during the World War II, refused to meet with Mussolini in 1936 and supported the Congress decision to send fifty volunteers to help the leftist struggle against fascism in Spain.

'NEHRUVIANISM'

Indians often refer to Nehru's foreign policy as 'Nehruvian' and one might as well describe the ideas behind that policy as 'Nehruvianism'. In his lifetime, Nehru avoided labels tied to his name, though he did speak of Gandhian principles. His mark on some ideas is so strong that they can only be associated with Nehru rather than with Gandhi or someone else. The key pillars of Nehruvianism were the concept that India was a great civilization that could regenerate itself at all times; the desire for independence and non-alignment in relation to great powers; a strong belief in economic autarky; and support for international institutions in maintaining global order and world peace. These ideas remain influential in Indian thinking to this day.

In his three-volume biography of Nehru, Sarvepalli Gopal, son of India's second president Sarvepalli Radhakrishnan, outlines Nehru's belief that 'India would develop an active concern in world affairs, pursuing an independent policy compatible with her own national interests – a statement of objective which remained true throughout his years in office'. However, according to Gopal 'at the start there was little precision and definiteness about this objective. It appeared to consist primarily of vague and rather grandiose hopes of closer ties between Asian countries and even the formation of two or three Asian federations.' In Gopal's words 'the foreign policy of a newly independent nation does not emerge overnight' and 'with the general directions clear in his mind, Nehru set about building up the foreign policy of India brick by brick, in the process discarding the generalizations which had taken the place of rigorous thought'.[14]

Echoing the views expressed by many of his colleagues and the feelings of fellow Indians, Nehru assumed that India was destined to play a major role in the globe because of its rich history, tradition, resources, location and population. In a speech in March 1949 Nehru stated: 'Remember that India, not because of any ambition of hers, but because of the force of circumstances, because of geography, because of history and because of so many other things, inevitably has to play a very important part in Asia.'[15] There was an inevitability to India's greatness, in his mind. 'India need only wait until others understand and accommodate to the Indian position,' he once declared. Nehruvianism implies waiting for the 'inevitable consequence of what India is and what a free India must be'[16] instead of scrambling to seek alliances or take advantage of global conflicts and crises.

Tied to the notion of India's inevitable rise was the view that India had a moral obligation to use her influence for good in the world. On the one hand, the claim to higher moral ground had an emotional appeal and connected India – and Nehru – to the father of the nation, Mahatma Gandhi, who had emphasized ethics in pursuit of politics. At another level, there was a realist rationale for painting India as a preachy, altruistic global actor. Nehru understood that until India built its economic and military potential, the only way it could punch above its weight was as a champion of smaller nations in promoting a just and moral order in the world.

Championing the eradication of imperialism and colonialism were part of this strategy to rally the world's weak and downtrodden nations and emerge as their leader. It followed closely from India's own anti-colonialist struggle and was helpful in building close ties with other former colonies. The moral imperative and strategic dimension went hand in hand. The British legacy of viewing India as the dominant power in South Asia, with its power extending to the Middle East and South-East Asia, was echoed in Nehru's early speeches when he referred to India and China as the rising powers of Asia. Indian leaders saw their country as the natural leader for Asia and Africa, especially for fellow newly decolonized nations. According to veteran Congressman Jivatram Bhagwandas Kripalani, India's 'prestige' ran high even though it had just emerged as an independent state because it 'stood for the freedom of all nations and peoples and against all colonial or racial domination of one people over another'.[17]

As subjects in a former colony, India's leaders saw anti-colonialism as the defining issue in the post – World War II world. They refused to be drawn into the cold war or to let fear of communism frame their world view. Nehru declared in his first broadcast to the nation that India was 'particularly interested' in the emancipation of all dependent countries [or peoples] and in decolonization'.[18] India's founding generation viewed the legacy of colonialism as a threat to India's security and territorial integrity. Nehru saw non-alignment as an element of a scheme to 'pre-emptively contain the spread of the Cold War' as, in his view, conflict would have hurt recently decolonized countries like India.[19]

Nehru's goal of seeking the end of imperialism and colonialism tied in to his policy of building closer ties between India and the rest of Asia. The desire to rekindle India's ancient economic, political and cultural influence with fellow Asian countries was the rationale for hosting the first Asian Relations Conference in New Delhi on 23 March 1947, just months before India's independence. Under Nehru's leadership, India championed regional initiatives (such as the Afro-Asian Conference, also known as the Bandung Conference) as well as international organizations (most significantly the United Nations).[20] British India was one of the signatories to the United Nations (UN) Charter in 1945 and in 1947 independent India inherited the status of being one of the UN's founding members.

An analysis of Nehru's pronouncements on international affairs reflects the influence of colonial rule and the British legacy on his world view. For Nehru, India's neighbourhood included not just South Asia but West Asia (India's term for the Middle East), Central Asia and South-East Asia. Nehru chose different policies towards India's immediate periphery than towards distant countries or those in the broader Asian neighbourhood. Immediately after Independence and through the initial cold war years, for example, India sought to continue the British policy of buffer zones around India, especially to the north. It built close ties with Nepal and Bhutan in order to 'fortify its Himalayan defense structure'.[21]

India under Nehru also sought to prevent neighbours like Nepal, Bhutan and Sri Lanka from joining military alliances with either cold war bloc and was particularly irked by Pakistan's participation in Western military alliances. According to former foreign secretary J.N. Dixit, Nehru's 'sense of history' and awareness that India's neighbours were critical to India's security led him to adopt this policy.[22] Dixit argues that Nehru was aware of the asymmetry in size between India and its immediate neighbours. He sought to reassure these smaller neighbours by attempting to build ties on the basis of Panchasheel or principles of equality, non-interference and respect for territorial integrity.

Former diplomat and writer S.D. Muni asserts that Nehru had a Curzonian mindset – derived from the British imperialist Lord Curzon – on issues relating to national security. According to this view, Nehru sought to 'retain the core British strategic framework' for India's defense while 'shedding off its imperial and colonial façade'.[23] Muni states that India treated each of the three Himalayan kingdoms with 'nuanced differences' in terms of sovereignty and degrees of independence. Sikkim was viewed 'as a protectorate' (which was later absorbed as a state of the Indian Union in 1974), Bhutan 'evolved' into a sovereign state and Nepal was always considered 'a fully sovereign' country.[24] The treaties India signed with each of these countries – Bhutan (1948), Nepal (1950) and Sikkim (1950) reflected these differences. Muni states that while minor changes occurred over the years, what remained intact was this policy of 'keeping the neighbouring countries free from adversarial strategic influences and forces'.[25]

Muni echoes views expressed as early as 1951 by international relations scholar Werner Levi. Levi stated that when it came to India's immediate neighbours Nehru was 'very much the realist' who understood that in a Westphalian system of states 'national survival is the primary aim of foreign policy'. For Levi, policies adopted towards Hyderabad, Kashmir, Afghanistan and Nepal demonstrate the realist aspect of Nehruvianism. Levi quotes Nehru as defending India's interference in the internal affairs of Nepal on the grounds that 'much as we appreciate the independence of Nepal, we cannot risk our own security by any happenings in Nepal which permit that barrier being crossed or which otherwise weaken our frontiers'.[26]

Beyond the immediate neighbourhood, Nehru wanted India to find its place in the sun by playing a leadership role in Asia and on the global stage. He acknowledged that India was too weak militarily or economically to stand up to the superpowers. India had to adopt a policy whereby it could maintain its independence and yet be part of the world, receiving support for its development from all major powers. Non-alignment – the notion of aligning with neither superpower while maintaining friendship with both and adopting positions on different international issues not because of alignment but on a case by case basis – appeared to be the way out. Michael Edwardes refers to non-alignment as Nehru's 'doctrine of defence by friendship', a policy that appealed to Nehru on both practical and moral grounds.[27] Nehru leveraged India's ties with former colonies to create a third bloc of nations refusing to join either bloc during the cold war. Burma, Egypt, Ghana, Yugoslavia and Indonesia joined India as the founding members of the Non-Aligned Movement in 1961.

Veteran diplomat, Kunwar Natwar Singh, who joined the Indian Foreign Service during Nehru's tenure, argues that while Nehru sought non-alignment he was not in favour of turning it into a movement as, for Nehru, non-alignment was 'a state of mind', not 'a dogma or doctrine'. According to Natwar Singh, Nehru treated non-alignment as 'an instrument' which would strengthen 'forces of peace, disarmament and economic cooperation' and 'provide a platform' for the recently decolonized nations of Asia, Africa and South America.

Like Murty, Natwar Singh asserts that for Nehru non-alignment meant retaining 'our thought, judgement and action under conditions of the Cold War' instead of becoming a camp follower of the United States or the Soviet Union. Being non-aligned, India could stay out of foreign entanglements it sought to avoid while speaking out on issues that mattered. A formal Non-Aligned Movement of states went beyond that by tying India to a group of other mid-sized and small powers, each with issues of its own. According to Natwar Singh, it was Krishna Menon, defence minister and Nehru's close confidant, who 'convinced' Nehru into agreeing to convert the non-aligned idea into a movement comprising several countries.[28]

On non alignment, Sarvepalli Gopal argues that Nehru was not 'priggishly parading principles and was determined to develop, at whatever cost, a policy of independent judgement of each issue because that was ethically the right position'. Nehru emphasized 'the practical advantages to India of non-alignment and judged its efficacy on a pragmatic basis'. According to Gopal, non-alignment 'was firmly based on the current realities of the world'. Nehru often expounded the moral virtues of non-alignment, especially in later years, and reportedly annoyed other governments by appearing to demand a lot for India. Still, his policy reflected utilitarian advantage as much as idealism. 'It was not so much a code of conduct as a technique to be tested by results,' Gopal explained that Nehru did not consider it 'a wise policy to put all our eggs in one basket' and considered an honest and independent policy the best option 'from the point of view of opportunism'.[29]

Americans, in particular, objected to Nehru's non-alignment, terming it 'neutralism' and suggesting that it was not a moral position in a world threatened by the spread of communism. Escott Reid, who served as Canada's high commissioner to India

(1952–57) did not agree with his American counterparts who considered Nehru's non-alignment as a heresy that benefited global communism. 'Mr Nehru is a man of very great intellectual ability, highly articulate and of great personal charm,' he wrote, adding, 'He is also, like other great men, sensitive and complex.' Reid argued that Americans 'should not only be conscious of Mr Nehru's difficulties but should also not expect him to behave as if he were a North American politician. It is important not to alienate Mr Nehru by treating his suggestions as second-class advice from a third-class friend. Democratic leadership in Asia can be developed only if the Western powers deal with Asian leaders as equals, seeking their counsel and occasionally deferring to their opinions.'[30]

Reid explained that by adopting non-alignment, Nehru was not tilting away from the Western powers, in favour of the Soviet Union and its communist allies. 'Nehru is, I submit, not neutral between our side and the USSR. He is a member of our side,' he insisted, pointing out that India as a whole saw the West with 'half reluctant admiration, half volatile resentment' as a result of 'the tutelage of the British'.[31]

According to Indian strategic thinker K. Subrahmanyam, non-alignment was an attempt to balance Indian foreign policy in a world of superpower dominance. For Subrahmanyam, it was a 'sound strategy in realpolitik sense and in terms of balance of power'.[32] According to Devdutt, Dixit and E. Malcolm House, non-alignment helped India achieve both 'internal stability' and 'external security' as it enabled India 'to speak in one voice' based on a positive consensus-driven policy.[33] Non-alignment also ensured that while India did not join either bloc, it maintained ties with both the camps and hence was able to obtain aid and technical assistance from both blocs, allowing it to build its resources without getting drawn into conflicts. According to Levi, following the policy of non-alignment enabled India to 'retain greater freedom of action to play its leadership role in Asia'.[34]

Paul F. Power attempts to analyse Nehruvianism through two broad principles, order and strategy. The desire for order led Nehru to pursue friendship towards all states; champion anti-colonialism, anti-racialism and anti-imperialism; seek economic self-sufficiency; and oppose military alliances, arms build-up and nuclear weapons.[35] Non-alignment provided the underpinnings of strategy or as Power prefers to call it, an 'independent' policy. For Power, like Murty, non-alignment was a calculated response to the prevalent international situation. It was not just 'an ad hoc response' to the cold war. It reflected the desire to accomplish what Nehru had stated in a September 1946 speech: Stand up to the existing system of world affairs which was framed by imperialism, military alliances and war making and in its place create a world with no camps where all worked towards global peace and prosperity.[36]

Pursuing non-alignment ensured a domestic consensus on foreign policy that might not have been possible had India aligned itself to either superpower. The strong Indian left would have objected to alignment with the West while a similar reaction would have ensued from the right in case of alliance with the communists. Averting polarization on foreign policy gave Nehru a relatively free hand in dealing with divisive politics over domestic problems. Nehru preferred cooperation and reasoning over confrontation and conflict. Nehru's speeches in the Constituent Assembly and later as prime minister reflect this desire for consensus and his hope that people 'who differ considerably in regard to our internal policy' would agree on a 'more or less unified foreign policy'.[37]

Subrahmanyam points out that Nehru had deployed non-alignment as a tactic specifically for the cold war but it became 'a moral code of conduct' for executing foreign policy in the post-Nehruvian era.[38] Journalist Inder Malhotra also echoed Subrahmanyam's views that for Nehru non-alignment was a policy, not a doctrine or a 'mantra to be chanted in season and out of season'. Malhotra recalls that on one occasion Nehru made a speech in the Indian parliament that 'he could not be non-aligned against himself'.[39]

In a recent book, Andrew Kennedy, professor, Australian National University, points out that Nehru's 'moralistic concern for world peace was not simply contrived for public purposes, it reflected his "genuine" concern about the world while protecting narrower Indian interests'. Non-alignment helped India diversify its relationships and prevent dependence on any one superpower. Kennedy also argues that Nehru sought to convert India into 'an industrial power in its own right' but knew that in the short term, India would need to be dependent on other countries. To prevent India from being involved in conflicts that would hurt her economic growth, Nehru chose the path of non-alignment. The idealist in Nehru, Kennedy argues, saw non-alignment 'as a means of maximizing India's influence' whereas the realist in him 'anticipated from the very beginning that a non-aligned stance would be difficult to maintain'.[40]

In a series of interviews conducted over several years, a majority of diplomats, both serving and retired, stated that while every country needs to adjust to changing environment, Nehruvianism is still the bedrock of Indian foreign policy. In the words of Natwar Singh, Nehru 'studied history, wrote history, made and shaped history'.[41] As an American political scientist wrote in 1958, the 'principal source' of Indian thinking on international affairs and the 'high emotional content' of Indian foreign policy are due to the 'omnipotent influence' of Nehru on the conduct of foreign policy and the 'immense popular support' given to his declarations.[42]

Most analysts agree Nehru's greatest legacy is the underlying framework of ideas and institutions that have governed India's external relations since 1947. Just as he received praise for laying the foundations, Nehru has also been criticized for being overly idealistic and for crafting a foreign policy with a strong moralistic tone. Under his successors, India came to be seen as a nation that judged and preached to others instead of accepting the dynamic of conflicting national interests that shapes international relations. Like the United States, India has often attracted the charge of hypocrisy in foreign policy because its proclaimed ideals do not always match its actions.

During what Paul Power describes as the 'Age of Nehru', moral concerns dominated a wide spectrum of diplomatic, ideological and strategic considerations.[43] Nehru's global stature and his role in organizations like the United Nations, coupled with his championing of the anti-colonial and anti-racist cause, won India recognition from other former colonies in Africa and Asia. However, Michael Edwardes asserts that Nehru mistook 'respect for Nehru' as being the same as acceptance of India as a major power on the world stage and as the undisputed leader of non-aligned nations. According to Edwardes, 'Nehru had created for India an international persona which was not congruent with her actual status as an underdeveloped country.'[44]

Nehru's knowledge of foreign affairs was so vast that none of his contemporaries or successors ever attempted to disagree with him. The dictum of 'Panditji [Pandit Nehru] knows best' often prevented disagreement with him. Veteran diplomat Katyayani Shankar Bajpai notes that his father Girija Shankar Bajpai, the first Secretary General of the Ministry of External Affairs, was one of the few advisers who were able to speak the truth to the powers that be. Nehru's successors simply followed in his footsteps because, in the words of B.M. Jain, political scientist and professor at Rajasthan University, 'they lacked either the intellectual stamina or political courage to tinker with the basic premises of the foreign policy as laid down by him'.[45]

G.P. Srivastava echoes Edwardes when he asserts that the claim that Nehru's foreign policy 'raised the moral prestige of India' and helped maintain world peace was illusory. Srivastava cited a letter to an editor written in 1951 by Sir Jagdish Prasad, former member of the Governor General's Executive Council. According to Prasad, India was left with no friends in the West because of 'self-praise', 'arrogant self-conceit' and the belief that India's foreign policy was 'superior to that of all other powers because it is claimed to be based on truth and non-violence'. He wrote: 'The great powers do not wish to be told by implication that in contrast to our foreign policy theirs is based on trickery and violence; that we are the only people in the world to handle international affairs on a moral basis, and that our superiority on this score is now universally recognized and receives worldwide homage.'[46]

Even J.B. Kripalani, Praja Socialist Party (PSP) leader and a Congress stalwart during the freedom struggle, admitted in an article in *Foreign Affairs* in 1959 that India's prestige built up under Nehru had not helped 'advance any vital interests of India or diminish tension on her borders'. Kripalani argued '...the Indian government thought that the whole business of diplomacy consisted in enunciating the principles of international policy. But international politics is not concerned merely with enunciation of abstract principles. It is very much concerned with international diplomacy, strategy and tactics.'[47] According to Kripalani, there was always 'a danger in overemphasizing moral and ideological principles in international affairs. There are bound to be contradictions in the actual conduct of nations in dealing with each other.'[48]

Whereas others criticized Nehru for his 'idealistic presumptions' in a Hobbesian world based on realpolitik, Dixit critiques Nehru for his naive belief that since India 'had no expansionist or aggressive designs against any other country, India would not face any threats to its unity or territorial integrity'.[49] Nehru apparently held the view that since India had decided to keep away from power blocs, it would be protected from negative implications of the cold war equations.[50] Dixit points out that India's neighbours joined the cold war – Pakistan in alliance with the United States, and China's initial alliance with the Soviet Union – and brought war to India's neighbourhood. India's lofty principles were not enough to deter others from pursuing cynical realism. Even though India was a status quo power, her neighbours China and Pakistan were revanchist as was amply demonstrated in the wars of 1948, 1962 and 1965.

Dixit and other analysts believe that Nehru's policies were reasonably successful until the India–China war of 1962. India was recognized as a major Asian power and as a leading voice on anti-colonialism and against racial discrimination in the United Nations. India was involved in the post-crises negotiations in Korea and Indo-China and was a leading contributor to UN peacekeeping operations in the Middle East. Even though the United States and its allies were disenchanted and 'estranged'[51] with India, they still maintained close ties and provided economic and technological assistance to India. Nehru's desire to build ties with fellow Asian countries was reflected in the 1947 Asian Relations Conference, followed by the Bandung Conference of 1955 and eventually the Non-Aligned Movement of 1961. But the war with China in 1962 exposed the chink in India's armour. Non-alignment and absence of superpower support had ended up encouraging Chinese aggression against India.

Nehru's biographer Gopal described Nehru's assessment of China's attitude to India as 'naive'[52] and said that there was 'much idealism in his China policy'. According to Gopal, Nehru had 'hoped fondly that friendship with the new China would not only maintain peace in Asia but start a new phase in world affairs with Asia giving the lead in a more humane as well as a more sophisticated diplomacy. The Chinese did not reciprocate India's trust, taking advantage of Nehru's favourable disposition and exploited the goodwill generated by the 'Hindi–Cheeni bhai bhai' (Indians and Chinese are brothers) rhetoric. 'The basic challenge between India and China,' Gopal points out 'ran along the spine of Asia,' something 'China never seemed to forget and Nehru could not finally help recognizing'.[53]

INDIAN REALISM

For all his idealism, and notwithstanding the validity of some of the critique of his China policy, Nehru was still a pragmatist and realist. When asked in 1947 to define his foreign policy, Nehru replied that India would have to maintain ties with all countries irrespective of whether or not India approved or disapproved of their policies. He emphasized that since India is not 'strong enough to be able to have our way' the policy to adopt would be that of 'peace-makers and peace-bringers'.[54] Nehru did realize that while India would seek to avoid any entanglement with power politics, realistically speaking that would not be completely possible.[55] India would therefore try to play the part of 'a bridge for mutual understanding' between the two cold war blocs.[56]

Nehru was also not completely blind to the challenge of China. In a letter in 1950 to British statesman and Labour Party politician, Ernest Bevin, he wrote 'Chinese psychology, with its background of prolonged suffering, struggle against Japan, and successful communist revolution, is an understandable mixture of bitterness, elation and vaulting confidence to which the traditional xenophobia and present-day isolation from outside contacts have added fear and suspicion of the motives of other powers.' He saw his role as 'inducing a more balanced and cooperative mentality in Peking' based on his understanding of the psychological factors affecting Chinese policy.[57]

Andrew Kennedy describes Nehru's foreign policy as an attempt to reconcile realism and idealism. According to Kennedy, Nehru 'was idealistic in the sense that he sought to transform international norms and institutions on the basis of moral principles. In doing so, however, Nehru also sought to secure advantages for India and in that sense his idealism often had a realist edge.' Kennedy argues that even if we focus on Nehru's 'most important "idealistic" preoccupations in foreign policy: the UN, non-alignment and nuclear disarmament' we see that he 'was both sincerely committed to what he saw as a moral cause and convinced that advancing it would serve India well'. Nehru did not support the UN simply out of an idealist desire to make the world a better place. He saw the prospect of a stronger UN advancing important Indian interests. [58] In Kennedy's view, Nehru saw the United Nations 'as an opportunity to reshape the international system in ways that were both morally desirable and consistent with India's interests in particular'.[59] Nehru saw the UN as a guarantor of India's sovereignty while promoting international peace and to him 'it offered a foundation on which India could establish itself and commence its rise to greatness'.

Nehru's realism also manifested in his stance on nuclear weapons. Nehru championed nuclear disarmament as a key part of his campaign for global peace. In Kennedy's words, 'While making the case against nuclear weaponry India's Prime Minister often sounded like an idealist who was both anxious about the threat of nuclear war and optimistic about the possibility of international cooperation.' However, Nehru's disarmament diplomacy reflected not only 'some degree of idealism' but also 'his perception of narrower Indian interests. Nehru was not willing to sign on to any sort of disarmament arrangement regardless of the implications for India.' Nehru believed that disarmament 'was very much in the interests of relatively weak powers like India' and 'hoped that the disarmament process would come to constrain India's rivals, particularly China.'[60] Further, Nehru's support for civilian nuclear energy and the work of Indian nuclear scientists demonstrated that he understood the need for India to have the requisite nuclear power potential just in case circumstances ever changed.

According to Murty, Nehru's foreign policy was 'cold and rationally calculated', bearing in mind that India, a country with 'pride in its glorious past and great civilization', was industrially and technologically backward and underdeveloped. Hence, democracy at home and global peace were critical if India sought to grow economically and build its security.[61]

Nehru led India from Independence in 1947 to his death in 1964. Although he forged a domestic consensus on foreign policy, support for his world view was far from unanimous. There were many who disagreed with his basic premises or with specific elements of his policies. Some criticized him openly while others voiced their views only in private. Some dissenters stayed in the Congress party and tried to reform it from within; others founded new parties after Independence to advance their alternative viewpoints.

A major rival to Nehru in defining India's external relations was Sardar Vallabhbhai Patel, India's first deputy prime minister and home minister. Patel was a foreign policy realist who often disagreed with Nehru though he expressed this disagreement in private or through letters the two wrote to each other until Patel's death in 1950. While agreeing that India needed to avoid being involved in power politics, Patel was amongst those who deemed a pro-Western orientation was to India's advantage. He argued that India needed strong ties with the United States more than the formal association with the British Commonwealth and asserted that 'we depend on the USA more than on the UK'.[62]

The Swatantra [literally Independent] Party of the 1960s led by veteran Congressman Chakravarti Rajagopalachari (or Rajaji as he was popularly known) also opposed Nehru's liberal internationalism and Fabian socialism. It reflected the views of the business community, former bureaucrats and former royal families from British India's princely states. Swatantra Party's major policy planks included support for free-market economics, desire for close ties with the US and not the Soviet Union during the cold war and realism, not liberal internationalism, as the basis of India's foreign policy. While these views had some support among intellectuals and elite groups, the party lacked a mass base. Moreover, different party leaders espoused differing views at times. Rajaji, referred to by Mahatma Gandhi, as the 'keeper of his conscience', was a pacifist whereas another leader Minoo Masani was vehemently anti-communist and pro-Western and was not prepared to forsake war.

The Swatantra Party offered a sharp contrast to Nehruvianism. It championed 'alignment' or building regional alliances including joint defence with non-communist countries from Israel in the Gulf to East Asia including Japan, Australia and New Zealand. [63] It is interesting that the foreign policy initiatives of Prime Minister Narendra Modi since his election in 2014 embrace some of the ideas championed by the Swatantra Party during the 1950s and '60s.

Like Patel within Congress, the Swatantra Party believed in the importance of having superpower backing and sought to align with the West, not the Soviet bloc. The Western democracies were viewed as having more resources and the Americans would be more likely to support India against China, which the Swatantra Party saw as the main threat to India. They turned out to be correct when in India's conflict with China in 1962 it was not the non-aligned countries but the West that came to India's aid. When critiqued for being willing to 'surrender their sovereignty' by joining military alliances, Swatantra Party leaders responded by saying, 'If economic assistance and PL 480 funds do not indenture a nation, there is less reason why military aid should.'[64]

Further, the Swatantra Party viewed communism – especially Chinese – not Western colonialism or racialism as the major threat to global peace. Thus, it did not support the idea of a third front of developing countries standing up to the two cold war blocs. For the Swatantra Party non-alignment neither helped India achieve its national interests nor helped India make friends. According to C. Rajagopalachari, 'never have we been more abandoned by friends and menaced by foes thanks to our airy foreign policy' and hence 'it is time to discard non-alignment, for it not only does not insure our national security but in fact imperils our domestic economy'.[65]

In Rajagopalachari's view, Western colonialism was 'a "dead horse" which Swatantra declines to beat, and Angola, Rhodesia, et al. are far from its concerns; communist colonialism, especially that of China, is the clear and present danger; racialism is of little concern; non-alignment is held to be both militarily and economically suicidal; the notions of a third force and of mediation in the "cold war" fall to the ground once alignment is accepted; and this receives further impetus from the conviction that the truth lies with the Western democracies'.[66]

The Swatantra Party died a slow death by 1974 because of lacklustre leadership and an inability to generate a mass following. Its electoral performance was far from impressive. However, another conservative movement, rooting itself in Hindu (as opposed to Nehru's secular Indian) nationalism, has managed to survive through various incarnations all the way to the present-day Bharatiya Janata Party (literally Indian Peoples Party). Inspired by the Rashtriya Swayamsevak Sangh (RSS – National Volunteer Organization), an ideological movement seeking revival of Hindu identity and culture, the Bharatiya Jana Sangh (BJS) (literally

Indian Peoples Association) was the first major incarnation of Hindu nationalist politics. The Jana Sangh emerged in 1951 and maintained that name until 1977 when it merged with the anti-Congress multiparty alliance, the Janata Party. In 1980, the Hindu nationalists broke from the Janata Party to become the Bharatiya Janata Party (BJP), which became the first right-wing party to wield power in India.

Like the Swatantra Party, the Jana Sangh and its successors have seen China as a threat, but unlike the Swatantra Party, the Hindu nationalists viewed Pakistan as an equal threat to India's security. According to Howard Erdman, an American political scientist who wrote one of the earliest books on right wing political parties in India: 'The basic instinct of BJS is to be chauvinistic and isolationist, building Indian power and involving India only when she is directly and immediately involved.'[67] While the Jana Sangh sought to be sufficiently distinct from the Congress, in some ways it was closer to specific aspects of Nehruvianism. 'The party's basic instinct is to be "Gaullist" and relatively isolationist,' explained Erdman, adding that for Jana Sangh, Western colonialism and neo-colonialism were not dead issues, nor were some racial considerations. The party accepted non-alignment 'but in a more negative sense', one that 'would still leave India freer to serve as an arbiter or as a third force' in international matters.[68]

A leading stalwart of the Jana Sangh, Atal Bihari Vajpayee, became minister for external affairs during the brief period of non-Congress rule from 1977 to 1980. In his inaugural address in May 1978 to the Foreign Service School, Vajpayee gave a speech titled 'Continuity and Change in India's Foreign Policy'. In the speech Vajpayee asserted that the main purpose of India's foreign policy was 'to promote harmony, trust and a cooperative spirit among nations'. He asserted that India's 'concept of security is not militaristic' but rather the desire to 'create around us an environment of peace, trust, and stability which would permit optimum utilization of our natural and manpower resources for economic, social and cultural advancement.' He stated that his government's policy was 'strict non-interference in the internal affairs and seeking cooperation of India's neighbours'.[69] The speech combined the Jana Sangh's 'India First' approach with Nehruvianism.

POST-NEHRU SEARCH FOR POWER

The Nehruvian framework secured India global attention and, in V.P. Dutt's words, ensured that 'a country with very little military muscle on the morrow of independence and with no economic clout either could still be a significant factor in the international arena'.[70] Notwithstanding right-wing criticism of Nehru's policies during his years in power most Indian intellectuals agreed even after his death that his vision reflected national consensus. A study conducted in the early 1960s of around 100 Indian intellectuals who worked on foreign policy showed that the majority (83 per cent) endorsed non-alignment as the basis of India's foreign policy.[71] After Nehru's death in 1964, his successors felt the need to assert Indian power though they insisted their actions did not deviate from the first prime minister's structural design.

Scholars such as Kennedy argue that Nehru's 'bold diplomacy reflected his belief that his country had a unique capacity to promote international cooperation, and that such sacrifices were therefore worth making'. This confidence in India's diplomatic prowess, was not shared by Nehru's successors, which to Kennedy explains why 'none of them have acted with as much ambition or achieved as much global renown as he did'. Kennedy acknowledges that Nehru's successors have not 'suffered such painful setbacks' as Nehru did because they pursued more modest and realistic foreign policy goals.[72]

In recent years, Narendra Modi reflects a passion resembling Nehru in his zealous focus on foreign policy. After winning the 2014 general elections in a landslide, Modi has expended a lot of time and political capital on travelling around the world, wooing world leaders and global corporate executives, hoping to boost India's stature and also to strengthen its economy and military. We have to wait and see how far he will succeed in this endeavour.

Nehru's immediate successor as prime minister, Lal Bahadur Shastri, remained in office rather briefly from 1964 to 1966. As a former colleague of Nehru, Shastri did not alter Nehru's policies during his short stint. India's second war with Pakistan, in 1965, was the key event during Shastri's tenure. By most accounts, Shastri handled the war and India's foreign and defence policies extremely well though he had no foreign policy experience before becoming prime minister. Until then, domestic politics had been his forte.

India's foreign policy evolved significantly when Nehru's daughter, Indira Gandhi became prime minister in 1966, two years after her father's death. She served in that job from 1966 to 1977 and then again from 1980 until her assassination in 1984. Indira had grown up amidst politics as the granddaughter of Motilal Nehru (1861–1931) and the daughter of Jawaharlal Nehru, both important figures in India's independence struggle. After her father became prime minister, Indira was, in Dixit's words, 'a personal witness to and participant in major political developments both domestically and in terms of India's external relations'.[73] She knew almost every leader of not just the Congress party but of the national movement since her childhood.

Indira served as her widower father's official hostess and companion during his years in power. She had interacted with many of the world's leaders and policymakers well before taking office as prime minister. But Nehru, reluctant to be seen as practising dynastic politics, avoided anointing Indira as his successor. It was only in 1959, twelve years after he took over as premier and after she had earned her spurs, that Indira was chosen president of the Congress party. Nehru also nominated her on behalf of India to the Executive Board of UNESCO on which she stayed from 1960 to 1964.

In her work on Indira Gandhi, international relations professor Surjit Mansingh analyses how Indira's childhood and youth framed her views on foreign and domestic politics as well as on governance. Indira, according to Mansingh, was convinced that 'she embodied the will of the Indian people' or as the then president of the Congress

Dev Kanta Barooah, in a fit of sycophancy, said, 'Indira is India and India is Indira.'[74] Just as Indira had a lonely 'insecure' childhood so India faced a global environment that was 'indifferent and often hostile.'[75] Asia and the world had been Nehru's focus and his scepticism of the superpowers had led him to maintain a healthy distance from both. Indira, on the other hand, chose the South Asian region as her focus, and suspicions of the intentions and policies of the superpowers, especially the United States, in India's immediate neighbourhood was coloured by her international outlook.

There were other differences between Nehru and Indira. Nehru's policies were shaped by his knowledge of history and sympathy towards socialism, whereas Indira did not have any ideological predispositions. Both pursued what they deemed to be India's national interest but their approach to the world was markedly different. Nehru's world view had a moralistic tinge because of the influence of Mahatma Gandhi and the strongly moral national struggle. Indira, on the other hand, one spoke the language of realpolitik and where she used moral slogans it was in her search for power and desire to boost India's status in the world. According to Dixit, Indira undertook a 'radical' change in India's foreign policy orientation by changing India 'from an idealistic player into a force to be reckoned with.'[76]

In a broadcast two days after becoming prime minister in January 1966, Indira asserted that the principles guiding India's foreign policy were based on 'national interest, honor and dignity.'[77] Thus, Nehru's policy of peace and friendship towards all countries would continue but India's security and territorial integrity would be the paramount concern.[78] Indira believed that only a stronger and more united India 'would we be able to stand up to other nations.'[79] Under her leadership, the Indian state became increasingly concerned about its security and defence, something that had not received Nehru's full attention.

Under Indira Gandhi, Indian strategists embraced the belief that India's security would be negatively impacted unless its smaller neighbours followed pro-Indian foreign policies. This led to what has come to be known as the Indira doctrine whose core principles were firstly that 'no foreign power should be allowed to cross the crest of the Himalayas' and secondly that 'India would consider the presence or influence of an external power in the region as adverse to its interests unless that power recognized Indian predominance'.[80] The Indira doctrine was in effect a South Asian equivalent of the US Monroe doctrine. It led to actions during the East Pakistan crisis leading to India's military victory in 1971 against Pakistan, which, as Dixit points out, 'restored national self-confidence' after the 1962 military loss against China.[81]

Indira explained the contours of what became known as the Indira doctrine in a 1970 seminar organized by the Congress party. Like her father, she insisted that foreign policy was based on both history and geography and hence the way India looked at things would differ from other countries. Indira stated that under her father India was able to make a mark on the international stage even though it lacked economic and military strength. This was because India was 'in the forefront of the freedom struggle' and had 'leaders of stature'.[82] The realist in Indira acknowledged that India no longer punched above her weight, as it had been able to do under Nehru. However, Indira's strategy for increasing India's international weight was not alignment with one of the superpowers. It lay in building India's economic and military strength, preferably indigenously. Under Indira, therefore, India's foreign policy became 'a search for power' and not for moral influence.[83]

A key part of building India's military strength and security was the nuclear dimension. Indira maintained the dual policy of Nehru with respect to championing disarmament while continuing to build India's nuclear potential. It was under Indira that India undertook its first nuclear test in 1974 and despite condemnation and threat of sanctions Indira continued with India's nuclear weapons programme. She saw it as the natural course for India as both its adversarial neighbours, China and Pakistan, were also building their nuclear weapons programmes.

The desire for an independent foreign policy remained strong under Indira as it did under Nehru. For her it meant both India's territorial integrity as well as economic autarky. A constant refrain in her pronouncements was that while India was 'politically free' but economic and technological dependence on other countries meant that it did not enjoy 'complete freedom'. She said, 'My idea of freedom is a self-reliant nation. It is true no nation today can be fully self-reliant. We shall have to have something from outside; but at least there should be a base of self-sufficiency and self-reliance.'[84] Her economic and security policies tied in to her particular take on non-alignment as well.

For Indira, non-alignment was not simply 'avoidance of entanglement' with the two blocs but rather 'preserving independence despite close relations with one or both of them.'[85] While India under Indira continued to champion non-alignment, Indira sought to narrow its focus more in terms of the interests of the developing countries. Under Indira's leadership, there was a growing 'insistence on autonomy' which was in sharp contrast to the reality – India's need for economic and military aid. The reduction or elimination of direct US aid was seen as 'a badge of honour'. Hence for Indira, deeper ties with the Soviet Union and even the 1971 treaty of friendship with the Soviets (concluded amidst US backing for Pakistan during the East Pakistan/Bangladesh crisis) did not mean that India was no longer non-aligned. As Indira often stated, India was too large a country to be part of any bloc but it needed economic, military and scientific resources to be able to follow an independent policy.

For Indira, non-alignment meant India reserved 'the right to judge each international issue on its merits and keeping in view our national interests and interest of world peace'.[86] Like Nehru, non-alignment for Indira was 'an assertion of our freedom of judgement and action' as it demonstrated that India was not a camp follower.[87] Indira saw non-alignment as 'the only hard-headed, practical path that is open to any country which wants to keep itself independent'.[88]

While India under Indira still talked about the need for global peace and prosperity, what Indira sought was a 'new international economic order' [89] where the developing countries had a say and where only a few countries – like the permanent members of the UN Security Council – did not determine the balance of power.[90] While Nehru saw colonialism as the major threat facing the world, Indira saw neocolonialism as the new threat that India had to stand up against. In Indira's view, the Western world was trying to impose neocolonialism on the developing countries and India as their champion had to fight back.[91]

Indira wanted India to play the role of a leader in helping create this new economic order. In this she echoed the views of her fellow Indians, most of whom believed it natural that India would be a leader or guide to other developing countries. Indira's speeches critique the superpower blocs for seeking 'overseas possessions', for carving out 'spheres of influence' and erecting 'cordon sanitaires'.[92] In a 1972 *Foreign Affairs* article Indira spoke of the need to destroy 'past colonial feudal structures,' stay away from 'spheres of influence' and safeguard India's independence as well as maintain global peace. [93] That the legacy of anti-colonialism still framed India's foreign policy long after Independence can be seen in Indira's speeches that referred constantly to the fears of colonialism and neocolonialism, the desire for economic autarky and aversion to the cold war blocs.

Like Nehru, Indira also tried, but failed, to reconcile India's claims to moral ascendancy with the realities of global power politics. According to Mansingh, Indira remained preoccupied with the question, 'how to be strong enough to prevent encroachment on national interests by outside powers and yet avoid intimidating small neighbouring states by an increase of power'. It did not help that there was disagreement on the proper status of India in the world.

'Was India a small power to be treated as a pawn in international politics because of its low per capita income?' Mansingh asked. That was not the only fully unanswered question though. 'Was

India a middle power by virtue of its size, capability and the middle position it occupied between competing blocs? Was India a regional power because of its strategic location and historic position in southern Asia? Or was India an emergent great power in aspiration and perhaps in fact?'[94] Some of these questions facing Indira still remain issues in India's foreign policy debate.

Indira tilted the scales of the 'morality or power' debate in favour of power. She also had a lasting impact on the organizational conduct of foreign policy. Indira followed Shastri's lead rather than her father's tradition by appointing a cabinet member as minister for external affairs. Subsequently, all prime ministers, with the exception of Inder Kumar Gujral, always appointed an external affairs minister and, if needed, held the portfolio themselves only for short periods of time. (Gujral, who served as prime minister briefly in 1997–98, saw himself in Nehru's mould and tried to run foreign policy directly from the Prime Minister's Office.) The influence of prime ministers on foreign policy remained profound even in the presence of a cabinet minister wielding the external affairs portfolio.

ECLIPSE OF COLD WAR POLITICS

Indira Gandhi led India in military victory against Pakistan and adopted a more robust posture in fighting various insurgencies within the country. Building Indian military might alongside its claim to higher moral ground in the cold war became essential elements of Indian foreign policy. Indira's assassination in October 1984 resulted in the passing of the leadership mantle to Nehru's grandson and Indira's son Rajiv Gandhi, who was chosen prime minister at the age of forty-four with little previous political experience. The third prime minister from the Nehru-Gandhi family left his own mark on India's external relations at a time when the cold war was in its last stages.

Rajiv had entered politics in 1980, after the death of his younger brother, and Indira's heir presumptive, Sanjay Gandhi. A former airline pilot, Rajiv soon became general secretary of the Congress party and was one of his mother's close aides for the next four years. Dixit argues that even though Rajiv 'came to power without any discernible or direct experience or knowledge of politics', he 'could legitimately claim absorption of general information and experience' from his grandfather and mother.[95] In her book on Rajiv's years in power, American writer Kathleen Healy made a similar point. She wrote that Rajiv 'lived with and learned from Nehru, his father Feroze Gandhi and his mother Indira Gandhi all of whom lived and suffered for India. Rajiv's personal knowledge of history has been and is a lived experience.'[96]

Before being thrust into the office of prime minister, Rajiv had overseen the functioning of the foreign affairs cell of the Congress party and had travelled around the world often with his mother. As prime minister, Rajiv's views on foreign policy reflected Nehru's idealistic and moralistic streak combined with a streak of pragmatism inherited from Indira.

In a recent book Srinath Raghavan argues that the 'incipient shift in foreign policy' under Rajiv 'stemmed from a conjunction of external and internal factors'.[97] Rajiv 'recognized the importance of foreign policy in furthering his domestic objectives'[98] as he spoke of the need to 'build for an India of the twenty-first century'.[99] In his speech soon after his mother's assassination, Rajiv laid out the key principles of his foreign policy which reflected Nehruvianism by emphasizing non-alignment, anti-colonialism, adherence to multinational institutions like the United Nations and a desire for good relations with all countries. 'Jawaharlal Nehru bequeathed to us a foreign policy,' he said, adding, 'I shall carry it forward. I reaffirm our adherence to the United Nations, to the Nonaligned Movement and to our opposition to colonialism, old or new ... We have always been friends with East and West as they are called and we want better relations with them.'[100]

A year later, in New York Rajiv stated that the basic principles of India's foreign policy were 'a logical outcome of our own experiences, needs and aspirations'. To him, standing with oppressed peoples was still important, as was the desire to resolve issues through peace. The streak of independence was important because India 'will not be a camp follower'. Sounding like Nehru, Rajiv stated in an interview on an American news show: 'We take a stand which is right.'[101] He also made it clear that he was seeking to create a balance between tradition and modernity. In his address before a joint session of the United States Congress on 13 June 1985, Rajiv spoke about India being an old country but a young nation. He emphasized the 'firm foundations' laid down by modern India's founders on which the future would be built. He spoke of the goal of a 'strong, independent and self-reliant' India.[102]

Rajiv's pragmatism was reflected in his desire to improve relations with Pakistan and China. In a speech given two weeks after the assassination of his mother, Rajiv emphasized that for him the first requisite for India's march forward was 'peace with our neighbours'.[103] In his inaugural address at the annual South Asian Association for Regional Conference (SAARC) Summit in 1986, Rajiv emphasized the importance of the geographical, historical, religio-cultural and ethnolinguistic ties that bound the various South Asian countries. He spoke of the need to increase interactions so as to boost each other's resources. Interestingly, Rajiv cites Kautilya and justified SAARC on the grounds that the *Arthashastra* spoke of the importance of having friendly neighbours.[104]

When Benazir Bhutto was elected prime minister of Pakistan after the death of military dictator General Zia-ul-Haq in 1988, Rajiv's hopes for peace with Pakistan were raised. Both Rajiv and Benazir were post-Partition leaders and did not carry the baggage of that tragic episode in the subcontinent's history. Both had popular support in their countries and could accomplish what earlier leaders had not been able to do. Rajiv travelled to Pakistan in 1989 to attend the SAARC summit in Islamabad and concluded an agreement with Bhutto on confidence-building measures between India and Pakistan. In the end, however, Benazir Bhutto's term in office was cut short when the president, backed by the military, dismissed her from office and dissolved parliament.

Sri Lanka was the other neighbouring South Asian country with which Rajiv attempted to alter relations. Sri Lanka had a large ethnic Tamil population, which the majority Sinhalese sought to suppress. The Sri Lankan Tamils, who received considerable sympathy from Tamil-speaking Indians, sought protection of their rights. Some demanded a federal system with autonomy for Tamil majority areas within Sri Lanka. All Indian prime ministers, beginning with Nehru, had attempted to solve Sri Lanka's Tamil problem but had not succeeded. In 1983, civil war broke out in northern Sri Lanka as Tamil hardliners pushed for independence after Sinhalese attacks on Tamils.

India's initial role was to ask the Sri Lankan government to protect its Tamil minority. Then, Rajiv went a step further by using the Indian Air Force to drop vital supplies for the Tamil population when the Sri Lankan government blockaded the Jaffna peninsula. As civil war intensified, Rajiv agreed to send Indian troops for peacekeeping after the 1987 Indo–Lanka accord that resulted in ceasefire between the Tamil guerillas and the Sri Lankan military. Dixit, who praised other policies of Rajiv, observed that his Lanka policy put Indian troops in the middle of two irreconcilable sides neither of which liked India's presence. 'It has to be acknowledged that he did not understand the physical complexities of the ethnic conflict in Sri Lanka,' Dixit wrote.[105] The Indian Peacekeeping Force (IPKF) had to be withdrawn in 1990 after it came under attack from both Tamil and Sinhalese extremists.

Rajiv had as much difficulty as his mother in balancing hard-nosed realpolitik with noble objectives of global peace and regional cooperation. For example, as he sought to improve ties with India's neighbours he also knew that India needed to protect its interests. Rajiv's policies towards Pakistan, Nepal and Sri Lanka reflected his view that while India was willing to accommodate its smaller neighbours, those neighbours also had an obligation to bear India's interests in mind. Unlike Indira, he did not voice his opposition to external powers getting involved in South Asia but he still stuck to the Indira doctrine in effect.

Representing a generation that grew up in an independent India rather than an environment of struggle against colonial rule, Rajiv was unencumbered by ideological scepticism of the West, including the United States. He started the process of repairing and rebuilding India–US relations both on the economic front as well as in foreign affairs. Rajiv's pragmatism was also reflected in his policy towards China. He was the first prime minister after Nehru to visit China, leading the first high-level delegation since the 1962 Sino-Indian war. Rajiv laid down the policy that has allowed India and China to deepen economic relations even though their border dispute remains unresolved.

Non-alignment remained one of the pillars of Rajiv's foreign policy, just as it had been for Nehru and Indira. In his 1985 address to the Council of Foreign Relations in New York Rajiv stated: '[Non-alignment] is rooted in our belief that the world is and has to be many-hued. It is an assertion of our own right to look at the world the way we see it. We do not think there is one and only one infallible path which all must follow. Independence is the core of the logic of non-alignment.'[106] Forty years after Independence, Indian leaders still sought to follow an independent foreign policy, and non-alignment continued to be seen as the way to maintain independence.

For Rajiv, as for his predecessors, non-alignment reflected India's fervent desire for independence as well as its quest for international peace.[107] Like Nehru and Indira, Rajiv saw non-alignment as the 'alternative' to military alliances and the pursuit of balance of power.[108] Speaking on the occasion of the twenty-fifth anniversary of the NAM in Harare, Rajiv echoed Nehru when he referred to non-alignment as 'an idea, a reality, a movement' and a major force 'that transformed history'.[109] Like Nehru and Indira, Rajiv emphasized the need for 'peaceful coexistence' instead of a 'vain and dangerous pursuit of confrontation and domination'.[110]

The membership of the Non-Aligned Movement had risen from twenty-two members in 1961 to around 100 in 1986. Even countries that previously belonged to one of the two cold war blocs now embraced non-alignment as, in Rajiv's words, the 'way out of the impasse in which conventional politics and civilization find themselves'. Rajiv asserted that India and its fellow non-aligned friends had not only 'withstood' the pressure of the blocs but also 'kept faith' in their principles. According to Rajiv, independence and non-alignment should be seen as the 'driving forces' behind India's domestic and foreign policies. This would boost India's economic strength that in turn would help India obtain respect.[111]

For Rajiv, non-alignment was not simply about uniting developing countries. It was a path towards economic cooperation and multilateralism. 'Complementarities of Southern countries offer possibilities of fruitful economic cooperation: resources in raw materials, manufacturing capacity, finance and credit, managerial and production skills and range of matching technologies,' he declared, adding, 'The scale of cooperation is still small but the potential is great.'[112] According to Rajiv, the 'leitmotif' of non-alignment was 'the assertion of our right to unity, self-determination and independence' by virtue of which we have the right to 'freely pursue' our 'economic, social and cultural development without intimidation or hindrance'[113] by major powers.

During his five years as prime minister, Rajiv undertook forty-eight foreign trips. In his speeches and travels to fellow developing countries, which like India were former colonies, Rajiv would touch on topics which resonated: history and old civilization, colonialism, imperialism, and racialism. According to Healy, Rajiv 'links the Indian heritage of culture and freedom stymied under colonialism with the prospect of a new democracy on the march'.[114] He pursued closer ties with the United States than under Nehru or Indira alongside close identification with the world's developing countries.

Rajiv often emphasized India's key role in the global anti-imperialist struggle. 'Long before our independence, we were the first to raise our voice against racial discrimination in international organizations,' he once remarked.[115] On another occasion he said, 'When Gandhiji and Panditji fought for freedom, they did not think of freedom of India only. They were concerned about slavery and oppression wherever it was present in the world. Their aim was to get freedom for all these people. India got freedom and thereafter gradually all other countries got freedom one by one.'[116]

Under Rajiv, India sustained its position as a leading nation of the world without being among the wealthiest or the militarily most powerful. Rajiv focused on economic issues more than his predecessors, paving the way for even greater interest in India's growth by his successors. According to Raghavan, Rajiv understood that if India sought to grow and become a modern economy it needed to increase its imports and exports and obtain access to the latest technology. At the heart of Rajiv's championing of modernization 'was the need to embrace high technology, particularly information technology, to transform the Indian economy and society'. Raghavan argues that Rajiv understood this would require 'greater and more adroit engagement with the world and that foreign policy had to be geared towards securing these objectives'.[117] Rajiv understood the importance of economic growth not only for domestic reasons but also to raise India's status in the world. He also tied this in with the desire to build 'a more equitable world economic order in which the developing countries will have a large voice'.[118]

In his speech at the Non-Aligned Movement (NAM) summit in Harare in 1986 Rajiv talked about the need for 'revolutionizing' the international economic order by 'tangible, broad-based cooperation' amongst the NAM countries. He spoke about the need to share skills, technology through an information grid and the need to set up a multinational system like the Global System of Trade Preferences. Rajiv believed this would strengthen 'the South's negotiating power in parleys with the North'.[119]

Thus, to the Nehruvian legacy, Rajiv added the need to use deeper economic and technological ties to create a new global economic order. Unlike Nehru and Indira, Rajiv trusted the market and did not see the state as the sole and key actor in the economic arena. Not only did he start economic reforms that were later taken forward in 1991, but he also voiced a desire to secure for India all advantages of globalization and the attending technological and economic changes. He sought an economic order in which all countries, including developing ones, would have 'a fair opportunity' to become prosperous.[120] Rajiv seemed to think that seeking greater power for the global South would help build India's global weight.

In Rajiv's lexicon, words like 'common humanity', 'human dignity' and 'peaceful co-existence' were combined with 'survival', 'security' and 'independence'. For him the ideal world was one where 'each of us, irrespective of size or wealth or military strength, is the equal of every other nation'.[121] Unlike his mother, Rajiv was prone to verbose speeches where he would state that the path India had chosen was 'unique',[122] that India's 'stock' in the world was high and that Indian policy was to 'carve out the right path and reach the principles and ideology of Gandhiji to all corners of the world'.[123] For Rajiv, India's Weltanschauung was 'shaped by our history, our traditions and values of our civilization'.[124]

The Nehruvian idealist in Rajiv championed disarmament with a passion, which echoed his grandfather. In November 1986, India and the Soviet Union signed the Declaration for a Nuclear-Weapon-Free and Non-Violent World. The declaration spoke of the need for peaceful coexistence, supremacy of human life, non-violence, political and economic independence and using resources for social and economic development, not military resources.[125] Still, as a pragmatist, Rajiv also stated that while India did not want to accumulate arms or build nuclear weapons, the international system was such that India had no option but to divert resources to strengthen itself. That is how he justified India's nuclear test of 1974, under his mother's leadership, and why India had not unilaterally abandoned the quest for nuclear weapons.[126]

Foreign policy under Rajiv Gandhi was a personalized affair in which the prime minister was the main actor. This echoed the conduct of his mother and grandfather. Rajiv changed his foreign minister often, going through five external affairs ministers and seven ministers of state for external affairs during his five years as prime minister. His lack of confidence in his first foreign secretary led him to discontinue the traditional weekly meeting between the prime minister and the foreign secretary and to even publicly dismiss his own foreign secretary in the midst of a press conference. Seeking to implement drastic change in a system that was oriented towards status quo and with which he was not very comfortable led Rajiv to seek outside advisers or trust his own views instead of those of an entrenched bureaucracy.

For his critics Rajiv was a dilettante who tried to combine what Nehru and Indira did but lacked the depth of knowledge and steadfastness to stay on course. His spur-of-the-moment decisions, like his decision to send troops into Sri Lanka, often created long-term problems. His detractors critiqued him for listening to a small group of advisers – both bureaucratic and political – who were concentrated in his office and in India's external intelligence services.[127] Dixit, however, sums up Rajiv's years in power by stating that despite lacking in experience and faced with a changing world Rajiv successfully navigated India's national interests.[128]

AFTER THE DYNASTY

Rajiv Gandhi turned out to be the last prime minister of the Nehru-Gandhi political dynasty. Changes introduced by him paved the way for India's next steps during the 1990s but these were carried forward under different politicians who did not inherit the mantle of leadership from blood ties to Nehru. Internal economic problems, the end of the cold war and collapse of the Soviet Union led the Indian government to implement a series of economic measures that led to liberalization and less government control. The opening up of the economy also forced a rethink of India's foreign policy even though the left wing opposed both economic reform and international realignment. Many politicians, even within the Congress party, preferred the state-led model of economic development and objected to the expanded role of the private sector as a harbinger of greater corruption. They did not consider the emergence of the United States as the world's sole superpower as a positive development either. By 1989, Rajiv could not retain the wide political support that had led to his election in 1984. Dissidents from the Congress party, led by Vishwanath Pratap Singh (known as V.P. Singh), joined other left-of-centre factions to form the Janata Dal, which challenged Rajiv's Congress in the general elections of November 1989.

The Congress failed to secure a majority in parliament during the 1989 election, resulting in V.P. Singh's ascent to the office of prime minister as head of a minority government. He lasted in power for only eleven months (from December 1989 to November 1990). During Singh's tenure, the government's weak grip allowed little room for major foreign policy initiatives. Singh's foreign minister, veteran Congressman Inder Kumar Gujral, ran foreign policy without much guidance from the prime minister. V.P. Singh was one of those prime ministers who had little knowledge or interest in external affairs, whereas Gujral was passionate about foreign policy. Gujral had served as ambassador to Moscow from 1976 to 1980. He later became external affairs minister again in 1996 and prime minister at the head of a coalition government in 1997–98. Gujral saw himself as reviving Nehru's idealism albeit with a vengeance. He is known most for his Gujral doctrine, forsaking reciprocity in relations with India's immediate neighbours and offering them unilateral concessions. [129]

Gujral's detractors fault him for his extreme idealism reflected in the Gujral doctrine as well as his belief that foreign and defence policy only meant diplomacy, not the hard side of intelligence gathering. Under Gujral, India's covert intelligence capabilities were drastically reduced and they hurt India's diplomatic potential. India's intelligence gathering offices in many countries, not only the neighbours but also beyond, were wound up. One immediate impact of this was felt when a coup in Fiji took place. India had a huge diaspora in that country and the winding up of India's intelligence capabilities meant India did not find out about the incident till much later.

The defining moment in Gujral's first stint as Singh's foreign minister came when Gujral chose to be photographed hugging Saddam Hussein while India wavered in supporting the US-led coalition against Iraq during the war over Kuwait. Iraq's invasion of Kuwait in August 1990 was almost universally condemned. Logic and rationality dictated that India too should have denounced the invasion. Strategically, India would have benefited from offering support to Kuwait though it also needed to protect 170,000 Indians working and living in Iraq and Kuwait.

Under Gujral's influence, V.P. Singh's coalition government appeared flummoxed and unsure of what to do. India chose to be neutral in the ensuing conflict, ignoring that one non-aligned member country had invaded another. Soon after the invasion of Kuwait, Gujral went to Baghdad and instead of conveying India's concerns about Saddam's actions ended up creating the perception of sympathy for Saddam Hussein. The government did succeed, however, in evacuating 110,000 Indian citizens from Iraq and Kuwait, leaving behind only those who chose to stay there through the war.

India's response to the Gulf War of 1991 had several consequences. Saddam Hussein's military was badly defeated and the Kuwaiti royal family was restored to power. While Saddam was in no position to advance any economic or political interest of India, the V.P. Singh government's neutrality cost India the goodwill of Kuwait and the Gulf Arab countries. Saudi Arabia and other Gulf Arab states reduced employment opportunities for Indians and showed their displeasure by withholding investment and job contracts. It took decades for India to overcome this setback. For an administration that lasted less than a year, the V.P. Singh government cast a long shadow on Indian foreign policy, especially in the Gulf Arab region.

V.P. Singh's short-lived government was followed by one for eight months headed by Prime Minister Chandra Shekhar (November 1990–June 1991). Chandra Shekhar had been in politics a long time and had a good understanding of both domestic and global issues. Presiding over a weak coalition government, he still managed to make major decisions. One such decision was to allow refuelling facility to US aircraft during the Gulf War, which served as some mitigation for the V.P. Singh government's errors.

Chandra Shekhar was not an intellectual like Gujral with high-flying ideas. He was a hard-nosed politician who had knowledge of global issues thanks to long parliamentary experience. According to a former confidant of his, Chandra Shekhar was a quick decision maker who did not like to dither. For example, he decided to allow refuelling facilities to US aircraft in exercise of his executive authority without seeking a decision from the cabinet committee. Even after criticism, Chandra Shekhar stuck to his decision as he believed it was in India's interest to help a friendly country. Once he took the decision he was strong enough to stand up to any criticism by parliament and public opinion.[130] It helped that he knew he could not survive in office after another general election, which was forced by the instability of coalition politics in the summer of 1991.

The 1991 election might have yielded another hung parliament had it not been for the tragedy of Rajiv Gandhi's assassination during the course of the election campaign. A sympathy wave catapulted the Congress party to power and a veteran Congress politician from India's south, P.V. Narasimha Rao became India's next prime minister. Rao was a consummate insider who had served as minister for external affairs under both Indira and Rajiv Gandhi (1980–84 and 1988–89). Now he led as prime minister at a critical juncture in Indian politics as the first person outside the Nehru-Gandhi family to govern for a full five-year parliamentary term (1991–96).

Dixit refers to Rao 'as one of the most effective and creative influences' on Indian foreign policy.[131] Rao became prime minister at a time of domestic upheaval. Rajiv Gandhi had just been assassinated, the Congress party faced divisions in the absence of a towering figure or a scion of the Nehru-Gandhi family and domestic politics was unstable as new regional parties emerged as power brokers. Rao also had to contend with far-reaching changes in the global order marked by the end of the cold war, the coming down of the Berlin Wall and the disintegration of the Soviet Union.

Added to all this were India's economic troubles that reached a climax around the time that Rao took charge. The disintegration of the Soviet Union meant that India's main supplier of military equipment – Soviet Union – was in too much disarray to be able to help. The end of the cold war marked the unipolar moment with the United States as the world's sole superpower. After decades of criticizing the West and invoking non-alignment to seek benefits from two contending blocs, India now had to find a way to rebuild ties with Western nations, especially the United States.

In some ways, Rao had an opportunity similar to Nehru's, to define India's direction for years to come. He initiated policies that continued under his successors, irrespective of their political affiliations. According to Dixit, Rao provided 'the required equilibrium' that India's foreign policy needed in the post-cold-war era.[132] Economic reforms constituted a key component of Rao's strategy. Realizing the importance of economic reforms, Rao provided the political support for his finance minister, Manmohan Singh, to implement a series of market-friendly restructurings that helped India move away from its mixed socialistic economy towards a liberal free market.

As early as 1947 Nehru had stated that talk of security was futile without economic strength. However, his successors focused more on the non-economic levers of hard power. With a massive population, India could have attracted foreign direct investment with the promise of access to its large domestic market. It could have become globally influential as the destination and source of investment, as a trading nation and as an innovator in various fields of technology. Instead, India chose to be the voice of the world's poor while seeking economic self-sufficiency and a government-led economy. The reforms of 1991 finally forced Indian leaders to understand that unless they changed their economic model and focused on building India's economic prowess, India faced being marginalized and sidelined by global transformations.

One of the major foreign policy initiatives of the Rao government was its 'Look East' policy, an acknowledgement of the economic success of Japan, Korea and other East Asian countries. Rao professed that India needed to look not just towards the developed countries of the West but also needed to learn from its eastern neighbours while deepening economic and security ties with them. Until then India's relations with East Asia had been largely political, based on Nehru's vision of Asian brotherhood and shared history.

Even after East Asia's economic boom in the 1980s, there had been no real attempt to bolster those ties with a different emphasis. India had even turned down an offer of membership in ASEAN at the time it was formed, a mistake in view of the grouping's later success. Rao understood that there was little he could achieve with India's immediate neighbours, especially Pakistan, which had stepped up support for Islamist militants in Jammu and Kashmir. Sri Lanka was in turmoil with its escalating civil war while Nepal and Bangladesh faced internal crises. In such an environment, Rao decided to build a legacy by expanding India's ties with South-East Asia while adjusting to the new American-led world order in which Russia had a diminished presence compared to the one in past.

In addition to enhancing relations with bourgeoning economic powers of East Asia, Rao's government also boosted India's ties with the Arab countries of the Gulf that had been annoyed by the V.P. Singh government's attitude during the war over Kuwait. India's existing cultural and economic ties with the Gulf and the presence of a large Indian diaspora worked to India's advantage. Rao sought to secure energy supplies from the Gulf region, given the increasing energy needs of India's growing economy. He also sought to ensure that the Arab Gulf countries would continue to be an avenue for employment for India's large working-age population. Rao's big idea in India's external relations was to weave in economic needs into foreign policy priorities.

When Rao sought re-election in 1996, the Indian electorate rebuffed him and the Congress party. The right-of-centre Bharatiya Janata Party (BJP), led by Atal Bihari Vajpayee, emerged as a major force but did not secure a majority in parliament and failed to find coalition partners. India went through two elections and a succession of coalition governments in three years, with Haradanahalli Doddegowda Devegowda (June 1996–April 1997) and Inder Kumar Gujral (April 1997–March 1998) serving as prime ministers before Vajpayee could form a coalition government for thirteen months (March 1998–October 1999). In late 1999 Vajpayee won a full five-year term as prime minister at the head of the National Democratic Alliance (NDA), an alliance of political parties led by the BJP. India's foreign policy drifted under the unstable coalitions before Vajpayee restored order to the conduct of external relations.

Vajpayee had been external affairs minister in the 1977–79 Janata Party government. His world view had been shaped by the Hindu revivalist movement Rashtriya Swayamsevak Sangh (RSS) of which he had been a lifelong member. Vajpayee had been a parliamentarian for the Bharatiya Jana Sangh before the party evolved into the BJP. He was considered a moderate within the Hindu nationalist movement, having avoided association with some of the most hard-line stances and actions of his own allies, such as attacks on India's religious minorities. The BJP's foreign policy accepted some strands of Nehruvianism, especially the belief that India is a great civilization and that it has a role to play in the global arena as well as belief in economic independence. It differed from Nehruvianism in emphasizing pursuit of economic and military power, not just invoking India's moral or civilizational greatness.

Vajpayee came to power expressing a desire to rebuild ties with India's neighbours, improve ties with the United States, build on

India's Look East policy and push for building India's military and economic resources. His critics point out, however, that Vajpayee left decisions to a small group of advisers and lacked support of his own party (and the wider Hindu nationalist movement) on key policies. Former officials who worked with Vajpayee, including some of his confidants, say that his principal secretary and national security adviser, Brajesh Mishra, was virtually his main adviser and executor of foreign policy.

The task of articulating the BJP's foreign policy views to the world fell to Jaswant Singh, who served as Vajpayee's external affairs minister. In his book *Defending India* (1999), Singh outlined the core elements of this world view. To Vajpayee and Singh, the US was a friend rather than a threat, China was not a natural ally of India (unlike what Nehru believed till 1962) and India needed to build its economic and military power because that is what would make India acceptable by the world as a major power.[133] It was not surprising, therefore, that tests declaring India as a nuclear weapons power took place under a BJP government in 1998. An assertive India was able to improve relations with Pakistan, China and the United States even though India and Pakistan fought their fourth war, the Kargil conflict, in 1999.

After five years in office, Vajpayee and the BJP lost the 2004 parliamentary elections, paving the way for the return to office of the Congress party, this time at the head of a coalition government, the United Progressive Alliance (UPA). Manmohan Singh, the technocrat and reformist finance minister in the last Congress government, was chosen as prime minister and he remained in office for two successive terms, spanning the decade from 2004 to 2014. Singh was known as the architect of India's economic liberalization, leading to a lot of expectations, especially in further opening up of India's economy. He was hemmed in by the fact that the Congress party chief, Sonia Gandhi, and not the prime minister wielded real power. Sonia controlled the Congress party machine and Manmohan Singh had no popular political base. In the end, Sonia's views on the economy and on India's role in the world prevailed.

These were reminiscent of early Nehruvianism, wedded to Fabian socialism, suspicion of the West, and non-alignment.

Manmohan Singh laid out what Indian analyst, C. Raja Mohan, described as the Manmohan Singh doctrine in speeches at the *Hindustan Times* Leadership Initiative Conference on 5 November 2004 and at the *India Today* Conclave on 25 February 2005. According to this doctrine the 'single most important objective' of Indian foreign policy was to 'create a global environment conducive to her economic development and the well-being of the people of India'. India sought 'greater integration with the world economy' especially with those in Asia. India's ties with major powers would be shaped by economic factors and especially energy security. India championed greater regional cooperation and deeper physical connectivity within South Asia. Like his predecessors, Manmohan also saw India as an example to the world of a country that pursued economic growth and yet remained a plural, secular and liberal democracy. India also had a 'global responsibility to assist societies in transition'.[134]

Nehruvian idealism was visible when at an annual conference of Indian diplomats Manmohan Singh asserted, 'Foreign policy is not defined merely by our interests, but also by the values which are very dear to our people. India's experiment of pursuing economic development within the framework of a plural, secular and liberal democracy has inspired people around the world.'[135] For Manmohan, as for every prime minister before him, the key priority was ensuring that India secured the requisite space to grow economically and occupy its place under the sun. But after the pragmatic approaches of Narasimha Rao and Atal Bihari Vajpayee, India's new prime minister reverted to idealistic proclamations on certain issues as a substitute for hard-nosed policy choices.

Nehru had emphasized the importance of economic foreign policy but it was only from Rajiv Gandhi onwards that Indian leaders really focused on this issue. As prime minister, Manmohan Singh carried this view forward, especially in his first five-year term. He also spoke of the importance of India's neighbourhood, the need for building regional institutions and deepening economic ties and building connectivity between the various countries of South Asia. He was unable during his ten years in power to implement many of his policies in the region even though he put forth a number of suggestions.

Manmohan Singh's decade-long stint as prime minister was not distinguished by new ideas or successful foreign policy initiatives. One major step during that period was the conclusion of the US–India civil nuclear deal, negotiations over which were started in the Vajpayee years and concluded in 2005. The deal separated India's civil and military nuclear programmes, allowed purchase of nuclear material under IAEA safeguards by India for civilian purposes and opened the possibility of India's membership of the Nuclear Suppliers Group (NSG) without signing the Non-Proliferation Treaty (NPT). The Manmohan Singh government had to overcome considerable opposition from within the ranks of its left-leaning coalition to secure parliamentary approval of this major agreement.

A MODI ERA?

The 2014 election brought the BJP to office after ten years in opposition, with Narendra Modi as prime minister. Unlike Vajpayee, who owed his position solely to the party, Modi's personal popularity was a major factor in his party's electoral success. This gave him considerable leeway in defining his own foreign policy. The Modi doctrine, though still evolving, appears to have elements of both continuity and change with his predecessors. Despite the desire to be different from the Congress and Nehru, Modi's foreign policy still has much in common with Nehru's, though he envisions a more powerful India than its first prime minister.

Modi, like Nehru and several other prime ministers, has so far ensured that foreign and security policy is formulated in the Prime Minister's Office (PMO) and not in the foreign ministry. Modi has risen to the office of prime minister from heading the state government in Gujarat, without earlier serving in the Union cabinet.

He is an outsider to Delhi's bureaucracy and traditional power brokers in the mould of Rajiv Gandhi and Vajpayee. Reflecting his position as the key, perhaps only, decision maker, Modi has handpicked both his ministerial colleagues as well as the key civil servants working under him.

His right hand man from Gujarat, Amit Shah, was chosen to head the BJP as party president. Senior party leaders above a certain age were forced into retirement while other potential contenders to power within BJP were incorporated into the cabinet. Emulating Rajiv, Modi changed his foreign secretary in order to nominate a candidate, career diplomat Subrahmanyam Jaishankar, whom he identified as sharing his own world view. Like Vajpayee, he depends on his national security adviser, former intelligence officer Ajit Kumar Doval, for advice on both internal and external security.

Modi is in charge of his foreign policy and seems to understand the intrinsic link between economic growth and projection of power abroad. Unlike Nehru, he does not seek stature for India solely through speeches in international forums though he is not averse to that variety of international attention. He actively pursues economic partnerships and investment and wants international and Indian business to collaborate in expanding manufacturing in India. His first act of foreign policy took place even before he was sworn in as prime minister. In May 2014, he invited all South Asian heads of government to his inauguration.

South Asia, India's immediate periphery, will perhaps remain critical to every Indian prime minister and every Indian administration. In his first two years in office, Modi emphasized his regional focus by travelling to a number of India's immediate neighbours including Afghanistan, Bhutan, Nepal, Mauritius, Myanmar, Sri Lanka and Bangladesh. During his visit to Dhaka, India and Bangladesh signed a land border agreement which was first agreed to in 1958 between Nehru and then Pakistani premier Firoz Khan Noon.

Indian leaders have coveted improved relations with Pakistan as their potential legacy. Given the record of discord and acrimony between the two neighbours, the idea of making history by resolving that conflict appeals to Indian politicians. Modi too started his tenure by reaching out to Pakistan, hoping to write a new chapter in the troubled India–Pakistan relationship. In December 2015, he made a short stopover in Lahore on his way back from Kabul to Delhi to meet with Pakistan's prime minister Nawaz Sharif. In a symbolic moment, Modi was photographed holding Sharif's hand, amid much fanfare reminiscent of Vajpayee's 1999 bus trip to Lahore.

The bonhomie ended with a terrorist attack on a military base at Pathankot, near the Pakistan border, in January 2016. A second terrorist attack on the Indian base at Uri in Kashmir in September 2016, which India blamed on Pakistan-sponsored jihadi groups, resulted in Modi's decision to break off talks with Pakistan without its concrete commitment to end support for terrorism. The 2016 SAARC summit, scheduled to be held in Islamabad, was cancelled after India (along with Afghanistan, Bangladesh and Bhutan) announced its boycott. India hinted at its desire to internationally isolate Pakistan in an effort to force policy changes over the terrorism issue. Indian special forces conducted what experts termed a 'surgical strike' aimed at terrorist camps across the Line of Control (LoC) in Pakistan-occupied Kashmir. This is not the first time that India had targeted terror camps inside Pakistan but this was the first time that the Indian government publicly announced such strikes.

Notwithstanding the setback in ties with Pakistan, Modi managed to forge closer relations with most of India's traditional friends around the world while adding some more to the list of global partners. In his first thirty-one months in office, Modi has travelled to forty-five countries including the United States, Japan, China, Australia, France, Germany and Brazil. One of India's former national security advisers, Shivshankar Menon, referred to this as India 'speed dating' the global powers.[136] Singaporean diplomat and scholar Kishore Mahbubani postulates that Modi's world view is made up of genuine non-alignment, an emphasis on economic growth and the desire to rebuild ties in India's 'regional backyard'.[137] According to Mahbubani, Modi's 'genuine non-alignment' is reflected in India's good ties with and ability to secure economic investment and defence equipment from diverse countries like the United States, China, Japan, Israel, Iran, Germany, France and Russia. 'It takes great political and psychological confidence to maintain equally good relations with such sharply divided leaders,' Mahbubani observed'.[138]

French scholar Christophe Jaffrelot attributes Modi's passionate focus on foreign policy to his being a nationalist leader, just like Vajpayee. In Jaffrelot's view economic interests and South Asia are Modi's two key foreign policy priorities.[139] Like Mahbubani and Jaffrelot, Harsh Pant acknowledges that Modi has focused on strengthening ties with diverse powers like the United States, Japan and China as well as South Asian neighbours.[140] But Pant asserts that Modi seeks to dismantle non-alignment and move beyond 'ideological rhetoric' to real action. To that effect, Indian diplomats have been provided with a detailed strategic evaluation of how the Modi government sees India's place in the world and have also been encouraged to deepen and push India's economic interests.[141]

Modi's foreign policy activism in his first two years in office is reminiscent of Nehru's travels soon after India's independence. Nehru, like most Indians, believed that India shouldered a great responsibility by virtue of its size and its history. He spoke of 'the responsibility of the freedom of 400 million people of India, the responsibility of the leadership of a large part of Asia, the responsibility of being some kind of guide to vast numbers of people all over the world'. Nehru had no doubt that one day India would 'play a part on the world stage, even on the narrowest plane of material power, and I should like India to play that great part in that plane'.[142]

Over the years, Indian leaders have lived by Nehru's belief that 'India has the right to lead because of her heritage, and also because of her present, when, in the face of the complexity of her own problems, she has stood up and estimated values and not let go all those ideals which she had placed before her'.[143]

Nehru's personality and charisma ensured that the basic tenets of India's foreign policy remained unchanged for over five decades.[144] Now Modi hopes to build on his own popularity and charisma for a similar lasting legacy. Nehru's impact resulted in defining the underlying principle of India's foreign policy as a desire for independence of action and autonomy of decision making. The belief that India, a great civilization, will one day be a great power has meant that not only has India sought a seat at the global high table but has been unwilling to allow the big powers of the day to dictate to India.

4

Principles and Interests

A DAY BEFORE Independence, on 14 August 1947, the president of India's Constituent Assembly, Rajendra Prasad, declared that India had 'a great part to play in the shaping and moulding of the future of a war distracted world'. It could play that part, he said, 'not by mimicking, from a distance, what others are doing, or by joining in the race for armaments and competing with others in the discovery of the latest and most effective instruments of destruction'. As an independent country, India now had the opportunity and Prasad expressed the hope that it would have 'the courage and strength to place before the world' an 'infallible substitute for war and bloodshed, death and destruction'.[1] Prasad became the first president of the Republic of India, serving from 1949 to 1962. His independence-eve declaration reflected values that have resonated in India's interaction with the rest of the world.

In the view of most Indians, their fervent desire to safeguard independence and autonomy of decision making is the most significant principle underlying their country's foreign policy. The colonial experience has left an indelible mark on India's collective personality. More than six decades after Independence, seeking freedom from external pressures is as much at the core of India's external relations as it was when India was a colony. Territorial integrity and economic autarky, championing of anti-colonialism, aversion to military alliances and seeking a South Asia free from foreign influence are deemed critical to India. These, above everything else, are the defining elements of India's national interest.

The pursuit of an independent path has always been tied to moral certitude that India ought to be a beacon not only for Asia but also for the entire world. India's policies have generally been framed to build a world based on ideals of peace and international friendship. To create this idealized world, India championed non-alignment; encouraged multilateral cooperation through the United Nations and regional organizations; and supported decolonization and disarmament, including nuclear disarmament.

The importance that India attaches to its place in the world is an essential theme of the annual addresses delivered by the president of India to the joint session of India's parliament at the start of the budget session. The presidential address, modelled on the queen's address to parliament in Britain, gains greater relevance when it is the first speech soon after elections as it lays out the policies of the incoming administration

In his first address as president of the Constituent Assembly, Prasad had voiced hope that the world needed India and would welcome it, unless the world was 'prepared to reel back into barbarism from which it boasts to have emerged'. He assured all countries of the world on behalf of India that 'we propose to stick to our historic tradition to be on terms of friendship and amity with all, that we have no designs against anyone and hope that none will have any against us. We have only one ambition and desire, that is, to make our contribution to the building up of freedom for all and peace among mankind.'[2] To modern India's founding generation, these were not mere platitudes but a description of substantive policy ideas.

Following Prasad's precedent, every presidential address to the joint session of parliament reaffirms the aims of India's foreign policy as being 'peace and friendship in the world, non-alignment and the building of a just and equitable world order'. Starting with discussion of ties with neighbours in South Asia, these speeches progress outward to other parts of the world: Central Asia, China, East and South-East Asia, Middle East and the Gulf, Russia, Europe, the United States, Africa and Latin America.[3] Also, the head of state reminds members of India's parliament that independence in making decisions on foreign policy remains India's topmost priority in external relations.

STRATEGIC AUTONOMY

The emphasis on independence and strategic autonomy is a throwback to the struggle against British rule. During the Raj, Indians were kept out of decision making and the key demand of India's freedom struggle was the right for Indians to make decisions that affect their lives and their future. The Raj forced Indians to fight distant wars with which they had little to do. While Indians were involved in local government and administration, they had nothing to do with foreign policy, which remained firmly in the hands of colonial officers and administrators.

'What does independence consist of?' Nehru rhetorically asked the Constituent Assembly in March 1949. He then proceeded to reply, 'It consists fundamentally and basically of foreign relations. Once foreign relations go out of your hand into the charge of somebody else, to that extent and in that measure you are not independent.'[4] Thus, freedom was only possible if you could think freely for yourself while making decisions of war and peace and regarding friend or foe. India's founding elite was adamant that independent India would make its own decisions, even if it resulted in occasionally treading a somewhat lonely path. Standing alone at times or standing up to the dominant superpowers has been perceived as a badge of honour by India's leaders.

India's championing of non-alignment followed directly from this desire to make decisions without having to take directions from others. Non-alignment meant India did not need to consider someone a friend or enemy because of the friendship or hostility of a superpower. It also enabled India to safeguard its territorial unity by staying out of disputes it might be drawn into through alliances. Above all, non-alignment provided a platform from which India could attempt to lead other developing countries at a time when India lacked resources to be a superpower itself. Nehru argued that other countries would respect India only if it was not 'a camp follower'.

The expansion of India's economic and military capabilities, coupled with the end of the cold war and the blocs it spawned, have diminished the need for India to emphasize non-alignment and to seek leadership through rhetorical moralizing. The pursuit of strategic autonomy, however, persists and has become the reason for a diverse foreign policy that enables India to deal with the world's major issues without being tied down to a single great power or set of powers.

In a recent article, Itty Abraham, disagrees with the view that non-alignment was the rational outcome of a calculated policy. According to Abraham, the Non-Aligned Movement (NAM) did not emerge 'fully blown from the collective minds of Nehru, Nasser and Tito in Brioni in 1956'.[5] Abraham asserts that NAM was rather the 'outcome of a sophisticated analysis of world order as well as the difficult political choices facing a leadership that was very much on the defensive in contemporary regional affairs during the late 1950s and early 1960s'.[6] Worried about global conflict arising from the two blocs, non-alignment was seen as the buffer that would reduce friction and allow peaceful outcomes.

Often critiqued for adopting a moralistic or preachy foreign policy, this policy actually served key goals: India sought leadership of Asia and believed it was a future great power but it lacked the resources to achieve this goal through military or economic means. As Werner Levi states: 'For a nation with few effective means and little spare energy to influence international events, the idea of making a virtue of staying out of international troubles is practical and wise.'[7] Following a principle-based moralistic foreign policy helped India project itself as a leader of fellow developing former colonies, and helped India punch above its weight. It also tied in to India's goals of decolonization, anti-racialism and disarmament.

While non-alignment fulfilled a moral dimension of India's policy it did not provide India with the critical support needed when faced with war and conflict. During the 1962 India–China war, the non-aligned countries remained non-aligned and it was the West that really supported India, both with economic and military resources. As Mansingh states, the Non-Aligned Movement ended up becoming 'an aggregation of states with disparate interests' that had nothing in common except that they were former colonies. This led to a 'dynamics of group behaviour' that was not always in tune with India's needs and interests.[8] While Indian leaders sought global peace and nuclear disarmament, other countries had their own set of problems.

Non-alignment also clashed with the reality of living in a world where a country could only defend itself with economic and military power. India's policy of non-alignment posed problems in achieving these goals. Non-alignment was more anti-Western capitalism and imperialism than it was against Soviet communism. Some analysts ascribe that to Nehru's sympathy towards Soviet socialism and scepticism and cynicism towards American capitalism. Others blame America's pro-Pakistan policy and Soviet support especially their veto on the Kashmir issue in the Security Council. The balancing act sought was how to receive economic and military aid from both blocs while not becoming too dependent on either.

With the end of the cold war and the break-up of the Soviet Union, India has built closer ties with the United States. Russia no longer occupies the position it did. Still the Indian elite remains suspicious and sceptical of American intentions. Knee-jerk criticism of American foreign policy and the desire to maintain autonomy often lead to a reluctance to describe India as an American ally, preferring to use the phrase 'strategic partner'.

Even today, when the world is no longer aligned the way it was during the cold war, India still remains a prominent member of the Non-Aligned Movement (NAM) and often uses that platform to demonstrate its independence from great powers. The anomaly led former Indian prime minister Inder Kumar Gujral to remark, 'It is a mantra that we have to keep repeating, but who are you going to be non-aligned against?'[9]

Over the years, the desire for decision-making autonomy that led to non-alignment has tied into the concomitant goal of ensuring India's territorial integrity and unity. As a country that was colonized piecemeal by a distant power that initially sought trading privileges, India has been vigilant about safeguarding its territory against foreign encroachment. The legacy of Partition reinforced the need for unity and cohesion lest the country be again divided in the name of religion or ethnicity. Independent India has consistently sought an international environment that would guarantee its independence, safeguard its territory, help build its economy, bolster its military resources and ensure domestic stability and social cohesion. A peaceful and stable global environment is seen as the precondition for India's development and evolution in pursuit of its historic place under the sun.

India's decision to stay away from military alliances and follow a path of non-alignment stems from the view that this path would ensure independence in decision making. While other newly independent countries opted to seek benefits of alignment with one or the other superpower, India chose to stay out of the cold war. India did not have the resources to participate in such a conflict, did not consider the inducements of aid and weapons offered by the superpowers as worth their price and feared that cold war alignment could tear its fragile nation apart.

India's policy on nuclear weapons was also framed by the desire to be independent, to be unique and to ensure full strategic space. Nehru championed disarmament – conventional and nuclear – and yet understood the benefits of nuclear energy as well as the wherewithal for a future nuclear weapons programme. His successors Indira and Rajiv continued with his policies and in 1974 India conducted her first tests. Despite international pressure, India continued to build its nuclear weapons programme independently and was ready to test by the early 1990s. For India, nuclear weapons represented a combination of prestige, security and capability. For India, nuclear disarmament is the ideal but as long as other powers possess nukes, India must maintain a nuclear arsenal too. At the same time, there has always been the view that India would disarm as part of global disarmament as India does not need weapons of mass destruction to bully or threaten other nations.

India's desire for economic autarky and self-sufficiency also has its roots in the almost zealous guarding of independence. The dominant streak among Indian policymakers and public has tended towards protectionism. While India as a developing country has always needed both foreign aid and foreign capital, it has never been comfortable with either. The fear of foreign capital and malevolence of foreigners goes back to colonial rule and the manner in which the East India Company transformed trade and investment into occupation.

The desire for self-sufficiency has also extended to the military arena, where India has sought to not only maintain large professional armed forces but also to equip them with weapons that can be manufactured at home. Nehru embraced the ideas of the German philosopher Kant and the internationalism associated with former US president Woodrow Wilson, but the Indian state veers towards a Hobbesian view of the world wherein India has to depend solely on itself.

Concerns about India's territorial unity and integrity have led India to try and build indigenous military capability instead of simply buying weapons off the shelf, which would make it dependent on other countries. The effort to indigenize weapons manufacturing has not been sufficiently successful to foreclose the option of massive purchases on the global market and India remains one of the world's top importers of military equipment and arms. Until recently, the Indian government was reluctant to allow even Indian corporations to enter the defence sector and preferred to rely exclusively on public sector enterprises. The private sector has now been invited into the field of defence production because state-owned manufacturers have not reached the production levels of their Chinese counterparts.

The 'Make in India' initiative of the Modi government carries forward the legacy of building an Indian defence capacity. The initiative expects that foreign firms will be willing to share their technology in return for access to the Indian market. The assumption is still that the size of the Indian market compensates for bureaucratic hurdles and other inconveniences that serve as a disincentive. The focus still remains on manufacturing locally rather than importing India's defence needs. In this case, the security imperative has been merged with economic nationalism as a principle of external relations.

INDIAN EXCEPTIONALISM

Many Indians see the role of Indian foreign policy as being a set of measures designed to safeguard Indian nationalism. The desire to find India's place in the sun, to project India as an example or guide to others, and the belief that as one of the oldest civilizations India was a future great power can all be traced back to the influence of nationalism. The moralistic dimension to India's foreign policy can also be traced back to the deeply high-minded and value-based independence movement, which was influenced by the views of the leader of the national struggle, Mahatma Gandhi, who is acknowledged as the father of the modern Indian nation.

These views are clearly visible in the Constituent Assembly of India debates from the first two years after Independence. Leaders like Purushottam Das Tandon, Sri Krishna Sinha, Vijaya Lakshmi Pandit and Algurai Shastri championed it to the notion that India would one day lead Asia and that India owed it to the world to work for global peace and prosperity.[10] In Nehru's words India had the 'responsibility of being some kind of guide to vast numbers of people all over the world'.[11]

Even Nehru's main rival as leader of the Congress during the 1930s, Subhas Chandra Bose, held views similar to Nehru with respect to India's role in Asia and its critical geographic location. For Bose, as for Nehru, it was the time for Asia to 'throw off the yoke of thralldom' and 'take her legitimate place in the comity of free nations'. Bose firmly believed that India had 'a mission to fulfil and it is because of this that India still lives'.[12]

The first and only Indian Governor General of independent India, C. Rajagopalachari, spoke about global citizenship and the mission that lay ahead for all Indian citizens. 'Not only the Prime Minister and I, but every enlightened citizen of India must now rise to the full height not only of national citizenship but of world citizenship,' he declared. According to Rajagopalachari, 'The world is watching India with goodwill. Our culture, our philosophy and our outlook on life have a new meaning and a new hope for the nations that have suffered and are suffering in the West. ... Being citizens of a free country we should now realize our mission as a nation and our place in world civilization. We must fulfil the obligations that arise out of our place in Asia and our long and intimate connection with the West.'[13]

It seems that a deep-rooted inheritance of India's long civilizational past is the belief that India's civilizational greatness trumps the current status of the Indian state. As a civilization, India historically possessed hard (military and economic) as well as soft (religious and cultural) power not just in its region but also in Asia and beyond. The Indian belief that historical greatness is manifest destiny persisted even during British colonial rule when Indians were subordinate subjects of a faraway sovereign. Despite being a developing country with limited economic and military potential at Independence in 1947, Indian leaders projected themselves as the inheritors of a great civilization and the trailblazers of a future big power. In his presidential address to the parliament in 1999, then president K.R. Narayanan restated something that has been said and resaid several times since the departure of the British. India, he announced, will secure 'a place, role, and position in the global arena, commensurate with its size and importance'.[14]

Under the influence of the founding fathers like Mahatma Gandhi and Jawaharlal Nehru, the average Indian has also believed that India was special, is special and will remain special. This 'Indian exceptionalism' – the term used by several public figures – rested on the faith that there was something unique about India, which enabled it to gain independence without violence, revolution or war. Other aspects of the same conviction are that

India is special because it is the land of Gandhi and Nehru or that India's ability to subsume various cultures under the rubric of Indian tolerance makes it unique. Indian discourse often speaks of an 'Indian character' that will overcome odds and circumvent difficulties. In the words of a former Indian president, 'The vision of a mighty India will be realized only in the actual lives of men and women who have strength of character.'[15]

'India stands tall as a nation because we are seen as a liberal and plural democracy, which has faced and overcome tremendous odds,' declared the current president, Pranab Mukherjee, in his presidential address of February 2013. According to him, 'The world recognizes India's demonstrable democratic and secular practices as a major achievement. While we should rejoice in the benefits that our plurality brings, the challenge is to relentlessly pursue our efforts to accelerate economic growth and widen opportunities within our democratic framework. It is only if we constantly renew and defend the democratic values that define our nationhood that we will be able to face the great challenges that lie before us.'[16]

Such pronouncements are not just the 'feel good' avowals of leaders trying to rally their people. In India's case, they reflect a deep-seated way of thinking almost identical to the messianic vision of the United States. It has repeatedly manifested itself in India's policies.

As India has become more globally connected and integrated, Indian exceptionalism has not diminished. In fact, it even lives on among the vast Indian diaspora, including second and third-generation non-resident Indians (i.e. immigrants to other countries). Conversations and interviews with politicians, civil servants, scholars and diplomats over the last decade reflect a continuing sense of destiny and sense of India's specialness. Like others who believe in national uniqueness and manifest destiny, Indians tend to stick to what they see as their principles and not give up on them as part of a compromise. An Indian diplomat remarked to this author in an interview that India needed to do things not simply because they were beneficial to India but because it was the right thing to do. Thus, compromises for self-interest are often looked down upon, and when they are made, a veneer of high-minded principle is maintained.

While India aspires for global great power status, in its immediate neighbourhood it already considers itself one. India's immediate neighbourhood – South Asia – is India's backyard where it does not like the interference of other major powers. The greater neighbourhood, extending from the Gulf to South-East Asia, is also part of India's sphere of influence, and developments in the region are deemed critical to India's foreign and security policy. As President Pranab Mukherjee observed in his annual address to the joint session of parliament in 2013, India seeks 'peace, stability, cooperation and economic development' in South Asia and attaches 'the highest priority to relations with our immediate neighbours'.[17]

The South Asian region has always received the greatest attention from the makers of Indian foreign policy. At Independence, India inherited borders or imperial fault lines that have impacted ties with all its neighbours. India is the largest and most populous country in South Asia, with the largest economy and the biggest armed forces. This threatens some neighbours and overwhelms others. India is also the only country in the region that shares land or sea borders with other member states of the South Asian Association for Regional Cooperation (SAARC), with the exception of Afghanistan.

India is sometimes described as the region's 'big brother' with whom several neighbours have border disagreements. Some of India's neighbouring states were once part of an Indian Empire while others emerged as separate kingdoms within a vast Indian civilization. India is the geographical, sociocultural and economic centre of South Asia and, in the words of former diplomat S.D. Muni, India's centricity in the region is because 'there is a bit of India in every other country of South Asia'.[18]As is often the case involving smaller neighbours of a large country, it is easy to fuel resentment or fear of domination among India's neighbours.

Concerns of neighbours notwithstanding, India has not pursued a hegemonic or expansionist policy under any government or leader. Some leaders have sought unequivocal peace with neighbours (e.g. the Gujral doctrine) while others have sought amity based on reciprocity or quid pro quo (e.g. the Indira doctrine). None, however, have sought to take over neighbours' territory. That has not deterred India's neighbours from viewing India as hegemonic or imperialist. Over time, such views have diminished among most of India's neighbours with the exception of Pakistan, which continues to suspect India of wanting to dominate South Asia. Islamist ideologues in Pakistan go so far as to allege that India's real ambition is to recreate a Brahmin empire across the subcontinent.

Ironically, it is not the ancient Hindu empires that inspire India's view of its immediate neighbourhood. Modern India's perception of its environs originates from the days of the British Raj. Different Indian leaders have seen the region stretching from the Gulf to South-East Asia as important to India, just as the officials of the Raj saw it, albeit with a different focus. For the British, India was the nucleus of an overseas empire, a base from which they could rule, control and defend lands distant from the British homeland.

After Independence, Nehru focused on Asia where he sought to act as leader of a vast continent that was just emerging from Western colonial rule. He did not think in security terms, at least until the war with China in 1962. In Nehru's view, bilateral treaties of friendship and peace with the three northern Himalayan kingdoms – Bhutan, Nepal and Sikkim – and an offer of a no-war pact to Pakistan[19] was enough to deal with South Asia, freeing him to seek prominence on the Asian and global stage.

The notion of the subcontinent as India's backyard attained centrality under Indira Gandhi. Under her leadership, India's goal in its immediate vicinity was no longer simply to protect India's security and strategic interests; India would henceforth also be interested in any incidents in the neighbourhood that had or could have an impact on India. The Indira doctrine was a South Asian version of America's well known Monroe doctrine. As writer Ashok Kapur states, Indian leaders, beginning with Indira, wanted India to be 'the only security manager in South Asia' and sought to reduce the role of external actors – primarily the United States and the Soviet Union – and their ability to influence regional politics 'to a level of economic and technological assistance that would not encourage Pakistan to pursue its irredentist claims.'[20] India was not always able to achieve this policy as Pakistan continually sought parity with its larger neighbour, drawing the United States into the region as its ally.[21]

Under Indira, India sought acknowledgement as South Asia's pre-eminent power, was willing to flex its muscle to assert its pre-eminence and did not want outside powers to involve themselves in the region's affairs without India's approval. The Indira doctrine manifested itself most prominently when, in 1971, India protested against the suppression of democracy in East Pakistan and went to war to prevent the genocide of Bengalis by the Pakistan Army. After assisting in the birth of Bangladesh, Indira withdrew Indian troops from erstwhile East Pakistan to show that India's assertion of power did not amount to coveting other people's territory.

India's desire to be the only major power in South Asia has not always been successful, partly because India could not step in with economic assistance or military hardware whenever its neighbours needed them. Managing a sphere of influence is not only a function of telling others what to do but being able to expend resources that deny space to competitors. Even Bangladesh, which attained independence with India's help, eventually had to turn to the United States and China for economic support because India alone could not bear the cost of its development. India's attempts in recent years to keep China's influence out of its periphery have not succeeded for similar reasons.

More recently, India has tried to use economic diplomacy to build better ties with its neighbours. It has offered trade concessions, such as zero tariff or removing non-tariff barriers, and concessional loans and credit to Afghanistan, Bangladesh, Sri Lanka and Nepal, primarily with geopolitical motives. Such initiatives have become possible because of India's economic growth. Any loss that India incurs in trade, lending or investment is deemed bearable as long as it leads India's neighbours to uphold India's security interests.

AUTARKY AND MULTILATERALISM

India's economic expansion has enabled India to deploy economic tools in managing national security and maintaining international influence. Major nations now look at India as a trading partner, destination or source of investment and as a market for their own products. It was not, however, always the case that India could use economic clout in the conduct of foreign policy.

For years, India's leaders and Indian governments did not accord economic foreign policy the same priority as security policy. The Indian Foreign Service, in its training and functions, traditionally treated economic matters as falling outside their essential role. Trade and commerce was a subject for consular officials, not for India's diplomats. As early as 1947, an Economic Affairs Division was created in the Ministry of External Affairs only to be abolished in 1950. Later, in 1961, that division was revived as the Economic and Coordination Division under a Joint Secretary.[22]

This reluctance to undertake economic diplomacy led to an interesting phenomenon in India's economic foreign policy: the role of business organizations like the Federation of Indian Chambers of Commerce and Industry (FICCI), the Associated Chambers of Commerce of India (ASSOCHAM) and the Confederation of Indian Industry (CII). Even before Independence, business groups started playing a critical role in India's external relations insofar as economic matters were concerned. Over the years, both diplomats and economic specialists have had to deal with economic issues, including trade with other countries, aid that India receives, foreign investment, relations with international economic institutions like the IMF, World Bank and Asian Development Bank, and finally with aid that India has started providing other developing countries.

India has also taken its time in figuring out its place in the global economy. Nehru and Indira spoke of changing the global economic order but through diplomatic means and through participation in organizations like the Non-Aligned Movement and the United Nations. Instead of building India's economic muscle under the existing rules of the game, they hoped that India could lead other poorer nations in demanding changes to the structure of the global economy. This, in turn, was supposed to raise India's weight in world affairs and also strengthen its economy. It is only from Rajiv Gandhi onwards that Indian leaders truly understood the dynamics of global economics. India's leaders now are well aware of the rise of China – which has built its international stature by enhancing its economic power.

According to Mansingh, India tried initially to achieve economic self-reliance by seeking three goals: concessional development assistance, diversification of trading partners and changing the international economic order.[23] The first would help India follow its own independent policies without being accountable to others. This tied into both non-alignment as well as the desire to avoid being part of any system or bloc. India sought aid from international organizations like the World Bank, International Monetary Fund (IMF) and even from the Aid India Consortium, viewing them as multilateral donors offering assistance with no strings attached.

By having several trading partners, India wanted to make sure that it had its eggs in many baskets and was not dependent on just one buyer or supplier. The belief that the international system was skewed in favour of the superpowers and discriminated against developing countries like India led to the desire to change the world order. India has frequently called for a new international economic order, for reform of the IMF and the World Bank and even for reform of the UN Security Council.

The Nehruvian approach to economics as well as economic diplomacy did not serve India well. Sumit Ganguly and Manjeet Pardesi point out that, 'The failure to develop ties with the global economy contributed to a paucity of foreign investment, important technological lags, a lack of innovation, and the stifling of entrepreneurship. In turn, these forces contributed to what the eminent Indian economist Raj Krishna mordantly referred to as the "Hindu rate of growth".'[24]

Immediately after Independence, the emphasis on economic autarky or self-sufficiency made it a concern of domestic, not foreign, policy. Self-reliance was seen as critical to ensuring India's independence and even now the fear of the East India Company's legacy is so deep-rooted that most Indian leaders would rather India not be dependent on any country. This desire has always conflicted with reality. India does not produce everything it needs and is one of the leading importers of oil and gas and defence equipment. According to data compiled by the US Energy Information Administration (EIA), India imports approximately 4.3 million barrels of crude oil per day and by 2040 it will need ten million barrels of oil per day.[25] According to data on international arms transfers published by Stockholm International Peace Research Institute (SIPRI), between 2010 and 2014 India accounted for 15 per cent of the volume of global arms imports, more than three times as much as China. This was up from the period between 2005 and 2009 when India accounted for 7 per cent of global arms imports.[26] India also requires large doses of foreign investment and access to the latest foreign technologies.

India resolved its dilemma of wanting autarky while needing external support with sometimes contradictory policies and even hypocritical practices. For example, foreign aid and investment are described as impinging on India's independence but that has not prevented successive governments from accepting both. In effect, self-sufficiency has been the aspiration even as pragmatic compromise has led Indians to get what they can from whatever source will let them have it. In the policy realm, the aspiration finds reflection in programmes such as 'import substitution' that India adopted in its initial years and the 'Make in India' slogan of India's current prime minister, Narendra Modi. In practice, however, exceptions and adjustments rule the roost and India has neither closed itself from the global economy nor refused to let principle come in the way of its immediate needs.

A major example of practicality in India's economic approach lies in the adjustments made over time to the country's agriculture policy. During the 1950s and 1960s India's wheat production was insufficient to meet domestic demand. India accepted US wheat under the PL-480 program, which allowed India to pay for wheat in local currency. The arrangement was useful because India had limited foreign exchange availability and wheat purchases would have depleted these further. US president Lyndon Johnson decided to slow shipments of wheat to India under PL-480 in what he regarded as an effort to end Indian complacency about improving wheat yields. The US would release wheat shipments only at the last minute in what came to be known as the 'ship to mouth' scheme.

Even though Johnson's intent was to force a positive change in Indian policy, India under Indira saw it as undue pressure. India started importing wheat from Mexico, considering purchase from a fellow developing country as preferable to an overbearing superpower's aid. India eventually improved its wheat yields, albeit with US assistance in the form of high-yielding variety of seeds and other technical inputs. That goal, however, was achieved only after a mix and match of approaches that included pursuit of autarky through external assistance. More recently, the controversy in India over the use of genetically modified (GM) foods has more to do with the desire not to be dependent on foreign seeds and to produce home-grown food.

Another example of India's aspiration for self-sufficiency can be found in the constant tension between India and the World Trade Organization (WTO) over trade issues. When India first joined the WTO, it sought an exception under the Trade Related Intellectual Property Rights (TRIPs) rules. Western countries granted 'product patents' on new inventions, which precluded the manufacture of a patented product by whatever means without permission of the patent holder. India, since 1970, started granting 'process patents', that allowed another inventor or manufacturer to make an already patented product as long as it was created by a novel process. The 'process patent' only recognized the uniqueness of the process of manufacturing, not the uniqueness of the end product. 'In pharmaceuticals,' the *New York Times* said of India's rules, 'that has meant that a tiny tweak in the synthesis of a molecule yields a new patent. Several companies can produce the same drug, creating competition that drives down prices.' According to the newspaper, India's colonial era patent laws had resulted in some of the world's highest drug prices whereas process patents on drugs, fertilizers and pesticides helped extend life expectancy and ended regular famines. In Africa, for example, Indian-made drugs helped drive the annual price of antiretroviral treatment needed for AIDS patients down from $15,000 per patient to about $200.[27]

By insisting on an exception to WTO rules on Intellectual Property Rights, India was able to build a successful pharmaceutical industry that manufactured drugs patented in the West using a different process than the patent holder. Once the Indian pharmaceutical industry was able to benefit from having both process and product patents, India changed its position. It now recognizes the WTO's patent rules, after having fought for distinction between product and process patent for years.

A similar economic nationalism can be seen in India's stance at the Doha round of WTO trade negotiations, where India seeks an exception for agricultural subsidies and policies regarding government storage, pricing and distribution of foodgrains. Behind India's difficult bargaining at WTO lies the belief that India is different, unique and sufficiently important for the rest of the world to accept its demands for exceptions. India's stubborn insistence on being granted an exception at every international venue creates the risk of India being left out of global trade arrangements in addition to the potential for countries like the United States simply walking away from international negotiations held up by India. A better policy for India might be based on give and take to ensure inclusion alongside the US and Europe, something that India appears to have done in relation to the UN Framework Convention on Climate

Change (UNFCC), by signing it to coincide with Mahatma Gandhi's Birthday on 2 October 2016.

Although self-reliance and self-sufficiency still remain a major theme in Indian national discourse, the country is much better integrated with the global economy now than at any time since Independence. India's ties with the Gulf, with South-East Asia, with Europe, with the United States and even with China now have a strong economic dimension. Economic growth has become a key national priority for India's government. Every prime minister over the last two decades has stated that India must maintain a growth rate of 8–10 per cent and foreign policy is expected to help India achieve this goal. When India's growth rate fell down to below 4 per cent between 2009 and 2013, it impacted India not just domestically but also affected its status and negotiating ability abroad.

While India seeks exceptions, especially in the economic arena, it has always supported the idea of creating global norms through multilateral institutions. Critics see a dichotomy in India's almost zealous insistence on absolute autonomy while simultaneously championing multilateral institutions. Indians, however, would argue that India fully supports multilateralism but seeks to keep in check the prospect of global institutions becoming instruments of renewed dominance by major powers. A global order that allows international organizations to simply echo the desires of Western powers would be too reminiscent of the colonial era. In some ways India and the US have a similar perspective: both want to be part of multilateral organizations but prefer bilateral or regional agreements. While both countries support and subscribe to numerous multilateral institutions neither would like their participation in these institutions to impinge on their autonomous decision-making abilities.

As a champion of cooperation between sovereign nations, India has sought membership of almost every major global and regional organization possible. It has sought to play an active role in all these groupings, seeking to advance not only its own interests but also to voice the collective interests of developing nations. India sees itself as an example for other poor and formerly colonized countries, primarily in Asia, but increasingly all over the world. India was one of the founding members of the United Nations, in 1945, even before Independence and played a critical role throughout the era of decolonization.

In recent years, Indian activism in the UN has focused on seeking change in the composition of the Security Council to reflect contemporary global power realities. At the time of the UN's creation, it might have made sense to give a veto to only five major powers. The United States, the Soviet Union, Britain, France and China were allies during the Second World War and, having defeated the Axis powers, were expected to be the key arbiters of global security. Much has changed since that time, however. Russia no longer wields power similar to that of the Soviet Union while Britain and France have diminished in stature. India along with Brazil, Germany and Japan is part of the group of four nations (G-4) that see themselves as worthy of permanent membership in an expanded Security Council.

Apart from demanding reform of the Security Council, India is currently also one of the major contributors of troops for UN peacekeeping missions around the world. India prefers not to station its forces outside its territory except as part of a UN peacekeeping force. Over the decades around 180,000 Indian troops have served as UN peacekeepers. India has participated in forty-four of the sixty-nine UN peacekeeping missions mandated by the UN and 156 Indian peacekeepers have been killed while serving the United Nations.[28]

A similar activism characterizes India's role in global financial institutions. India has been a member of International Bank for Reconstruction and Development (IBRD), known as the World Bank, since its creation in 1945. One of the twenty-five executive directors on the World Bank board is from India. For years, India was among the World Bank's leading borrowers, utilizing loans for infrastructure development such as construction of dams and canals or for poverty alleviation programmes. Since 2006, India has also contributed financing for projects in other parts of the world. India's direct lending through the World Bank stands at $10.5 billion.[29]

India's membership of the International Monetary Fund (IMF) also dates back to its inception. India has drawn on IMF funds on three occasions, once in the 1980s and twice in the 1990s to address balance of payments problems.[30] India has drawn more on technical assistance from IMF than seeking actual financial assistance. This has included training of Indian officials in monetary policy and tax administration, assistance in foreign exchange market reform as well as in tax and customs administration. Mirroring its stand in the United Nations, India has also sought reform of the IMF quota system so that developing countries – like India – have a greater voice in the IMF.

More recently, India has supported two new financial institutional arrangements – the New Development Bank (also referred to as the BRICS Bank) and the Asian Infrastructure Investment Bank (AIIB). India is a founding member of both institutions. The BRICS Bank was announced in 2013 as a bank that would provide investment for infrastructure development in BRICS and other developing countries. The bank is to be headquartered in Shanghai with an Indian, K.V. Kamath, as the first chief executive.[31] India has also shown interest in the concept of an Asian Infrastructure Investment Bank with around fifty-seven or so founding members including Turkey, Australia, Austria, Israel, Portugal, France, Germany, South Korea and the United Kingdom. For India, inclusion in global financial bodies is a way to demonstrate India's place under the sun in addition to securing economic benefits.[32]

Although deeply involved in international financial institutions (IFIs), Indians are wary of the potential for political and strategic factors influencing their decisions. For example, the Asian Development Bank (ADB), under Chinese pressure, has turned down Indian requests in the past for financing of projects in Arunachal Pradesh, the Indian state that China claims as its territory. India has sought a greater voice for itself and other developing nations in the

Bretton Woods system while also helping to lay the foundations of new institutions like BRICS Bank and AIIB where the developing world might have greater say.

India's position in multilateral institutions, from the United Nations and its specialized agencies to the IFIs, has been consistent since India's independence. India supports multilateralism but it also seeks to reform global agencies, which it feels are influenced heavily by the world's major powers. Seeing itself as a future major power, India has positioned itself as the voice of equity in international bodies, demanding that more powerful nations voluntarily cede some of their power for the sake of greater fairness in international affairs.

GLOBAL DIASPORA, GLOBAL INTERESTS

Part of seeing India as a future great power has been the gradual recognition that India's interests are not limited to its immediate geographic vicinity but are spread all over the globe. India's vast diaspora, from Africa and the Americas to Fiji and Australia, is now considered an asset in exercise of global influence though, unlike some other countries, it is only in recent years that the Indian government has strengthened ties with and tapped into the potential of Indian communities spread all over the world.

Interestingly, the Indian National Congress had passed a resolution as early as 1925 to set up a foreign department that would 'look after the interests of Indians abroad and to carry on educative propaganda in the country regarding their position in the British Empire and foreign countries'.[33] In 1940, the Congress created an Indians Overseas Department.

The view championed by the leaders of the Congress in the early twentieth century with respect to the Indian diaspora was: 'make Burma thine home', 'make Ceylon thine home' and 'make Malaya thine home'.[34] As explained by a former foreign secretary, 'Gandhi and Nehru and the Congress did not want the overseas Indian to want or claim the best of both worlds. If you lived in Burma, treat Burma as your home, live and move and have your being in Burma, do not cast covetous eyes on India, not all the time. Your loyalties were to be towards the country of your adoption. When the Congress came into power in 1946–47 the entire outlook on overseas Indians was based on this theoretical viewpoint.'[35]

Before championing the Indian independence struggle, Mahatma Gandhi fought for the rights of Indians and other immigrants in South Africa. It is interesting that he fought for their rights to be treated as South African subjects of the British Crown, not as Indian citizens.[36] Both Gandhi and Nehru believed that once someone left their country and based themselves in another homeland, they should be expected to integrate themselves with their adopted country. An Indian living abroad would remain Indian in a cultural and civilizational sense but he or she was now the responsibility of their new country, not of India.

Nehru voiced that view whenever the issue of the Indian diaspora was raised in the Constituent Assembly right after Independence, resulting in discussions on Indians in South Africa, Burma and Sri Lanka. In his speeches, Nehru praised those who went abroad as merchants, traders, workers, indentured labourers and students, worked hard and managed to do well in life. 'They worked hard for themselves, and for the country of their adoption. They made good themselves and the country they had gone to also profited. It is a romance and it is something which India can be proud of.'[37]

The first prime minister of India recognized the perils of xenophobia in many of the countries to which Indians had emigrated. 'India is a country which in spite of everything has abounding vitality and spreads abroad,' he said. 'We tend to overwhelm others both by virtue of our numbers, and sometimes by virtue of the economic position we might develop there. That naturally frightens others who may not have that vitality in them and they want to protect themselves against it.'[38] While asserting that the Indian government wished to protect the interests of Indians abroad, the principled Nehru asserted 'we cannot protect any vested interest which injure the cause of the country they are in'.[39]

During the Constituent Assembly debates, when the issue of citizenship was discussed with respect to the Indian diaspora, Nehru remarked that only those could be offered citizenship who chose to be exclusively Indian citizens. If they chose another citizenship, he said, 'our interest in them becomes cultural and humanitarian, not political'. Nehru argued against dual citizenship for overseas Indians, telling the Constituent Assembly that it could not treat them as Indians while also demanding complete franchise for them in the countries where they lived. 'Of course, the two things do not go together,' he observed, adding, 'Either they get franchise as nationals of the other country, or you treat them as Indians minus the franchise and ask for them the most favoured treatment given to an alien.'[40]

This view resulted in India's decision to not offer the option of dual citizenship even though it is widely practised by many countries. In recent years, India has offered a lifelong visa and access to their country of origin for Indians settled abroad, giving them an identification card as an overseas Indian or a person of Indian origin (PIO) though they are not given an Indian passport and cannot vote in India though they may own property there.

Over the years the Indian diaspora has grown, especially in the Gulf, the United Kingdom and North America. The NRIs serve as a source of economic benefits to India, providing employment to a large number of Indians and making India one of the top recipients of remittances. New Delhi took time to grasp the enormous economic, strategic and diplomatic benefit of having a large and generally prosperous diaspora. Now, however, the Indian government views the diaspora as an extension of India's influence abroad and an additional source of prestige. A separate Union ministry dealing with non-resident Indian affairs was set up early in the first decade of the next century. The first conference for overseas Indians (Pravasi Bharatiya) sponsored by the Government of India was held in 2003 during which ten eminent persons of Indian origin were officially honoured. The idea of giving some form of dual citizenship – overseas Indian citizenship – is also of recent origin.[41]

These days, foreign citizens of Indian origin play an active role in determining policy towards India in countries such as the United States, the United Kingdom, Australia and Canada. Indians were always described as global ambassadors and were asked to uphold India's name and honour internationally. Nehru once remarked, 'If you cannot be, and if you are not, friendly to the people of that country, come back to India and do not spoil the fair name of India.'[42] It is unlikely that he envisaged a time when Canada's federal cabinet would have six members of Indian origin, including the defence minister, as happened after the 2015 election that resulted in Justin Trudeau becoming prime minister. At the same time, both Canada and the United States had persons of Indian origin as ambassadors to India.

In 1947, there were 3,410,215 persons of Indian origin in the British dominion and colonies: 700,000 in Burma, 700,000 in Ceylon, 700,000 in Malaya, 282,400 in South Africa, 184,100 in British East Africa, 271,640 in Mauritius (64 per cent of population), 125,675 in Fiji (47 per cent of population), 406,000 in British West Indies, 30,000 in Indonesia, 4,000 in the Persian Gulf (Oman, Kuwait, Bahrain), 2,500 in Iran, 1,000 in Egypt, 700 in Iraq and 200 in Afghanistan.[43] As of 2015, there are over twenty-seven million people of Indian origin, including temporary migrants, with the vast majority in the Gulf and in Western countries. Annually, India receives $70 billion a year in remittances, the largest for any expatriate group and this contributes to 3.5 per cent of India's GDP.[44]

Concomitant with the growth of Indian economic and global influence, the Indian government has sought to display its power by playing a direct role in the well-being of overseas Indians. For example, during outbreaks of violence in the Middle East (the 1991 Gulf War, the 2003 Iraq war, the 2012 Libyan crisis and the Syria–Iraq civil wars since 2013), India has sent military airplanes and ships to the region to rescue its migrant workers. Further, the Indian government has signed agreements with Arab countries in the Gulf to protect the rights of its workers and to help them when necessary.[45]

Matters that were considered internal affairs of other countries during the Nehru era, such as issues of wages or living standards for Indian workers to visas and immigration policies of countries which affect Indian migrant labour, have now become part of India's foreign policy concerns. This contrasts sharply with Nehru's view that Indians settled abroad were the responsibility of the countries they had made their homes, not India's.

Nehru had argued that Indians abroad got into difficulties that could not be helped, nor was it India's business to help find employment for Indians abroad. 'The tendency of any country is to reserve its employment for its own nationals,' he said. 'It is difficult to criticize that tendency.'[46] A similar attitude about Indians working overseas or settled abroad permanently is no longer possible. Today, the impact of American immigration policy on Indian companies and Indians studying and employed in the United States has become one of the key issues in bilateral discussions. The issue of employment visas for Indians (H-1B and L-1) was a key topic of discussion between former president Obama and Prime Minister Modi and will remain one when President Donald J. Trump meets with Premier Modi.[47] India now proudly considers persons of Indian origin all over the world as purveyors of its interests in other countries.

5
Institutions and Strategic Culture

FOR SEVERAL YEARS after Independence, India's leaders saw external relations as being mainly about diplomatic stature, not about competing interests and strategies. Nehru waxed eloquent about India's special position in the world but as K. Subrahmanyam points out, 'the much needed synergy for effective national security management', involving interaction of different components of the security establishment, was totally absent.[1] India's vision of its place in the world, its historic civilization, the writings of its ancient philosophers and actions of its medieval kings, as well as the policies of its Western colonizers, failed to bequeath a uniquely Indian strategic culture.

Jaswant Singh, who served both as minister of defence and as minister for external affairs at different times, pointed out that India sits at the crossroads of four collapsed empires – the Chinese, Ottoman, British and Russian – while its security challenges are defined by four lines – McMahon Line, Durand Line, Line of Actual Control, and Line of Control.[2] Influenced by other empires and circumscribed by boundaries drawn by outsiders, India lacks a clear set of beliefs, attitudes and norms about the use of force or defining its frontiers that could be described as exclusively Indian.

Most of the institutions currently engaged in shaping India's foreign policy are built on the edifice of the British Raj. They function with varying degrees of efficacy in different situations but cannot be said to represent an Indian strategic ethos. Subrahmanyam, India's leading strategic analyst, argued that the key reason for this was the absence of a strategic culture from the pre-British era. Prior to British rule various princely states focused on their own security in an ad hoc manner and there was little emphasis on global strategy. Since the princes saw a threat only from one another and not to India as a whole, they did not care to think about a strategy for the defence of the subcontinent. During British rule, the Raj framed its interests in terms of what benefited the empire and no Indian took part or was allowed to be involved in formulation of strategy.[3]

Subrahmanyam goes on to argue that after 1947, India saw itself as a status-quo-oriented, non-expansionist power. It, therefore, did not have the 'paranoid sense of insecurity' that leads to serious strategic planning.[4] The country's early post-British era leaders assumed that if India does not threaten others, others will leave India alone and refrain from threatening its security. In addition, civilian control of the military under domestic-policy-oriented politicians prevented the development of a large Indian military–industrial complex. India was thus denied the post-Independence institutional structure that could encourage strategic thought, which in its essence is about national security. More than strategic security it is national pride that defined India's foreign policy in the immediate aftermath of Independence.

Under Nehru, the military and intelligence apparatus were treated as tactical executors of policy and kept away from decision making. This ensured civilian supremacy but did not create vertical and horizontal integration in planning for national security. The Ministry of Defence, manned by civilians, kept the three uniformed services – the army, navy and air force – out of policymaking. Most of the proposals considered by the highest defence body – the Cabinet Committee on Security (CCS) – dealt with procurement proposals for necessary supplies or issues relating to soldiers' emoluments, not with real strategy.

At the time of India's independence in 1947, the Indian military's officer corps was unacquainted with national security management. The British started giving commissions to Indians as officers in the military only in 1920, having reserved officers' ranks exclusively for British of Caucasian descent until then. This meant that the Indian officers' corps was only twenty-seven-years-old at the time of Independence. India had inherited an army from the Raj but with inexperienced junior generals, some of whom were excellent field commanders but lacked proficiency in leading a larger force. Only three Indian generals had experience of commanding a brigade during World War II. Nehru refused to retain British generals, pushing Indians into senior command positions without adequate prior preparation.

The situation was exacerbated when generalist civil servants, with little knowledge of security issues and international relations, came to dominate the Ministry of Defence. Diplomats at the Ministry of External Affairs soon insinuated themselves into all aspects of national security. In an interview a former head of the defence department noted that for decades even the introductory chapter of the annual report of the defence ministry was traditionally written by the foreign secretary, not the defence secretary.[5] Thinking on defence and national security was seen as prerogatives of civil servants and diplomats, not of the uniformed military. Moreover, while Nehru was interested in economic planning, defence planning really started only after 1964 under American insistence in the backdrop of India's military defeat in 1962 at the hands of China.[6]

Subrahmanyam cites 'serious systemic flaws in the Indian national security structure and processes' that began under Nehru, which he believes were never fully redressed even under his successors. In his book *Defending India* (1999), Jaswant Singh joined criticism of India's early leaders, including Nehru, for personalizing foreign policy and for not developing and institutionalizing 'strategic thinking, policy formulation and implementation'.[7] Subrahmanyam asserts that in matters of national security India followed the instincts of its leader rather than practising democracy in debating and determining policy. 'Monocracies of all prime ministers of India from Jawaharlal Nehru to Atal Bihari Vajpayee in matters of national security appears to be largely due to this absence of strategic culture and tradition,'[8] he wrote. To some extent this remains true to this day. Despite the creation of a National Security Council with a national security adviser and secretariat, India's strategic decision-making process is still centred on the personality of the prime minister.

Jaswant Singh criticized Nehru for simply managing a system of external relations inherited from the British instead of defining clear underlying principles for India's foreign policy. This criticism contrasts with the view that Nehruvianism represented a strategic vision for India. The 1998 presidential address spoke of the need to follow the path laid down by Mahatma Gandhi and Nehru, of India recovering 'her traditional, historical place in the vanguard of human civilization'.[9] By then thirty-four years had passed since Nehru's death and a half-century had gone since Gandhi's assassination. Critics such as Jaswant Singh saw much of Nehru's contribution to India's foreign policy as grandiloquence rather than substantive strategic decisions.

High-sounding oratory has definitely been a strong feature of India's approach to international relations. The 2003–04 presidential addresses to parliament talked about India forging ahead in the world by 'drawing on the strength of our civilizational and historical ties with countries across the globe'. Ignoring the large number of poor in the country, the huge gap in GDP and other indicators with China and the serious lag in maintaining a modern military force, India's president declared the twenty-first century as 'India's century' and insisted that strategic autonomy and independent decision making were the hallmark of Indian foreign policy.[10]

Using poetic language, President K.R. Narayanan described India's foreign policy as 'alchemy' of 'the thirst for Independence, the desire to safeguard our national interest, the desire to pursue peace and cooperation in our environment and in the world as a whole'.[11] In reality, however, India's approach was one of maintaining the status quo while, in the words of a retired Indian official, 'preaching to others what we don't practise ourselves'.[12] Over the years, critics point out, India has generally only reacted to whatever the rest of the world does instead of taking many initiatives. Indian leaders and diplomats take pride in India being 'one of the few countries that is able to talk on reasonably friendly terms with everybody in the world',[13] a reflection of policies designed to muddle through instead of charting a new course.

PRIME MINISTERIAL PRE-EMINENCE

After Independence, India chose not to discard or disrupt the structure of state created during British colonial rule. Instead, the existing institutions of government were only slightly modified and adapted to work for a sovereign nation instead of serving a colonial regime. India's decision making on foreign policy too rests on the set of institutions most of which can be traced back to the Raj.

Within two years of the departure of the British from the subcontinent, India adopted a constitution in 1949 modelled on the Westminster form of parliamentary democracy. The first general elections on the basis of universal adult franchise were held in 1951–52. As in most democracies, members of parliament reflected their constituents and were more concerned with local issues than global ones. As prime minister, Nehru was the country's chief executive and, in effect, provided continuity from an era that vested all authority in the office of the viceroy. Thus, the office of prime minister in India started out wielding even greater clout than in other parliamentary democracies. In conduct of foreign policy, Nehru concentrated authority in the prime minister's position, which continues to be the focal point of India's international engagement to this day.

Almost all Indian prime ministers have sought to leave their mark in the arena of foreign policy. Some of them were powerful enough to craft and implement the policies they wanted; others had to learn how to take the system along with them. Even prime ministers lacking in knowledge of bureaucratic functions quickly mastered the art in order to push for their initiatives. Nehru and his early successors conveyed their decisions through the various ministries while maintaining relatively smaller staff directly working for the prime minister. Over the years, the Prime Minister's Office (PMO) has emerged as a bureaucratic machine in its own right that has helped cement the prime minister's centrality.

In addition to the PMO, several other key institutions and offices are also engaged in Indian foreign policy. These include: the Ministry of External Affairs (external affairs minister, foreign secretary, Indian foreign service and diplomatic missions), the recently created National Security Council (national security adviser, Strategic Policy Group and National Security Advisory Board), the parliament (standing and consultative committees), and the Cabinet Committee on Security. Several ministries, especially the Ministry of Defence, the Ministry of Home Affairs, the Ministry of Finance, and the Ministry of Commerce also weigh in on matters that relate to their portfolios. India's military and intelligence services, political parties, media and think tanks have, in varying degrees, influenced India's positions on international affairs at different times in India's recent history. The input of professional civil servants and specialists outside the formal bureaucracy, however, does not change the fact that the prime minister remains the final decision maker.

The Westminster system has an in-built tension between elected politicians and the permanent civil service. Most Indian civil servants would argue that they are implementers of policy and not policymakers. According to a senior diplomat, every prime minister has his or her own ideas and when they ask for advice from civil servants they pick up what they want and ignore what they do not wish to hear. Realistically speaking, the prime minister has strong views on a handful of issues and limits the permanent bureaucracy's input to methods of implementing his/her ideas. On most other issues, proposals originate in the relevant ministry and move up the hierarchy to the PMO for a decision. Most diplomats interviewed by the author stated that issues relating to India's immediate neighbours or critical countries such as the United States, Russia, the United Kingdom, China or major European Union states are often personally considered by the prime minister.

Even the decisions on non-critical issues depend on how much prominence the prime minister is willing to allow to the external affairs minister. Nehru did not appoint a Minister of External Affairs, preferring to maintain total policy control. Subsequent prime ministers have calibrated the level of freedom of their external affairs ministers depending on personality and political circumstances. Normally, if the prime minister gets along well with the external affairs minister or if a matter does not interest the prime minister, the external affairs minister would have the final say. No prime minister would have an external affairs minister in whom he or she does not have implicit trust though sometimes there is an unwillingness on the part of prime ministers to allow decision-making autonomy to ministers, especially in strategic matters.

Jaswant Singh described the relationship between the prime minister and the external affairs ministry with a pithy anecdote. The external affairs ministry and the PMO in Delhi are both housed in the same building, known as South Block. The prime minister's office is connected to the offices of the Ministry of External Affairs by a small door. 'If the door is open,' Singh observed, 'they are working closely together. If the door is closed they are not.'[14] As prime minister, Nehru used that door frequently as he was his own foreign minister. The door continues to be used but the frequency with which foreign ministry officials can access the PMO, or vice versa, through that door has come to symbolize the extent of cooperation between the two bureaucracies.

In some ways, interaction between the Indian chief executive's political team and the cadres of permanent state functionaries resembles the relationship between 10, Downing Street and Whitehall in Britain. India's adaptation of the Westminster model was heavily influenced by the towering personality of Nehru, who led India as prime minister for seventeen formative years. Nehru overshadowed his cabinet, the parliament and the permanent bureaucracy. He also saw himself as his own best civil servant.

Impatient by nature, Nehru often took decisions on his own and even sent replies to diplomatic cables.

Nehru's passion for and interest in foreign affairs meant that by the time he became prime minister he had rather firm views on international affairs. Other leaders of the Indian independence movement paid much less attention to foreign affairs than Nehru. Although he consulted some of his top officials, Nehru tended to make decisions on the basis of his own knowledge and instincts. According to Jayantanuja Bandyopadhyaya, who served in the Indian Foreign Service for several years, the advisory role of the missions and the foreign office under Nehru was minimal for two reasons. The first of these was Nehru's belief that he seldom needed advice. The second, and more significant, was the fact that Indian foreign policy was still being crafted in the early years of Independence and dealt more with 'broad generalities and problems of international relations rather than with detailed and specific problems' requiring an Indian response.[15]

Nehru's handling of foreign affairs on a daily basis is described in detail by former foreign secretary, Yezdezard Dinshaw Gundevia, whose memoirs offer details about the prime minister's routine. Nehru would start his day by meeting the public who had gathered in the lawn of his official residence, Teen Murti House, the former palatial home of the commander-in-chief of the British Indian Army. He would then go to his office in South Block where for the first twenty minutes he would meet with four government secretaries: the Secretary General, foreign secretary, Commonwealth secretary and special secretary. According to Gundevia, 'Each of us carried his own sheaf of pink and yellow telegrams on which we wanted instructions or orders. Jawaharlal had his own collection of telegrams and sometimes one or more letters with him properly sorted out.' Nehru would ask questions and then the officers would be allowed to ask theirs.[16]

Among his political peers, Nehru had to contend mostly with the views of his deputy prime minister and home minister Sardar Vallabhbhai Patel whom many saw as a potential prime ministerial candidate in his own right. Although Patel was primarily concerned with domestic politics and with integrating the princely states into the Indian Union, he disagreed vehemently with Nehru's foreign policy in relation to China. Cabinet members other than Patel rarely questioned Nehru on foreign policy and a saying of the era was, 'Panditji [Pandit Nehru] knows best.'

Nehru maintained the appearance of formal consultative mechanisms even when he made decisions individually. Other prime ministers have also used cabinet committees to share responsibility for decisions, based on the idea of collective cabinet responsibility in parliamentary governments. The number of cabinet committees has varied over time but the key cabinet committees are: Cabinet Committee on Political Affairs, Cabinet Committee on Security, Cabinet Committee on Economic Affairs, Cabinet Committee on Parliamentary Affairs, Appointment Committee of the Cabinet and Cabinet Committee on Accommodations. For many years the Cabinet Committee on Political Affairs also dealt with foreign affairs but in recent years the Cabinet Committee on Security has emerged as the key formal body.

Under Nehru, the Cabinet Committee on Foreign Affairs comprised the prime minister, defence minister, home minister and finance minister. There were Cabinet Committee on Defence and Cabinet Committee on Economic Affairs as well though none of them were 'particularly effective' in influencing the formation of policy.[17] Not only did Nehru dominate the proceedings but he often came to meetings already having decided the policy. According to Krishna Menon, Nehru 'was not a person who sought consultation' and at cabinet meetings would first lay down the issue and then in the end state 'everyone was agreed' on the policy.[18] Many non-Congress ministers in Nehru's first cabinet, like B.R. Ambedkar, resigned because they felt he took crucial policy decisions outside of the cabinet. Seeing himself as an educator for his people, Nehru was impatient to make decisions and viewed the committee process as laborious.

Currently, the Cabinet Committee on Security is the key decision-making body with respect to foreign and security policy. It is comprised of the prime minister, external affairs minister, defence minister, home minister and finance minister. It is the prime minister's prerogative to invite other cabinet ministers to these meetings. Depending on the issue being discussed, other ministers can be invited as well. The services chiefs participate whenever defence-related issues are discussed. The top bureaucratic heads – secretaries – of the ministries that are a part of the committee are also present, as is the head of the civil service, the cabinet secretary. According to protocol, a cabinet committee meeting cannot be held unless the prime minister and the cabinet secretary are both present, unless of course the prime minister designates someone in his or her place.

By the time Nehru died and Lal Bahadur Shastri became prime minister in 1964, decision making on foreign policy had become extremely personalized. The prime minister and his office were the key policymaking institution for foreign affairs. As a domestic politician with little interest in foreign affairs, Shastri gave more leeway to his external affairs minister Sardar Swaran Singh, who influenced foreign relations between 1964 and 1966.

Unlike Nehru, Shastri was not a prime minister willing to do everything himself. He needed someone he trusted to explain the content of voluminous diplomatic cables and administrative files. Thus, Lakshmi Kant Jha, a member of the Indian Civil Service from the British era, became secretary to the prime minister. Jha set up the prime minister's secretariat (PMS) that over time grew in power and size. During Shastri's time the permanent bureaucracy regained lost ground and, as Surjit Mansingh points out, Shastri made the prime minister's secretariat into 'a kind of super-ministry'. Diplomatic traffic was now routed through this secretariat and those serving in it had the prime minister's ear.

Indira Gandhi renamed the prime minister's secretariat as the Prime Minister's Office (PMO), which grew further not just in size but also in power and influence. The office now comprised officers, including those from the foreign service, who were deputed to the PMO to be the prime minister's eyes and ears. Missives and phone calls from the prime minister's office carried more weight than those from the Ministry of External Affairs (MEA). Indira Gandhi maintained control of foreign policy even as she appointed a succession of heavyweight Congress party leaders as her foreign ministers. These included Mahommedali Currim Chagla (1966–67), Dinesh Singh (1969–70), Sardar Swaran Singh (1970–74), Yashwant Rao Chavan (1974–77) and Pamulaparti Venkata Narasimha Rao (1980–84). The prime minister entrusted evaluations to a small group of advisers while Indira's foreign ministers simply implemented her decisions.

Indira's well-known advisers included Principal Secretary Parameshwar Narayan Haksar, Chairman, Policy Planning Committee Durga Prasad Dhar and some journalists such as G. Parthasarathy and Inder Malhotra. For advice, Indira chose people whose views aligned with hers but she was also known to be paranoid about loyalty. The slightest suspicion of disloyalty or perceived attempt to outgrow one's shoes would lead to even senior politicians or advisers being barred from even meeting with Indira. 'Indira Gandhi used men of ability almost as errand boys,' wrote Surjit Mansingh, who is known otherwise for being sympathetic to Indira Gandhi. 'When she valued their advice, trusted their discretion and had confidence in their loyalty to her person, she set them a variety of tasks, irrespective of their institutional position.'[19]

Indira's son, Rajiv, carried on his mother's tendency of accumulating power in the PMO when he stepped into office after his mother's assassination in 1984. He was not a traditional politician and was, therefore, not as interested in domestic politics. Rajiv was, however, impatient to bring about change in India and saw foreign policy as an important instrument of integrating India with the modern developed world. Faced with an entrenched bureaucracy and unsure of whom to trust in the domestic sphere, he found it easier to deal with foreign than domestic politics.

Reluctance to trust a bureaucracy that he saw as an impediment to change led Rajiv to concentrate even more authority within his office. Not only did he increase the number of foreign service officers attached to the PMO but he also sought out civil servants he could personally trust. Rajiv retained the foreign affairs portfolio for some time, like his grandfather, but ultimately appointed politicians from the Congress party as external affairs minister. Kunwar Natwar Singh, a former foreign secretary who had grown close to Indira, was appointed as minister of state for foreign affairs.

Rajiv often turned to Natwar Singh, not the cabinet minister for external affairs, for advice on key policies. For example, Rajiv's decision in 1987 to use the Indian Air Force to air drop emergency supplies to besieged Tamils in the Jaffna area of north-east Sri Lanka is attributed to advice proffered by Natwar Singh and not the cabinet minister or the professional bureaucracy. The Indian Air Force violated Sri Lankan sovereignty in conducting the ostensibly humanitarian mission. Later, Rajiv decided to send Indian peacekeeping troops to Sri Lanka without consulting his cabinet. In fact, even External Affairs Minister Narasimha Rao was informed of the decision after it had been made.[20]

For twenty-nine of India's seventy years of Independence, Indian prime ministers have also held the portfolio of external affairs. Even when external affairs ministers have been appointed, they have operated only under their prime minister's shadow. This runs contrary to the Westminster model of parliamentary system of government in which, according to Bandyopadhyaya, the foreign minister is 'the pivot' of the decision-making process in foreign policy.[21] The Indian practice of the prime minister playing a more direct role in making and executing foreign policy made India's foreign ministers less important than in most parliamentary democracies. A former foreign secretary lamented, 'I have even served foreign ministers who when I went for orders would say, "Why come here, just go down the corridor," pointing to the prime minister's office.'[22]

The pre-eminence of prime ministers in shaping India's foreign policy has endured over the years. As prime minister, Rao navigated his way in the post-cold-war world by boosting ties with the United States. He also initiated economic reforms to restart India's economy and championed the 'Look East' policy that was aimed at encouraging economic and trade ties with India's East Asian and South-East Asian neighbours. Rao was a polymath and a lifelong politician who had served as external affairs minister under Indira and Rajiv. He knew foreign service officers well and they expected him to give greater say to the professionals in the ministry and in diplomatic missions abroad. Instead, Rao continued to concentrate decision making in the prime minister's office.

Another prime minister with prior experience as foreign minister under his belt was Inder Kumar Gujral, who was passionate about foreign policy like Nehru and retained the post of foreign minister during his short tenure as prime minister. Gujral came to power intent on leaving a legacy in foreign policy especially with respect to India's immediate neighbourhood, South Asia – the Gujral doctrine. Without weakening the PMO, Gujral distinguished himself from his predecessors by relying heavily on outside experts and academics. This led to frequent clashes between the prime minister and the permanent foreign service.[23]

The BJP's Atal Bihari Vajpayee restored a semblance of consultation in the making foreign policy. He had served as external affairs minister during the Janata Party government (1977–79) and, after short stints as prime minister in 1996 and 1998, presided over a full five-year term as prime minister beginning in 1999. As a consummate politician, Vajpayee knew almost all opposition leaders and was able to reach out to them to build consensus on external relations. On certain issues he consulted his cabinet, his party and other members of the coalition government and even members of the opposition Congress party. One such issue was US president George W. Bush's request in 2003–04 for Indian troops for the war in Iraq. The decision to not get militarily involved in Iraq reflected a wide consensus. On other issues, for example his decision to extend a hand of friendship to Pakistan while giving a speech in Kashmir, Vajpayee acted alone and without too much consultation.

Under Vajpayee, a major institutional change occurred when the BJP-led government created the National Security Council (NSC) Secretariat headed by a national security adviser (NSA). Vajpayee appointed his trusted adviser, former diplomat Brajesh Mishra, as India's first national security adviser. Mishra was also principal secretary to the prime minister. This dual position combined with Vajpayee's total trust in him meant that after Rajiv this was the first time the prime minister's office fully ran foreign and domestic policy. According to former officials, the depth of the intrusion was demonstrated even with respect to administrative issues like appointment of ambassadors.

Two incidents during the Vajpayee government illustrate the prime minister's role as the key decision maker, with only a secondary role for his cabinet. The first of these occurred when in May 1999, while India was engaged in peace talks with Pakistan, its military was caught off-guard by Pakistani troops that captured mountainous territory across the line of control in Kashmir in the Kargil region. This marked the beginning of the Kargil crisis, which is said to have brought India and Pakistan to the brink of a nuclear exchange. The Indian Army eventually beat back the Pakistani intruders and international public opinion was unanimously on India's side. Even China joined the United States and other countries in demanding Pakistan's withdrawal from territory it had surreptitiously captured.

Several official reports have detailed India's intelligence failure (both human and technical) that led to the Kargil crisis. Once the crisis had presented itself, the prime minister made the major decisions about militarily confronting the intruders as well as to mobilize world opinion against Pakistan's stab in the back. However, Vajpayee was mindful of likely criticism at being caught napping and over-trusting Pakistan without putting in place mechanisms for verifying its trustworthiness. He, therefore, ensured that the Cabinet Committee on Security met daily, often a couple of times every day, during the course of the crisis. These meetings were attended by all service chiefs and intelligence heads so that no one could absolve himself of responsibility for decisions taken during the period.

The second major crisis where Vajpayee needed to create an appearance of collective decision came when, in December 1999, an Indian Airlines flight from Kathmandu to Delhi was hijacked by Pakistani terrorists. Once again, the Indian government was taken by surprise. Even though time was of the essence, the government was unable to make quick decisions from the first landing of the aircraft in Amritsar, to its subsequent landing in Lahore, Dubai and finally Taliban-controlled Kandahar. According to Kanchan Gupta, who was then an aide to Vajpayee, the prime minister and his team were on a flight and had no information about the hijacking for over an hour.[24] Former Research and Analysis Wing (RAW) chief A.S. Dulat in his book *Kashmir: The Vajpayee Years* has referred to the incident being characterized by 'a blame game' while others refer to its handling as 'mismanagement.'[25] The then external affairs minister Jaswant Singh wrote later in his book *India at Risk*, '...the failure to organise the logistics [during the hijacking crisis] is one bureaucratic muddle that still amazes me.'[26]

The terrorists demanded the release of several terrorists held in Indian prisons and threatened to kill all passengers on board if their demands were not met. They killed one passenger to demonstrate the seriousness of their threat. The cabinet decided not to give in to the demands of the terrorists but the media and public opinion led the government to reverse their initial determination. India released three terrorist leaders in return for the safe release of all Indian hostages. The three terrorists returned to Pakistan after being escorted to Kandahar on a special plane by the foreign minister and

India's intelligence chief. They were subsequently found engaged in terrorism again, albeit with enhanced clout for winning freedom through a daredevil act.

Vajpayee's prestige was seriously dented by his concession though he shared blame with his cabinet. During both Kargil and Kandahar, while Vajpayee discussed the issues with this entire cabinet, the decision at the end of the day was his alone. His NSA, Mishra, was most likely the only other person involved in the difficult choices. Due to the omnipresence of Mishra and Vajpayee's implicit trust in him, the role of the foreign minister had already become limited to those areas where the PMO was simply not interested.

The situation changed considerably when well-known economist Manmohan Singh became prime minister. As a former civil servant Manmohan Singh was known for following rules and he had experienced a cabinet position while serving as Rao's finance minister. Unlike other prime ministers, Manmohan Singh did not hold office in his own right but rather as a nominee of Congress president Sonia Gandhi. During his ten years as prime minister, real power lay not in his PMO but in the office of the president of the Congress party. The prime minister had his own outlook on world affairs. He sought better ties with India's neighbours, including Pakistan, as well as with the United States. The limitations of his authority coupled with the demands of coalition politics severely limited Manmohan Singh's ability to drive the agenda of the government he headed.

Manmohan Singh's close advisers recall that during his tenure the Cabinet Committee on Security (CCS) met every week but the prime minister rarely spoke or intervened during its proceedings. Instead of the CCS, key decisions were discussed in the weekly meeting of the Congress party's core group comprising Sonia Gandhi, Manmohan Singh, Defence Minister A.K. Antony, Finance Minister P. Chidambaram and close Gandhi loyalist Ahmed Patel. While the CCS met on Thursdays, it was the Core Committee's meeting every Friday that acted as the policymaking body. The

National Advisory Council (NAC) headed by Sonia Gandhi was another 'parallel policy structure' that further diminished the power of the cabinet and the prime minister.[27]

Narendra Modi does not face Manmohan Singh's constraints. His election in 2014 was seen as a personal mandate for drastic changes in foreign and domestic policies. Modi's experience as a state chief minister has made him aware of how the permanent bureaucracy might slow down policy change. As a pro-business conservative from one of India's states, he distrusts the Delhi-based machinery of state and has sought to concentrate even greater power in his PMO.

Like Nehru, Modi appears passionate about foreign policy and like Rajiv he is sceptical of the existing set-up and seeks to use his own key advisers. Like Indira he has a small group of advisers he trusts and like Vajpayee he has appointed someone dependable as his national security adviser. Modi prefers to deal directly with his officers, instead of through their ministerial superiors, a practice similar to that of Nehru. He has also built a direct relationship with the Indian public, using both traditional media and modern instruments like social media.

THE ROLE OF PARLIAMENT

India's parliament plays a lesser role in formulation and execution of foreign policy than in other parliamentary democracies. This is not what the founders of modern India envisaged. The record of discussions in the Constituent Assembly soon after Independence shows that India's founding elite wanted parliament to be supreme in the conduct of international affairs. H.V. Kamath, a member of the Constituent Assembly, argued: 'I am sure that Parliament will ultimately decide our international relations. It is neither the executive nor the President but Parliament which will have the final word on what out foreign relations are going to be, what our international policy is going to be.'[28] Kamath's sentiment was shared by other Constituent Assembly members and, as a result, Articles

246 and 253 of the Indian Constitution empowered parliament to legislate all aspects of foreign affairs including implementation of international treaties, agreements and conventions.

In practice, however, the conduct of Indian foreign policy rests with the executive branch of government even as the Ministry of External Affairs is subject to parliamentary oversight like all government ministries. Parliamentary oversight is exercised through discussions and debates on the floor, as well as through question hour – the time set aside during parliament's deliberations for MPs to question ministers on their department's performance. Parliamentary Committees on External Affairs and Defence also act as instruments of parliamentary oversight.

The parliament discusses and approves bills introduced by the Ministry of External Affairs, asks questions on issues and also studies and discusses the annual report of the Ministry of External Affairs before approving it. Officials of the Ministry of External Affairs say that a lot of their time is taken up in preparing answers to questions raised by parliamentarians during the period when parliament is in session. Questions are sometimes tied to a media report (say, on Indian hostages in Iraq) while on other occasions relate to the government's policy towards a certain country or specific international issue.

Those who criticize parliamentary oversight note that in almost every democracy most politicians are oriented towards domestic issues and they have relatively little knowledge or awareness of foreign affairs. As a result, parliamentary debates on foreign policy are not always based on hard facts or an objective assessment of reality. They often become an opportunity for the opposition to criticize the government or the party in power.

One way of building up a group of politicians who are knowledgeable about and have experience of foreign policy is through the committee system. There are two committees for external affairs, the consultative committee and the standing committee.

The origins of the consultative committee come from a practice started by Nehru who used to periodically consult with close parliamentary colleagues on aspects of foreign policy before he introduced that policy in parliament.[29] Lal Bahadur Shastri continued this policy. However, there was a backlash from members of parliament who demanded the establishment of formal consultative committees instead of informal consultation. In 1969 parliamentary consultative committees were set up.

The consultative committee is ideally supposed to be comprised of representatives of all political parties roughly in proportion to their strength in parliament. The current Parliamentary Consultative Committee on External Affairs and Overseas Indian Affairs is chaired by the minister for external affairs and overseas Indian affairs. In addition, there are the two ministers of state for external affairs and two ex-officio ministers – the ministers of state for parliamentary affairs. Other members include eleven members of parliament from the Lok Sabha (Lower House of parliament) and seventeen members of parliament from the Rajya Sabha (Upper House of parliament).[30] This committee is consultative and advisory in nature. It is chaired by the external affairs minister and is a body for the minister to consult.

The standing committees too have proportionate representation from both the Houses of parliament. The current Parliamentary Standing Committee on External Affairs is chaired by a member of the opposition, and has nineteen members of parliament from the Lok Sabha and eight from the Rajya Sabha.[31] The standing committee has the power to call the officials to testify before it. It looks over the annual reports of the Ministry of External Affairs, can ask questions about budgetary allocations and also has a veto over the budget of the Ministry of External Affairs. This committee submits its annual report to the parliament.

Supporters argue that the standing committee is like a mini-parliament and through it the parliament exercises control over the conduct of foreign policy. They argue that these committees enable detailed discussions of issues, create an environment where a small number of people, politicians and bureaucrats, can sit and discuss issues.

Critics assert that what the committee achieves depends upon how interested parliamentarians are in foreign policy issues and how willing they are to contribute to discussions on foreign policy. According to former diplomats most parliamentarians are interested not in broad issues of foreign and security policy but rather in issues like passports, visas, cultural exchanges, and of course on any issues to do with India's neighbours because all these have a domestic dimension. While the committee can call officials it does not have the power to call a minister or the prime minister.

According to most analysts, parliamentary oversight is not as intense as it used to be in the early years. According to academics and former diplomats, Nehru would always be in parliament to answer questions and would never miss question hour unless he was out of town. After Nehru, however, most prime ministers including Indira have preferred to avoid parliament when they can. Further, while all ministries, including Ministry of External Affairs, provide answers to parliamentary questions, accountability is not what it used to be or what it should be. Thus the only time the parliament is really interested in foreign affairs is when it is a critical issue.

'THE STEEL FRAME'

Even though India's prime minister, his cabinet and parliament are the major pillar of India's government, it is the professionally trained civil service that is described as the 'Steel Frame' of government in India. That depiction dates back to a 1922 parliamentary speech by British prime minister David Lloyd-George. The Indian bureaucratic system and especially the foreign service is a legacy of British colonial rule with a history dating back to the British East India Company.

In 1783, the East India Company's board of directors had set up what later became the Indian Foreign Department, the forerunner to today's Ministry of External Affairs. In 1843 four key departments were set up at the federal level: foreign, home, finance and military. After 1858, when the British government took over running India's affairs directly, the Indian Civil Service (ICS) was created, initially with the nomenclature of Imperial Civil Service and as the British Indian Civil Service after 1886. The civil service was broken into separate tracks dealing with diplomatic affairs, home affairs, Indian affairs and colonial affairs, each with its own designated officers. Candidates for all four services were recruited through a combined entrance examination and underwent a one-year training programme at a university in England. The civil services were exclusive to British men until the early twentieth century when Indians were allowed to enter. The training period for Indian civil servants was two years.

India was the engine that sustained the British Raj and a huge bureaucratic establishment was set up to serve the Raj. Schools were set up to train civil and military officials to maintain the empire's interests, locally as well as internationally. Under the East India Company, its military officers and civilian administrators were company employees and their roles were interchangeable. The company used the same personnel for domestic, diplomatic and military work and British policies in relation to India were framed on the basis of reports of these employees. Even after the Crown took over from the company, the foreign and political department's function was not purely restricted to the foreign affairs of British India but also included internal and imperial matters.

The Department of External Affairs based in Delhi framed policy for Persia, Afghanistan, Tibet, Burma, Ceylon and Malaya in addition to selecting personnel for implementation of these policies. The frontier areas of the British Raj were also under the jurisdiction of this department. An Act of the British parliament in 1937 ended this dual responsibility, creating a department for domestic affairs and another for external affairs. Until independence in 1947, the external affairs department was controlled directly by the Governor General of India. Indians fighting for independence from the British did not look favourably upon civil servants advancing the cause of the empire.

At Independence, there were differing views in the Congress party about whether or not independent India should retain the British civil services. Nehru supported abolition of the permanent civil service inherited from the Raj and wanted to replace it with a cadre of political appointees. In his view, this would be a more democratic system and, in addition to removing the vestiges of colonialism, would create a more patriotic governing class. Ironically, it was Patel who argued in favour of retaining the permanent bureaucracy created so carefully over almost two centuries by the British. In a letter to Nehru dated 27 April 1948, Patel asserted that 'an efficient and disciplined and contented service, assured of its prospects as a result of diligent and honest work, is a sine qua non of sound administration under a democratic regime even more than under an authoritarian rule'.[32] According to Patel, the bureaucracy 'must be above party' and a system should be laid out that minimizes 'political considerations either in its recruitment or in its discipline and control'.[33]

Patel's view prevailed and India's founding fathers were able to rise above the resentment resulting from mistreatment by the bureaucracy during colonial rule. India retained the broad British civil service system though, over time, numerous changes were introduced. Today the Indian civil services are divided into three broad categories: the Central Services (which include forty-three services including the Indian Foreign Service), All India Services (three services, including the Indian Administrative Service) and the various state services. Upon becoming prime minister, Nehru appointed Girija Shankar Bajpai, an ICS officer and India's Agent General to the US, as the head of the external affairs ministry with the rank of Secretary General, the highest possible position under the structure of civil service left behind by the British. The Indian Foreign Service (IFS) was formally established in October 1946.

From 1947 to 1964, the senior-most bureaucrat in the Ministry of External Affairs was the Secretary General. In 1948, the ministry's organization was relatively simple. While the Secretary General was in charge overall, a foreign secretary looked after Europe, the USA, Latin America, China and Japan and was assisted by two joint secretaries, two deputy secretaries and two undersecretaries. The Commonwealth secretary handled relations with the United Kingdom, British dominions and colonies and Asia.[34]

Former foreign secretary Gundevia narrates how the Ministry of External Affairs functioned in India's early years. According to him, the Secretary General presided over a meeting of all senior officials at 10:30 a.m. every morning. Secretaries and joint secretaries 'trooped in strict order of precedence and sat down in strict order of precedence and marched out in the same order when the session was over. It was a coordinated meeting at which, mostly, telegrams that had come in overnight were discussed. You got precise instructions, always, from the Secretary General on what to do and what not to do.'[35]

After Nehru's death in 1964, the office of Secretary General was abolished. The administrative head of the Ministry of External Affairs since then is the foreign secretary. There were initially two other secretaries, earlier called secretary EA I (External Affairs I) and secretary EA II (External Affairs II) later redesignated secretary, East and secretary, West. The two other secretaries in the current organigram who are relatively recent appointees are secretary DPA & ER (Development Partnership Administration and Economic Relations) and special secretary (Americas), indicating the increasing importance of the United States and the Western hemisphere in Indian foreign policy.

An important but less well-known aspect of India's foreign policy is India's aid for other developing countries. The annual budget outlay for the Ministry of External Affairs for 2014–15 was US $2.3 billion (INR 14,370.39 crore), of which 64 per cent accounted for aid given to other countries under the International Technical and Economic Cooperation (ITEC) programme.[36] For the year 2015–16, India's development aid budget stood at US $1.6 billion, most of which, around 84 per cent, was allocated to South Asian countries.

The budget apportioned 63 per cent of the aid for Bhutan, while giving Afghanistan 7 per cent, Sri Lanka 5 per cent, Nepal 4 per cent, Bangladesh 3 per cent and the Maldives 2 per cent.[37] Pakistan is the only South Asian country that does not accept Indian aid.

Within the Ministry for External Affairs, responsibilities for managing relations with various countries are divided on a territorial basis between the three senior-most civil servants – the foreign secretary, secretary (East) and secretary (West). As part of a tradition started many years ago, until recently the foreign secretary dealt directly with the United Nations and the permanent members of the UN Security Council (the US, the UK, China, Russia and France) as well as India's South Asian neighbours. Secretary (West's) remit is Europe, Latin America, North America (but not the US), Africa and the Gulf while Secretary (East's) responsibility covers East Asia but not China.

This tradition has not always been strictly adhered to and over time, foreign secretaries have accumulated more subjects and regions under their direct control. Modi has presided over subtle changes in the management of the Ministry of External Affairs, allowing greater concentration of policymaking at the apex of the pyramid. For example, Foreign Secretary Jaishankar delegated the UN portfolio to Secretary DPA & ER Sujata Mehta to free the foreign secretary to focus on India's pursuit of a permanent seat on the Security Council. This marked separating India's larger political objectives from the humdrum of India's role at the UN and was interpreted by one analyst as a sign 'that old turf and territories may no longer be sacrosanct'.[38]

Notwithstanding the changes in the foreign office's organization at various times, the training of civil servants remains as stringent as it was under colonial days. In case of the Indian Foreign Service, Bandyopadhyaya points out, well trained professional diplomats are crucial for India's international relations. 'However rational the broad goals and principles of foreign policy determined by the political executive may be,' he writes, 'there will be a wide gap between theory and practice if the personnel responsible for the various major aspects of policy are not properly selected, trained and utilized.'[39] Since 1926, recruitment of India's civil servants has taken place through the Union Public Service Commission (UPSC) – formerly Federal Public Service Commission – an independent body that conducts annual examinations for recruitment for various Indian administrative services, including the Indian Foreign Service and the Indian Administrative Service (IAS).

Once selected, new recruits (or probationers as they are called) train first along with colleagues from other services at the Lal Bahadur Shastri National Academy of Administration in Mussourie before heading to the Foreign Service Institute (FSI) in Delhi for specialized training. The training period lasts for three years after which each officer is assigned a compulsory foreign language. After a brief attachment to the Ministry of External Affairs in New Delhi, the young IFS officer is posted to an Indian mission based on language skills. At the end of the three-year training period, officers must pass an examination before being allowed to continue further in the service.

British India had no embassies but at the end of World War II, two offices of agent general were set up, one in the US and one in China, whose duties were limited to consular affairs including issuance of visas. After 1947, India's international presence grew rapidly and by 1953 India had opened sixty missions, and forty-two countries had their diplomatic representatives in Delhi. By the 1970s India had 112 missions abroad, which grew to 140 foreign missions during the 1990s. As of 2015 India has 162 embassies and consulates abroad.[40]

Retired diplomats often complain that, unlike the United States and some others, India lacks a formal system to train its diplomats for service in specific countries. Training by the Ministry of External Affairs provides a broad framework, leaving several things – such as learning languages, local customs and history – to the discretion of individual diplomats. Envoys are supposed to return to Delhi before taking their next appointment but it is not mandatory. Most diplomats lament the relatively small size of the foreign service, which does not allow foreign service officers reorientation time between postings. They argue that diplomats must be given an opportunity to return to Delhi and brainstorm with key stakeholders (not only at the ministry and the PMO but also at other ministries) during and between serving abroad. The counter-argument is that the ministry cannot micromanage a diplomat's understanding of the country where he or she serves and officers must be allowed to learn on their jobs.

There are approximately 770 IFS officers manning 162 Indian missions and posts abroad as well as at headquarters in New Delhi. For a country of its size and the demands of global engagement, India has a relatively small foreign service. The Ministry of External Affairs also has 400 support staff, including interpreters and lawyers who are not foreign service officers. These numbers do not compare favourably with other major developing countries. China has 6,000 diplomats while Brazil's foreign service comprises 3,000.[41] 'For every Indian diplomat there are four Brazilian diplomats,' Foreign Secretary Shivshankar Menon told a parliamentary committee in 2007. 'For every Indian diplomat there are seven Chinese diplomats,' he said and added, 'Now we might be wonderful and very efficient, but we are not that efficient or that good. The strain is telling on us.'[42]

The relatively smaller foreign service is the result of decisions made right after Independence. At that time, Indian leaders were more concerned about India's domestic problems than foreign policy and were reluctant to commit too many resources for the conduct of external relations. As early as the 1950s, a foreign secretary noted: 'No one in Delhi was prepared to accept that there had to be a reasonable increase particularly of senior posts in the Ministry for the maintenance of a balanced ratio between the posts abroad and the officer cadre at home.'[43] Nehru, while keen to expand the number of Indian missions abroad so that India's international presence grew, was not in favour of the Ministry of External Affairs 'bulging at the seams'.[44]

Starting off as a small elite service, the IFS only recruited 5–10 people each year for several years. The exclusivity and small number of Indian diplomats led to the view that they were better than others. Quality was believed to be a substitute for numbers. Over time, the foreign service has realized their personnel crunch. Had the Ministry of External Affairs been strategic consistently and added to their numbers on a regular basis, India could have doubled the number of its diplomats in fifty years, keeping pace with demand. Bad personnel management for decades has led to the difficulties Shivshankar Menon identified before the parliamentary committee sixty years after Independence. The Indian government has now decided to double the number of people working for the foreign ministry to 1,500 and recruitment rates have now gone up. Thirty-two 'officer trainee diplomats' were inducted in 2014, as against 8–15 some two decades ago.[45]

Increasing recruitment is only one way to boost the size of the service on a permanent basis; another could be lateral entry of candidates for specific positions. The Indian Foreign Service has generally opposed lateral entrants into diplomatic jobs from other services or from universities and think tanks. Critics of inducting non-foreign service officials argue that it does not make up for the paucity of well-trained diplomats. Opening the doors for such induction would only open doors for patronage politics polluting the purity of a highly admired professional service. While opposing experts from other fields being assigned diplomatic tasks, Indian Foreign Service officers often favour training of their own in a broader range of technical skills from energy issues to cultural diplomacy.

In an effort to bring fresh blood into the Ministry of External Affairs, the Modi administration is encouraging lateral entry. In a deposition before a parliamentary committee in 2015, Foreign Secretary Jaishankar stated that the MEA would fill positions in its Policy Planning Division by recruiting from outside the government.[46]

It is unlikely, however, that the Modi government will revert to appointing too many outside candidates in senior diplomatic positions. The ambition of every foreign service officer is to rise to the position of ambassador, and most capable officers manage to fulfil that ambition in India's case. To ensure that it continues to attract talent and that entrants believe they will all one day become ambassadors there is an internal reluctance to either recruit too many candidates or appoint non-career diplomats as ambassadors. Unlike several countries, India tends to limit the number of political appointees it sends as ambassadors. The vast majority of Indian ambassadors are career diplomats. The only exception until recently were ambassadorial appointments in the US, the UK and the Soviet Union, which were offered to ruling party politicians. In recent years that has changed, opening these previously 'political' positions for career diplomats.

In the first few decades after Independence the people who joined the services, especially the Indian Foreign Service, were driven either by their passion for foreign service or a desire to follow parents who had served in the civil service under the British. The Indian Foreign Service was considered a more exclusive service as those ranking highest in the competitive examination were selected for foreign service. K. Shankar Bajpai, who served as ambassador to the United States and also as foreign secretary narrated to the author that he joined the service because he was attracted to it even though his father (Girija Shankar Bajpai) wanted him to become a lawyer.[47] One of the lures of the Indian Foreign Service was the prospect of living in other countries and also to study in the world's elite universities. In his 2016 book *Choices: Inside the Making of India's Foreign Policy*, former foreign secretary Shivshankar Menon states that he joined the foreign service so that he could travel the world.[48]

Things have changed somewhat in terms of the calibre of recruits for the Indian Foreign Service, in particular, and India's civil services, in general, since the 1990s. The civil service no longer attracts the crème de la crème of Indian society as private sector jobs now offer higher pay and benefits. Indians can travel the world on their own, while doing other jobs, and do not need to be Indian Foreign Service officers to get that opportunity. There has also been a decline in those who joined the services, military or civilian, immediately after Independence out of patriotic motivations. None of this stops the Indian Foreign Service from considering itself an elite within India's elite bureaucracy.

After selection through a highly competitive national exam, Indian Foreign Service officers consider themselves as being among India's best and the brightest. They often view foreign policy as the domain of the Ministry of External Affairs and not something to be left to the whims of capricious politicians. According to professional civil servants, the function of the MEA is to evolve, frame and implement policy. Despite the centrality of the prime minister and the PMO, the day-to-day conduct of foreign policy and routine administrative work remains with the MEA and its professionals. These officials serve as key institutional input providers.

The relationship between the political structure and the 'steel frame' puzzles observers of India's decision making. The question is often asked as to how professionals at the ministry know what issues to handle on their own and at what stage do they send them to the PMO for decision. Diplomats assert that it is often a judgement call based on one's experience. 'How does the doctor know when to do this or that?' observed a foreign service officer, adding, 'they learn through experience and from their seniors.' Routine matters are disposed of at a junior level within the hierarchy while sensitive issues require attention up the chain of command. Careers are destroyed by errors of judgement in assuming a question is unimportant when later it becomes crucial.

Some diplomats deny that the relationship between the PMO and the Ministry of External Affairs is in any way competitive. According to the official version, the ministry's role is to serve the political leadership. The job of civil servants is only to list options for the prime minister along with their opinion as to the most practical course under given circumstances. In reality, permanent civil servants in the Ministry of External Affairs often complain that with decision making increasingly centred in the Prime Minister's Office, the bureaucracy's role is only to take blame for mistakes or public relations disasters. An increasing number of interest groups – political parties, state governments, local elites, corporate groups and media – now exert influence on foreign policy, primarily through political channels that influence the prime minister. The civil service in the MEA sees this as intrusion in their sphere, insisting that apolitical bureaucrats are better suited to make above-board choices and decisions on merit.

The appointment of a national security adviser since 1999 is designed as an institutional bridge between the foreign service, intelligence services and the PMO. Now, the Indian national security apparatus approximates the American model. It comprises the national security adviser (NSA), the National Security Council Secretariat (NSCS) led by the deputy national security adviser and the National Security Advisory Board (NSAB) that enables unofficial voices on foreign policy to be heard by the government.

India's National Security Council comprises the prime minister, the national security adviser, the external affairs minister, the defence minister, the finance minister and the vice chairman of the NITI Aayog (earlier the deputy chairman of the planning commission). The composition of the National Security Council and the Cabinet Committee on Security is the same, except for the addition of the national security adviser and vice chairman of the NITI Aayog. It is argued that the Cabinet Committee on Security always has three or four issues to deal with and has to make quick decisions. It does not have time for elaborate presentations or brainstorming on any issue. The National Security Council, on the other hand, is designed to discuss one issue at a time in greater detail. In practice, however, the National Security Council meets infrequently, often only once or twice a year, and spends most of its time on dealing with strategic issues tied to nuclear command and control.

Organizationally, the National Security Council comprises the Strategic Policy Group (SPG), the National Security Advisory Board (NSAB) and a secretariat represented by the Joint Intelligence Committee (JIC). The deputy national security adviser heads the National Security Council Secretariat. The Joint Intelligence Committee (JIC), originally set up in 1948, analyses intelligence data from all intelligence agencies, domestic and foreign, civilian as well as military. It was originally headed by an MEA officer and rarely fulfilled its role of collecting, coordinating, processing and evaluating intelligence inputs and reports from all ministries. It was reconstituted in 1965 with officers both civilian and uniformed military. When the National Security Council system was set up, along with the appointment of a national security adviser, the Joint Intelligence Committee was included within it.

India's National Security Council has the advantage of being able to tap into the National Security Advisory Board as an in-house think tank. The Indian system has, in the past, failed to use local think tanks for inputs, and the NSAB is now tasked with analysing issues of critical importance for the National Security Council. Over the last several years, the NSAB, like the national security adviser, has spent the bulk of its time on issues of internal security. It has also written reports on defence preparedness, on the threats from China, the growing importance of Myanmar and even a draft national security doctrine. Ideally, the think tank's reports should find their way to the Cabinet Committee on Security for consideration in policy discussions. However, incumbent officials tend to ignore the analysis of non-governmental experts and retired officials who make up the NSAB, making it less effective as an advisory body than was intended.

COORDINATING NATIONAL SECURITY

The reluctance of an entrenched bureaucracy to yield space is the reason why India took so long after 1947 to create additional structures for policymaking. For example, the idea of an adviser to the prime minister on foreign and security policy issues is not new and has been around since Independence. Nehru's appointment of a Secretary General at the Ministry of External Affairs was meant to put in position someone having trust of the prime minister and knowledge of the Indian system. Nehru rarely sought advice and the Secretary General ended up becoming just another tier in the MEA bureaucracy created by the British. Indira Gandhi created the position of chairman of the Policy Planning Committee to help her formulate foreign policy while other prime ministers relied on advisers within the PMO. However, it took several decades before a national security adviser could be appointed and the edifice left in place by the British was subjected to any serious revision.

Even now, bureaucratic rivalries persist as to whether the national security adviser should always be a foreign service officer or the task can be handled by someone other than a civil service mandarin. Those favouring reservation of the position for an eminent former diplomat claim that it is natural to appoint a former Indian Foreign Service officer as national security adviser, given that the job entails conducting diplomacy on behalf of the prime minister. The problem with that argument manifests in the fear that the national security adviser would end up encroaching on the powers of the foreign secretary and would end up like the erstwhile Secretary General, a kind of super foreign secretary.

In any case, the Ministry of External Affairs is not the only remit of the national security adviser. Internal security issues also take up a large part of their daily routine. This includes internal security and intelligence matters as well as defence and nuclear issues as the national security adviser is part of the nuclear command and control structure. Since 1999 there have been five NSAs, of whom three came from the foreign service while the other two – including the current one – were police service officers with intelligence backgrounds. Officials complain that just as former diplomats tend to meddle in the working of the Ministry of External Affairs while serving as national security adviser, former police or intelligence officers end up acting as super cop or super intelligence official.

Over the years the national security advisers have attempted to take powers, especially those related to intelligence, away from the Ministry of Home Affairs and a power struggle has periodically ensued between the national security adviser and the home minister. Like all bureaucratic fights, the outcome of that battle has varied depending on the strength of individual actors. One arena for contention relates to whomever gets to brief the prime minister on a daily basis. Former police officers designated as national security adviser have sought to wrest control of the daily briefing from the heads of the Intelligence Bureau (IB – the domestic intelligence service) and Research and Analysis Wing (R&AW – the external intelligence service). Prime Minister Manmohan Singh, tired of having to decide the dispute, discontinued the practice of being briefed daily by his intelligence chiefs and instead asked them to brief his national security adviser.[49]

The emergence of the national security adviser has created a new centre of power in addition to the Prime Minister's Office and the Ministry of External Affairs. The national security adviser is an all-round adviser to the prime minister. He handles foreign and security policy as well as domestic issues. As the key foreign policy adviser to the prime minister, the NSA participates in all high-level talks and often accompanies the prime minister on his foreign visits. An example of the role of the NSA in such talks was the start of conversations between India and the US on the civil nuclear deal. The idea of the India–US nuclear deal, for example, originated during a conversation between Indian NSA Brajesh Mishra and his US counterpart, Condoleezza Rice.

Direct and constant access to the prime minister enables the national security adviser to be better informed about current events than even the minister for external affairs. The creation of the office of the NSA has resulted in an erosion of authority for both the foreign secretary and the external affairs minister, which is what the permanent civil service feared all along. It has, however, paved the way for better coordination between different branches of government and made decision making as well as implementation easier. Critics argue, however, that the concept of national security adviser is better suited for a presidential system of government than a parliamentary one.

The national security adviser does not have any executive authority and can only advise the prime minister. In India the national security adviser is, in the view of critics, simply an extension of prime ministerial intrusion into affairs of the foreign ministry.[50] The first NSA, Brajesh Mishra, was principal secretary to the prime minister, in addition to being national security adviser, and therefore carried weight within the bureaucratic structure. His successors, however, have had to invoke the authority of the prime minister as their office does not derive any from the Constitution or legislation. The national security adviser is not answerable to parliament and the position is considered superfluous by those averse to greater executive privilege within a parliamentary system. 'The cabinet secretary is a bureaucrat and the national security adviser is a political appointee,' observed one retired civil servant, explaining why the job might have been created. 'You can get the political appointee to do what they want; the cabinet secretary goes by the rules,' he added.[51]

The Indian civil service's culture of jealously guarding its turf has resulted in classic stovepipe decision making. Foreign policy in the contemporary world involves dealing with myriad issues ranging from climate change to trade, defence and energy. This means the involvement of what is termed in Indian bureaucratic parlance 'the line ministries'. The Ministry of External Affairs must increasingly consult the Ministry of Home Affairs (MHA), Ministry of Defence (MoD), Ministry of Finance (MoF), Ministry of Environment and Forests (MoEF), Ministry of Science and Technology, the Atomic Energy Commission and Ministry of Commerce. Normally, the ministry concerned is the driver of policy whenever international issues relate to its sphere. Policy proposals go to the prime minister's office or the Cabinet Committee on Security for approval after an inter-ministerial process.

Sometimes the nature of India's relationship with a specific country makes a ministry other than the Ministry of External Affairs salient in relations with it. The Ministry of Finance always has a say in dealings with Japan because Japan is one of India's largest aid donors. With a potential civil nuclear deal in the offing, the Department of Atomic Energy is also weighing in heavily in bilateral ties with Japan. Similarly, the presence of a large diaspora and the extent of energy ties makes ministries of energy and overseas Indian affairs significant players in dealing with Gulf Arab states.

The Ministry of Defence is always a key ministry involved in decision making on foreign and security policy. It plays a critical role in ties with countries from which India purchases weapons, such as Russia, France, Israel and even the United States. The presence of the Indian military in several countries as part of United Nations Peacekeeping Missions requires coordination between the Ministry of Defence and the Ministry of External Affairs in dealing with both the UN and the countries concerned.

The role of the Ministry of Defence in foreign policy is likely to expand as India tries to modernize its forces and plans to spend around US $250 billion on acquisition and building of military equipment. The subject has led to some tension between the Ministry of Defence and the Ministry of External Affairs. Diplomats often advocate weapons purchases as a means of enhancing ties with countries such as the US whereas defence officials prefer building weapons at home. The MoD's policies have led to India supporting local public sector enterprises even when they produce costlier weapons that take a long time to deliver. The Modi government's emphasis on 'Make in India' even in the defence sector reflects this indigenization policy that is often criticized by diplomats and national security experts.

India's defence ministry establishment is even less flexible than the foreign service mandarins. Unlike the US or the UK, the civilian-led Ministry of Defence plays a greater role than the services headquarters. This has led to a growth in the role of the Ministry of Defence in foreign and security decision making but civilian bureaucrats, not uniformed officers, exercise that influence. Service headquarters have always complained that the civilians in the ministry and even the diplomats of the Ministry of External Affairs have more say on strategic issues than their uniformed counterparts. Unlike the American system, the Indian services have rarely been allowed a structured vertical and horizontal role to send input into the system.

Civil–military separation is so deep that the training programme of Indian Foreign Service probationers does not include training in military affairs. There is no arrangement for specialization of at least some foreign service officers in military affairs even at a later stage in their career. 'India's approach to international politico-military problems has generally been based on a political and even ethical assessment,' wrote one observer in 1970, adding that it was 'largely divorced from any objective understanding and evaluation of the military and technical implications of a given situation'.[52] This imbalance favouring political platitudes over hard-nosed politico-military analysis has continued.

The uniformed services have demanded for years that India should create an organizational set-up similar to that of the American joint chiefs of staff. The latest government committee to recommend this was the Naresh Chandra task force on defence in 2012.[53] Critics argue that keeping the uniformed military out of policymaking and strategic thinking has resulted in a situation where the uniformed military does not really know how to make policy if it were asked to do so. India's generals are said to have no clue about foreign policy because they have been marginalized by the civilians. Instead of working a way out of that marginalization, the military has embraced it and remains unaware of events and decision making outside its immediate sphere.

The Indian Navy is the only service that has been proactive on strategic issues. Starting around 2004, the navy produced a naval doctrine in addition to preparing analyses on maritime security, countering piracy and protecting India's sea lanes of communication (SLoCs). The navy has also built ties with navies of other countries including the US and the Gulf regions. In the words of a former diplomat 'the navy has muscled its way into the foreign policy realm', possibly because it is by nature outward-looking. It will, however, take more than the Indian Navy's efforts to integrate uniformed services in formulation of foreign policy.

NEW STAKEHOLDERS

The fragmentation of India's national political parties and the rise of regional, identity-based formations have changed India's foreign policy discourse drastically since the days when the Indian National Congress held sway over the country's politics. Political parties are critical to setting agendas in every parliamentary democracy. The rise of coalition governments and the gradual devolution in the social and economic arenas to the states within the Indian Union has resulted in states becoming new stakeholders even in the realm of foreign policy.

India is the only state in South Asia that borders all its neighbours and hence those states that share a border with India's neighbours have often treated ties with those neighbours as a domestic issue. What this has often meant is that the vagaries of domestic politics now affect foreign policy. India's ties with Sri Lanka and especially the Tamil question have been affected by the views of the party in power in the southern state of Tamil Nadu. Similarly, it took India decades to resolve the land border issues with Bangladesh and sign the border agreement in June 2015.[54]

Devolution of financial power to the state governments and economic growth in states has led some states, like Gujarat, Tamil Nadu and Maharashtra, to have a higher economic growth rate than the federal government. These states have also started building their own ties with not only neighbouring countries but also with countries far away. For example, when he was chief minister of Gujarat, Narendra Modi travelled to China and Japan. Singapore is the leading investor in the construction of the new capital of Andhra Pradesh after the creation of India's twenty-ninth state Telangana.[55]

New technology and methods of communication have had their impact on foreign policy as well. Today governments do not wait for long telegrams or dispatches from their embassies when television, smartphones and social media provide them with the latest information. Critics may argue that 'diplomacy cannot be practised simultaneously at the marketplace and in the chancelleries'[56] but diplomacy in a democracy means that the public will often force the government to take decisions based not on logic but on emotion. The media, both old and new, is thus a key medium for agenda setting and framing which issues will be prominent in the eyes of the public.

The growing involvement of the media and public opinion in foreign policy led the Ministry of External Affairs to set up a public diplomacy division in 2006. In recent years the MEA has become increasingly active on social media, both Facebook and especially Twitter. Both Prime Minister Modi and External Affairs Minister Sushma Swaraj are extremely active on twitter and the latter especially has been extremely responsive to queries and calls for help from the Indian diaspora around the world.

An insular focused system of institutions with a permanent bureaucracy that is reluctant to accept outside expertise has meant that for decades there was an absence of think tanks and external research institutions in India. It is only in recent years that these institutions have developed, and still more recent for them to be privately funded. Even though India has a number of well-regarded universities, significant discussions in these academic institutions on foreign policy issues has been negligible.

One area in which it has been easier to accept outside expertise is the economic arena. Economic foreign policy has been an area that the government has been slow to enter and has allowed private entities, including the corporate sector to play a role. Indian business organizations like the Federation of Indian Chambers of Commerce and Industry (FICCI), Associated Chambers of Commerce and

Industry of India (ASSOCHAM) and Confederation of Indian Industry (CII) have played a role in economic foreign policy right from the 1950s and have been accepted as collaborators by the various ministries.

A key challenge facing outside experts working on foreign and security policy issues is the issue of classification. As one expert noted, almost nothing gets declassified and so those in the government or in government-affiliated think tanks have an advantage. The Ministry of External Affairs has the Indian Council of World Affairs (ICWA) at Sapru House and Research and Information System for Developing Countries (RIS). The Ministry of Defence has the Institute for Defence and Strategic Analysis (IDSA) and the United Services Institute (USI).

Most outside experts as well as retired and serving diplomats and officials agree that compared to a decade ago there is more outside input or as one stated, there is greater osmosis between universities, government and think tanks. As a former foreign minister noted, you cannot depend on the brilliance of an officer or a minister or prime minister, you need outside inputs for difficult policy decisions. The same politician pointed out that he was a subscriber to intelligence publications like *Jane's Defence, Oxford Analytica* and others.[57]

One of the reason for recent changes is that a majority of the analysts in think tanks are former civil servants, even diplomats, and so it is easier for them to ensure that their views reach their peers. However, experts cautioned that it still depends on the individual and is not institutionalized. As an example many stated that when Indira called upon someone of the calibre of K. Subrahmanyam, who was then director, Institute for Defence and Strategic Analysis, for advice it was in his individual capacity. As a former foreign secretary noted cynically, everything in India is personal.[58]

Although India has come a long way since the days of Nehru's idealism, it is still more a nation hoping to be a great power than a great power with a well-defined strategic culture.

6

Outlook for a Future Power

'THE RISE OF India' is the subject of considerable discussion both among Indians and the international community. India's size and significance have positioned it to be a major world power but so far it lacks the wherewithal, military capacity and institutional structure to act as one. The British Raj trained Indian civil servants as writers of first drafts, not as policymakers. After Independence, these bureaucrats have jealously guarded their positions at the expense of India's coming into its own. India's political leaders have invoked history, more precisely historical imagery, to forge national unity and create an aspiration for India's place under the sun. The country now needs a pragmatic strategic outlook coupled with forward-looking institutions that can make India into a contemporary version of Chanakya's Chakravartin.

In the years immediately after Independence, India's priority was ensuring its territorial integrity and unity, carving out strategic space for India in the global order and securing a South Asia free from foreign influence. Underlying India's engagement with the world was the belief that India was a great civilization and a future great power. Emerging from colonial rule, wherein all key decisions about its fate were made by foreigners, India wanted autonomy in decision making and economic self-sufficiency. India was willing to occasionally tread a somewhat lonely path just to be able to stand up to the dominant superpowers.

Since the end of the cold war, close relations with the United States notwithstanding, India remains resistant to being referred to as a US ally, preferring instead the term 'partner' or 'friend.' Both

India and the United States share strategic goals like a stable and secure South Asia and Middle East, countering global terrorism and a common security architecture for the Indo-Pacific region. India now hosts joint military exercises with the United States, and the US is fast becoming one of the top defence suppliers to India. Yet, Indian leaders still view occasional disagreement with the US publicly as critical to India's autonomy in decision making. Not even partnership with the US in dealing with China's rise can deter India from continuing to seek leadership status of the smaller non-Western nations.

Although India demands absolute autonomy in bilateral relations with various countries, it is strongly committed to multilateral institutions. For India, global institutions are a mechanism for building solidarity with the developing countries and to present India as a role model for former colonies. During the 1950s and '60s India championed decolonization across Asia and Africa. Multilateral institutions are the venue for the demand by India's leaders that the leadership of these primarily Western-led institutions reflect changed global realities. This is the premise behind India's claim for a permanent seat on the United Nations Security Council and its demand for reformulation of the Bretton Woods financial institutions. India's often-defiant stance in international institutions like the World Trade Organization (WTO) also stems from its desire for a multipolar world that is no longer dominated by Western powers.

There is a lot in common between both the US and India. Both countries have a somewhat inward-looking, even quasi-isolationist sentiment while at the same time seeking the benefits of globalization. For both, their region – the Americas for one and South Asia for the other – is an area where they resent outside interference or military. Each has its own intellectual framework for exclusion of outside powers, the Monroe doctrine in case of the United States and the Indira doctrine for India. Both have a deep national identity and strong sense of national exceptionalism. Both also see themselves as being different from the old imperialist powers. Finally, both India and the US emphasize bilateral autonomy in relations with countries and yet are deeply involved in multilateral institutions like the United Nations.

India's first prime minister, Jawaharlal Nehru, and his colleagues in the Indian independence movement sought inspiration from ancient and medieval India. Ancient philosophers taught them that the subcontinent was one civilizational and geographical entity. These philosophers also provided moral attitudes – both idealist and realist – that were adapted to proclaim that contemporary India can only grow under the shadow of its past. This general principle, of the present being guided by the past and the future only reflecting it, has applied strongly to the realm of external relations. Ancient Indian philosophers emphasized the importance of avoiding disengagement from other peoples and advised against encroaching on or taking over territory that was outside the subcontinent. India's founding elite embraced the belief that South Asia is central to India's external relations and yet India needs to be a vital player in global politics. This followed from the ancient philosophers' views, and has been a consistent pillar of India's world view since Independence.

The influence of ancient India's most famous political philosopher Chanakya lies not only in the symbolism of naming the diplomatic enclave in New Delhi after him but in the way in which India has sought a system of layered relations coupled with the mistrust of other nations – the core of Chanakya's mandala theory. Chanakya explains why, despite close relations with Western countries, India still maintains ties with Russia, old friends in the developing world from the Non-Aligned Movement and is an active participant in the BRICS grouping.

In South Asia, Indian leaders view themselves as the dominant power. India is the geographical, socio-cultural and economic centre of South Asia. New Delhi expects not just its neighbours but even external powers like China, the United States and the West both to accept Indian dominance as well as bear in mind India's interests in the region. Modern India expects its neighbours to consider India as the Chakravartin; South Asia is the only region where India has been willing to send its army or use force to defend its interests. The principle was applied during takeovers of the princely state of Hyderabad in 1948 and the Portuguese colony of Goa in 1961, while sending the Indian Peacekeeping Force to Sri Lanka in 1987, and also fighting four wars with Pakistan.

Yet, as ancient philosophers noted, the Chakravartin asserted primacy but never forcefully took over territory. Modern India too has never taken over territory that belonged to another neighbour. After the 1971 war with Pakistan that led to the creation of Bangladesh, India withdrew its forces within a short period of time from the territory of the new country.

India faced several challenges to being viewed as the dominant power in South Asia and its desire that neighbours look only to India and not to outside powers. Slow economic growth for decades meant that India did not have the economic clout to provide its neighbours with the assistance they needed. Fabian socialism, a mixed economy and the principle of economic autarky meant that until the 1990s India only grew at 3 per cent a year, a growth rate that precluded India's ability to assist neighbours. The growth of India's economy in the last two decades has opened the way for India offering aid to neighbours as an instrument of influence.

India's effort to woo its poorer South Asian neighbours with aid now face competition from China under the One Belt One Road (OBOR) initiative. China launched the China Pakistan Economic Corridor (CPEC) and has promised to invest US $46 billion in Pakistan over the course of the next few years. Economic incentives are also being offered by China to Nepal, Bangladesh and Sri Lanka. Indian leaders are aware that managing a sphere of influence is not only a function of telling others what to do but being able to expend resources that deny space to competitors.

India's neighbours complain that India has a history of big promises and extremely slow follow-through on aid projects. The gap between promise and delivery is seen in Bangladesh, Nepal, Sri Lanka and even Afghanistan where India is currently the largest regional bilateral donor. Under Prime Minister Manmohan Singh, and especially since the election of Narendra Modi, India has sought to offer trade concessions, such as zero tariff or removing non-tariff barriers, and concessional loans and credit to Afghanistan, Bangladesh, Sri Lanka and Nepal.

As prime minister, Modi has articulated a more assertive vision for India's external relations. South Asia, India's immediate periphery, is as critical to India under Modi as it was under his predecessors. Modi invited all South Asian heads of government to his inauguration and has travelled to Bhutan, Nepal, Mauritius, Myanmar, Sri Lanka, and Bangladesh within less than two years of coming to office. He even attempted a strategic thaw in relations with Pakistan through his short stopover in Lahore in December 2015 to meet with Pakistani prime minister Nawaz Sharif though that effort remained unfruitful.

On the first stand-alone bilateral tour to Sri Lanka since 1987 by an Indian prime minister, Modi pushed for reducing non-tariff barriers, encouraging economic cooperation, promised to address Colombo's concerns about trade, offered US $315 million in a line of credit to upgrade Sri Lankan rail infrastructure and promised to help the port of Trincomalee to become a petroleum hub. Modi also sought to reassure Sri Lanka over New Delhi's policy on the Tamil issue, stating, 'We stand with you in your efforts to build a future that accommodates the aspirations of all sections of society, including the Sri Lankan Tamil community, for a life of equality, justice, peace and dignity in a united Sri Lanka.'[1]

Modi visited Nepal twice in the space of six months – August 2014 and November 2014. On the first bilateral visit by an Indian prime minister to this critical Himalayan neighbour since 1998, in August 2014, Modi spoke of the old civilizational relationship between India and Nepal, referring to them 'as old as the Himalayas and the Ganga'. Like Sri Lanka, here too Modi tried to assuage resentment of India as big brother by saying, 'We have not come here to interfere in your internal matters but we want to help you to develop.'[2] During his November 2014 trip, $1 billion line of credit was offered for building Nepalese infrastructure and hydropower. Regular bus services between the two countries are now envisaged in addition to creating ease of travel for private vehicles across the border, promoting trade, tourism and regional connectivity.[3]

While relations with Sri Lanka have improved, those with Nepal seem to have their ups and downs. In late 2015, political unrest over the new Nepalese Constitution resulting from disagreements between Madhesis (ethnic Indians who have lived in Nepal for centuries) and the Nepalese government adversely impacted India–Nepal ties. The subsequent unrest and violence also resulted in Madhesis blocking all entry points from India into Nepal. Given Nepal's dependence on transit trade through India, the blockade lasting several weeks hurt landlocked Nepal and was perceived as having been supported by New Delhi.[4] Nepal offered to sign a fuel deal with China during Prime Minister Oli's maiden trip to Beijing in an obvious effort to get India's attention. Instead of signing a fuel agreement with China, the Nepal government preferred seeking a meeting of the Eminent Persons Group (EPG) created in 2014 to review the gamut of India–Nepal relations including the 1950 treaty of peace and friendship.[5]

Regional connectivity – trade, tourism and travel – between the South Asian countries has been key to Modi's push for South Asia. It would require building infrastructure within India and connecting it to the neighbouring countries. That would be a long-term endeavour requiring consistent investment and policy support. Further, for this connectivity to actualize, a South Asian Association for Regional Cooperation (SAARC) agreement along these lines would be needed. That is still a long way away. In November 2014, the inking of the SAARC connectivity agreements, including the motor vehicles pact, was stalled as Pakistan asked for time arguing 'it was yet to complete its internal process'.[6] Seven months later, in June 2015, India, Nepal, Bhutan and Bangladesh signed a Motor Vehicles Agreement 'for the regulation of passenger, personnel and cargo vehicular traffic'.[7] India is thus trying to build connectivity with its neighbours even if Pakistan remains unwilling to cooperate. New Delhi believes that sooner or later Islamabad will understand that if it doesn't participate it will be left out.

On Modi's first trip to Bangladesh in June 2015, the two countries resolved their boundary dispute by signing the Land Boundary Agreement (LBA) that had been negotiated for four decades. Agreements were also signed on cooperation in maritime safety, curbing human trafficking and checking counterfeit Indian currency allegedly circulated by Pakistan's intelligence service through Bangladesh. India offered Bangladesh $2 billion in line of credit and the two countries agreed to set up special economic zones(SEZs). Dhaka also promised to adopt a policy of 'zero tolerance' against terrorists and insurgents operating in India's north-east.[8]

India's relations with Afghanistan have also deepened. In December 2015, Modi inaugurated the new building of the Afghan parliament in Kabul that was constructed with Indian aid. In his address to the Afghan parliament Modi referred to ties with Afghanistan as 'timeless' and 'ancient', and pointed out that 'in the shifting contours of history, there were times we have been one. There were times we saw wars. But, through the ages, we have always enriched one another.' Emphasizing strategic bonds but attempting to reassure Pakistan, which looks on India–Afghan relations with suspicion, Modi stated, 'You know that India is here to contribute, not to compete; to lay the foundations of future, not light the flame of conflict; to rebuild lives, not destroy a nation. You know, as we do, that Indians and Afghans have always stood for each other, never against another.'[9]

South Asia is not the only region where India seeks to expand its influence. India offers other developing countries technical and economic assistance provided through the International Technical and Economic Cooperation (ITEC) programme. Almost 64 per cent of the annual budget outlay of the Ministry of External Affairs is spent as international aid under this programme.[10] Other avenues of Indian assistance to developing countries are educators, teachers, doctors and technical trainers. An immensely successful mode of expanding India's civilizational sphere of influence has been the export of Bollywood movies, which have access to a global market.

In addition to defining South Asia as its virtual sphere of influence and asserting leadership in the developing world, India has always taken pride in its civilizational inheritance and made it an integral part of its world view. This pride has also created a sense of Indian exceptionalism: the belief that India is unique, it is special, was one of the centres of the ancient world and will, once again, find its rightful place. India's rise is seen as an inevitability, an eventuality that is waiting to happen and that nothing and no one can prevent. During the national struggle for independence, Indian leaders and thinkers also emphasized the idea of India as a beacon for the world, both because of its ancient past but also because of the expected future.

In this iteration of India's exceptionalism, other developing countries could learn from India and benefit from the Indian experience. Because India is different, it would not be a leader like the former colonial powers or the cold war superpowers; India would be different because of its unique history and civilizational experience. Such beliefs are not just the 'feel good' avowals of leaders trying to rally their people but something believed by the lay Indian. Its deep-rootedness is visible in the presence of this belief even in the global Indian diaspora. Like other nations, including the US, who believe in national uniqueness and manifest destiny, Indians tend to abide by what they see as their principles and not give up on them as part of a compromise. This means firmly hanging on to non-alignment in a world that no longer has differing ideological blocs as well as seeking an independent position in the World Trade Organization that is often starkly opposite that of the Western countries.

India's external relations reflect India's view of self, which, in turn, is derived not just from ancient Hindu philosophers but has also been influenced by other developments through subsequent history. Medieval Muslim sultans added religious and cultural pluralism to Indian life. This legacy helped modern India shape its relations with Muslim countries to the west and north-west of India. Another heritage from the medieval era was the intense personalization of administration. The Mughals bequeathed to the British Raj a political culture focused on absolute personal power rather than on permanent institutions. The Raj left behind strong institutions with personality-driven administration to modern India.

The country was deeply influenced by almost two centuries of British rule, 110 years of it under the East India Company and another ninety directly under the British Crown. The British brought to India modern education, technology and institutions. They also made Indians more aware of their greater neighbourhood, stretching from the Middle East to South-East Asia and contributed to Indian understanding of contemporary global affairs. British Raj saw India as the jewel in its crown and the heart of its overseas empire. India provided a large supply of recruits for the colonial army; it was a low-cost producer as well as a captive market for British manufactured goods and a critical geo-strategic location for Britain to ensure its global presence.

The ancient belief in India's civilizational sphere of influence spreading from the Middle East to South-East Asia and beyond was translated during the British Raj into a strategic reality. The British viewed India as the springboard for the security of the entire region from the Persian Gulf to South-East Asia. As early as 1943 Indian strategists like K.M. Panikkar championed the British world view to argue for India to step in as the security provider for this vast region. India under Nehru, however, was reluctant to be seen as continuing the policies of a colonial power.

Nehru and his successors did not create a large military presence in the Indian Ocean littoral. Yet, even the idealist Nehru was realist enough to understand the importance of this region to India's security and ensuring India's future as a great power. Thus Nehru built close ties with his peers in Egypt and Turkey and reached out to Arab and Persian politicians and intellectuals. Further, Indian leaders sought to build India's stature through groupings like the Non-Aligned Movement and even the United Nations. In recent years, however, with the growth in Indian economic and military power concomitant with the rise of China, there have been demands that India play this role.

The United States and its allies in East Asia like Japan, South Korea and even Australia appear open to the idea of India as a major power in the Indian Ocean. During the days of the British Empire this had meant a military presence and Britannia ruling the seas. India has so far preferred to build on its cultural ties, boost its economic relations and gradually emphasize strategic ties including military exercises. Slowly, the Indian Navy is emerging as a blue-water navy that might play a role beyond just protecting India's territorial waters.

Modern India is cognizant of President Roosevelt's maxim of speaking softly while keeping a large stick. Yet her leaders have demonstrated a preference to high words instead of quiet actions. Nehru understood the importance of maintaining a large military and he was not averse to the use of force as was demonstrated in 1948 in Kashmir and 1961 in Goa. Yet, he banked more on India's stature in global politics as insurance than on investing in Indian defence. Similarly, while Nehru knew the importance of a strong economy as the backbone of foreign policy, he created a paternalistic state apparatus that, over time, especially under Indira Gandhi, suppressed the growth of India's economy. This, in turn, meant that it was only with the liberalization of the economy in the 1990s that India was able to have the economic wherewithal to demand a seat at the global high table and also invest in its military apparatus.

Now, the primary objective of Indian foreign policy is to create a global environment that ensures India's economic development. While India's leaders continue to emphasize autonomy in decision making, the leverage obtained by India's deepening economic clout has ensured that it is easier for India today than it was in the early years after Independence. Narendra Modi has brought an activism to India's foreign policy that was missing for some time. In his first thirty-one months in office, Modi has travelled to forty-five countries including the United States, Japan, China, Australia, France, Germany, Brazil, the United Arab Emirates (UAE) and the United Kingdom.

Although they represent somewhat different outlooks, Modi is as passionate about foreign policy as Nehru. Modi conducts foreign policy with the help of a small group of advisers he trusts. He prefers to deal directly with his officers, instead of through their ministerial superiors, a practice similar to that of Nehru. He has also built a direct relationship with the Indian public, using both traditional media – his monthly *Mann Ki Baat* (literal translation 'Stray Thoughts') via radio – and modern instruments like social media; Modi has over twenty-nine million followers on twitter.

The Modi world view is underpinned by the intrinsic link between economic growth and projection of power abroad. Modi does not seek standing for India solely through speeches in international forums though he is not averse to that variety of international attention. For example, Modi championed the International Yoga day at the United Nations, taking pride in yoga's Indian origins and universal popularity. During his visit to the Central Asian countries in July 2015, Modi spoke of the ancient relationship based on India's Islamic heritage 'defined by the highest ideals of Islam – knowledge, piety, compassion and welfare'. Emphasizing the links of religion and culture, Buddhism and Sufi music, yoga and the Hindi language used by Bollywood, Modi pointed out that India and Central Asia 'have a special place in our hearts for each other. But, we have not paid as much attention to each other as we should. This will change.'

Modi's foreign policy has also honed in on the Indian diaspora. During the freedom struggle, the Indian National Congress sought the assistance of its diaspora and yet, after Independence, the Indian policy was that an Indian living abroad, while culturally and civilizationally Indian, was now the responsibility of their new country, not of India. During the 1960s Burma expelled Indians and

Sri Lanka forced Tamils to leave. During the 1970s Indians living in Uganda for years were forced to leave. The Indian reaction was to preserve bilateral relations with the country in question instead of standing up for their citizens of Indian origin.

In the last two decades, however, Indian governments have devoted attention to the demands and problems faced by the Indian diaspora, recognizing their potential as instruments of global influence. A Union-level ministry was set up in the first decade of this century to take care of the needs of the overseas Indians or Pravasi Bharatiya. There is an annual Pravasi Bharatiya Divas (Overseas Indian Day) and successive Indian governments have wooed their diaspora with awards and incentives. For decades, Indian labour abroad did not find anything more than moral support from Delhi. Now, when Modi and a foreign leader meet, the needs of the Indian labour is one of the issues discussed. Thus, what under Nehru were deemed internal matters of another country have become part of India's international relations.

In his speeches and travels, Modi has specially appealed to the Indian diaspora in every country he visits. Economic partnerships and investment by both international and Indian business to collaborate in expanding manufacturing in India are declared goals of Modi's foreign economic policy. The highlight of Modi's first trip to the United States in September 2014 was his speech at New York City's Madison Square garden where he addressed an enthusiastic Indian-American diaspora. Modi promised overseas Indians ease of travel, spoke of the ties between the oldest (United States) and the largest (India) democracies in the world, promised an end to bureaucratic red tape and sought investment by this diaspora in India's future economic growth.[11] On his second trip to the United States in September 2015, Modi travelled to the west coast, the first time an Indian prime minister had travelled since 1982. In San Jose, Modi appealed to the Silicon Valley technology industry, dominated by the Indian diaspora, seeking help for his Digital India initiative which provides 'an opportunity to transform lives of people in ways that was hard to imagine just a couple of decades ago'.[12]

Modi is keen to use the advantage overseas Indians bring to their ancient homeland. On his monumental trip to the United Arab Emirates, the first time an Indian prime minister visited in thirty-four years, Modi embraced the huge Indian diaspora that helped build the UAE and continues to live and work there. Modi offered the diaspora ease of visa and travel and sought investment and tourism in return. Modi spoke of the 'change in India' with respect to policies and bureaucratic red tape and sought investment from the UAE.[13] For its part, the United Arab Emirates government showed its interest in the welfare of Indians there by announcing the construction of a Hindu temple in Abu Dhabi, the first in the Gulf region.

During his Pacific Islands trip in November 2014, the first visit by an Indian prime minister in over three decades, Modi announced the setting up of a $1 million fund and visa on arrival facility for Indians settled in Fiji and other islands. In an attempt to boost trade with these islands New Delhi will set up a trade office and also raise the annual grant-in-aid for community projects to each Pacific Island country from $125,000 annually to $200,000.[14]

Subsequently, at the second Forum of India–Pacific Islands Cooperation (FIPIC) held in Jaipur on 22 August 2015, Modi pitched for stronger cooperation with the fourteen islands by offering to set up an Institute for Sustainable Coastal and Ocean Research, provide naval support for coastal surveillance and hydrographic surveys as well as set up Space Technology Application Centres in these island nations.[15]

China is both a major trading partner and a potential competitor for India. On his first trip to China as prime minister in May 2015, Modi spoke of the 'ancient spiritual and cultural links' shared by the two countries. He emphasized that India's ties with China are one of its most important strategic partnerships as the 're-emergence of India and China and their relationship will have a profound impact on the two countries and the course of this century'.[16] In a speech before twenty-two top Chinese CEOs, Modi pitched his 'Make in India' agenda and during his trip twenty-one business agreements were signed worth US $22 billion. Modi sought investment in India's infrastructure plans – from railways, to highways to road and port building – emphasizing that India had changed and was now 'more transparent, responsive and stable'.[17]

Among world leaders, Modi has a close personal relationship with Japanese prime minister Shinzo Abe, who like Modi is a centre-right nationalist politician attempting to revive his country's economy, revolutionize its defence policy and seek a role for it in a world challenged by a rising China and a less assertive America. On his maiden trip to Japan in September 2014, Modi wooed Japanese investment by remarking that he had converted Indian red tape into a red carpet while the two countries upgraded their ties to a special strategic global partnership. Tokyo promised to invest US $35 billion in India over the next five years and talks are ongoing about a civil nuclear deal between the two leading Asian nations.[18] On Abe's return visit to India in December 2015, agreements were signed to finalize Japanese companies building India's first bullet train connecting the industrial hubs of Mumbai and Ahmedabad. If Abe is able to change Japan's post–World War II policy restricting sale of defence equipment, India will also be able to purchase Japanese US-2 amphibian aircraft.

Modi's landmark economic programme is the 'Make in India' scheme under which he seeks to balance the desire for economic self-sufficiency with the aspiration of building a world-class economy. The fear of the East India Company's legacy is so deep-rooted that even today most Indian leaders would rather India not be dependent on any country. However, India needs foreign technologies and massive foreign investment if it seeks to become a global economic powerhouse. Modi has invited investment from corporations and businesses in every country. Foreign investors are eager to access India's large market but the drastic changes they expected are yet to be adopted.

India's economy has tremendous potential and there is a huge demographic divided which is waiting to be harnessed. Modi's administration has a once-in-a-lifetime opportunity to build on this by harnessing the Indian and global corporate sectors to spur Indian economic growth. This, however, will require as much attention to the domestic economy as Modi has given to foreign policy. In both spheres, the prime minister has to contend with entrenched views that characterize the Indian bureaucracy's way of thinking as well as the exigencies of domestic politics. While politics in India has come a long way, governments still believe they need to appeal to identity politics and that economic reforms do not win elections.

In the sphere of foreign policy, India is still wedded to old ideas and British-era structures. 'Institution building has not been our strength,' observed a former foreign secretary.[19] But as Subrahmanyam stated, 'Ours is a ritualistic society. We are used to creating institutions and formulating processes without any intention of putting them to use.'[20] According to K.S. Bajpai, Indians believe in individuals rather than institutions. It is a legacy India inherited from the Mughals through the British down to present times. Although institutions were ostensibly developed, and India has many, but 'as far as policymaking is concerned, it is still a handful of people who decide in a somewhat ad hoc manner'. Bajpai felt that he didn't know of any country, other than the United States, 'where so much expertise is brought into policymaking to so little effect'.[21]

Indian policymaking depends on the vision and will of its leader of the time and is run through networks of personal relationships. Since his election in 2014, Narendra Modi has articulated a new vision, demonstrated the will to change things and is creating the networks that might bring about that change. But the institutions of governance created by the British, including the civil service and the armed forces, were trained to think within predetermined parameters. Leaders, from Nehru to Modi, have promised to 'restore' India to its eminence.

India is, by all measures, an extremely significant country. However, the experience of the last seventy years leads one to wonder whether greatness as envisaged by India's leaders can be made to materialize by institutions designed to maintain a colonial enterprise. India's bureaucrats are wedded to the status quo even when India's people want to enter the twenty-first century as part of a new global order. India's history is its asset as well as a great burden. The fact that the country has existed for millennia creates hubris and the belief that, in the final analysis, India will go on. Why bother with building a new framework for global engagement and international leadership when the legacy is massive enough to enable muddling through? India's success as a twenty-first-century global power might depend on jettisoning that way of thinking.

7
Afterword

IN THE THREE years since the publication of *From Chanakya to Modi,* its core arguments have only been reinforced by events. India's foreign policy shows more consistency than change. Prime Minister Narendra Modi's focus on foreign policy is reminiscent of India's first prime minister Jawaharlal Nehru. Some institutional changes within the foreign and security establishments aside, India's way of conducting foreign relations remains constant. Strategic autonomy and its immediate neighbourhood remain the focus of India's engagement with the world.

India faces even greater challenges today than it did in 2017. The internal struggle for the Idea of India, between a secular democratic India versus a majoritarian Hindu rashtra, have exacerbated social discord and slowed economic growth. India's image has also taken a battering, not only in the United States and the West, but even in its own neighbourhood.

Many friends and admirers of India around the world are worried that the idea of India they supported since India's independence is changing and, in their view, not for the better. At a time when New Delhi would like the world to root for a rising India, the country is in the news for student protests and their violent suppression, attacks on minorities and weakening of India's democratic and pluralist credentials.

The passionate focus on foreign policy that defined Modi's first term in office has continued in the second term as well. Between 2017, when *From Chanakya to Modi* first came out, until the end of 2019, Modi continued his international travels. He went to thirty-eight different countries across five continents, including twice to the US and three visits each to Russia, France and China.[1]

Modi has often used his foreign policy speeches to inform the world about his views and goals. In every speech, whether at the World Economic Forum (Davos) in January 2018 or the annual strategic Shangri-La Dialogue in Singapore in June 2018, there is an emphasis on how India seeks to reclaim its place on the world stage, references to ancient India's civilizational ties, and an emphasis on the economic and cultural ties that bind India and that particular region or country.[2]

External Affairs Minister S. Jaishankar, who earlier served as foreign secretary, has also spoken over the last four years on how India seeks to be a leading power. He has argued that 'The India Way' going ahead would be to 'use' its 'capacity to bear on the international system for global good' and that India sought to be 'more a decider and shaper than an abstainer', in the global arena.[3]

At the structural level, there have been changes within the Ministry of External Affairs, with a move away from the current pyramid-style structure into a more decentralized one. The aim is to create a series of verticals with each vertical being headed by a policy director of the rank of additional secretary. This is in addition to the rise in lateral entry – direct appointment of experts to senior positions from outside the career foreign service – and creation of new divisions like the Indo-Pacific division, emerging technologies division, and others.[4] The national security apparatus too has undergone change. Not only does the national security adviser (NSA) now hold cabinet ministerial rank but there are also three deputy NSAs and one military adviser to the prime minister.[5]

For India, South Asia has always occupied primacy. The 'Neighbourhood First' policy of Modi is a continuation of this consistent attempt by Delhi to reassure its smaller South Asian neighbours that, in return for assistance, they must yield to India's security concerns. The initial enhancement of relations with all South Asian neighbours, excepting Pakistan, has given way to some diminution in bonhomie with most neighbours. Even good friend and partner, Bangladesh, has reacted unfavourably to the communalist turn in Indian domestic politics.

India can ill afford to antagonize critical allies like Bangladesh at a time when it needs their help to combat China's deep economic and strategic infiltration in South Asia. At some point, a course correction would be required to balance the demands of domestic vote-gathering and the expectation of external partners that India will continue to adhere to the secular principles enshrined in its Constitution.

At the same time, there has been a growing understanding in New Delhi on the need to expend resources not just in South Asia but also in India's greater neighbourhood, from Asia to Africa. This is reflected not just in the setting up of an Indo-Pacific division but also in the allocations for development assistance. South Asia retains primacy under the ITEC (International Technical and Economic Cooperation) programme but its percentage share in budget allocations has declined in recent years. From a high of 85 per cent allocated to South Asia in 2016-17,[6] two years later only 66 per cent was apportioned for the region.[7] Within South Asia, Bhutan occupies top spot. In both 2107-18 and 2018-19, Delhi increased the development assistance for Bhutan while Nepal received 10.42 per cent of ITEC, bearing in mind Beijing's overtures to Kathmandu.[8]

India's relations with Pakistan have been on a downward spiral since the high of Christmas 2015 when Prime Minister Modi and the then prime minister Nawaz Sharif walked hand in hand in Lahore. Pakistani civilian leaders have often sought better relations with India, but the country's foreign policy remains in the hands of the military-intelligence establishment for whom India continues to be an existential threat. The Pakistani military continues to use jihadis as a lever of foreign policy to ensure that India remains tied down to the region. This policy has continued unabated despite the Modi government's readiness to climb the escalation ladder each time there is a terror attack inside India originating from Pakistan.

The 2019 Pulwama terror attack,[9] where a Jaish-e-Muhammad suicide bomber attacked an Indian paramilitary convoy, led the two countries once again down a path of sabre rattling, military strikes, and counter strikes.[10] In the end, both sides realized their limits as nuclear-weapon powers and de-escalated. India may or may not have won the game of brinkmanship, but Pakistan's global isolation was demonstratable. Pakistan's loss of friends abroad, both in the West and even in the greater Muslim world, will have strategic consequences that Islamabad–Rawalpindi still prefer not to ponder.

In the Gulf, or West Asia as Indians refers to the region, the last few years have seen a further bolstering of economic and strategic relations with India. Part of it has to do with changing global realities: with the United States turning more isolationist, many American allies around the world are looking to expand relations with global players like India and China. Bolstering ties with India (unlike China) also does not hurt ties with the United States. India's economic potential, its large Muslim population (the second largest in the world), and its large military are all appealing for the Gulf Muslim states.

For Delhi, the Gulf Arab Muslim states are not only strong trading partners[11] and key sources of oil, gas[12] and remittances, but also potential allies on the regional and global stage. Increasing military exercises, collaborations at global fora and exchanges of high-level delegations have strengthened India's ties with the Muslim Middle East in the last few years. In March 2019, India's then external affairs minister, Sushma Swaraj, addressed the fifty-seven-member body of Muslim countries, the OIC (Organization of Islamic Countries), leading to Pakistan's decision to stay away from the meeting. The host, United Arab Emirates (UAE), historically close to Pakistan, chose India as the preferred guest at the OIC meeting within a couple of weeks after the Pulwama terror attack and just a few days after an Indian air strike inside Pakistan.[13]

Indians and Indian leaders have always believed that India's millennia-old civilization, critical geostrategic location and population size guarantee it a place under the sun. They see the growing partnership with the United States and expanding global support for India as validation of their belief. But the reasons for India's global role may have less to do with the civilizational factor than with contemporary realities. The world's renewed interest is more a function of India's democratic and pluralist credentials, its rapid economic growth after the 1990s, its large military base and potential, and the rise of China.

At the 'Howdy Modi' event in Houston, Texas, in 2019 and the 'Namaste Trump' gathering in Ahmedabad in February 2020, the symbolism of an American president walking hand in hand with an Indian prime minister was a victory for Prime Minister Modi and his administration.[14] But at the end of the day, the strength of the relationship between any two countries lies in substantive economic and strategic bonds. India considered itself the leader of the non-aligned world under Nehru, only to realize that symbolic gatherings of disparate nations do not confer tangible power. Under Modi, India runs the risk of mistaking hugs of an American leader for a real partnership, which might be more conditional than is being currently understood.

The Asia–Pacific, and later Indo-Pacific, strategy of successive American administrations has sought to counter the economic and military rise of China. This American strategy rests on renewed engagement with its partners and allies across the region – India, Japan and the states of South-east Asia – to construct a configuration that will be able to check China's march.

Americans consider India central to the security architecture aimed at stopping China from transforming its considerable economic clout into threatening military muscle in the Indo-Pacific. But hesitation on the part of India to confront China could unravel current US affections for India relatively quickly.

For its part, Washington has sought to help build India's security capacity through commercial and defence cooperation between the two militaries, viewing India as a potential regional security provider in South Asia. India is key to the US–Indo-Pacific Strategy, the US-South Asia strategy and is mentioned prominently in the US National Security Strategy (NSS) document. The US even renamed its Pacific Command as the Indo-Pacific Command. But differences in security priorities persist between India and the US.

India deems the Indian Ocean more important than the Pacific because India's interests are primarily in South Asia and the Middle East. For the US, China and the South China Sea are more important. India and the US also differ to some extent on Afghanistan. A stable Afghanistan that has control over its territory and is not ruled by extremists such as the Taliban is critical for India, while the US seems willing to walk away from Afghanistan as long as it does not provide a safe haven for global terrorist groups.

On the economic front, nationalist sentiment and demands of domestic politics are also driving the two countries in a direction where the divergence of economic priorities could undermine strategic convergence. Trade issues have come to the fore under the Trump administration, which claims that India has extremely high tariffs and demands that India import more American products. India's response is that its tariffs are not as high as those of others, including the US, and India is not alone in imposing high tariffs on certain products. But the Modi government understands that it cannot dismiss American concerns. There has been a steady decline in India's trade deficit with the US over the last three years. India has increased its purchase of oil, gas, civilian aircraft and defence equipment from American companies. The India–US bilateral trade, which stood at $126 billion in 2017, rose to $150 billion in 2019.[15]

Economic issues remain critical to success in the realm of foreign policy. India's phenomenal rate of economic growth over the last two decades made it an attractive partner for the US and many other countries. The slowing down of the economy might be taking away some of that allure. As a result of lacklustre economic policies, India's rate of growth has declined to 4.5 per cent in 2019, down from 7 to 7.5 per cent in 2017.[16] What was once described as the fastest growing economy in the world is now in its worst phase in forty-two years.

Unemployment in India is at an all-time high, industrial production is not growing and investment is declining. The agriculture sector is in distress and productivity has slowed even in the consumer goods sector. For a nation of more than one billion people, such stagnation does not augur well. Moreover, instead of jettisoning socialism, fear has been generated that India was in the process of abandoning its democratic credentials. India's performance in the economic realm, which is below expectations, coupled with concerns about illiberal majoritarianism limits India's ability to play the role it seeks globally.

The economic and military rise of China had led many around the world to woo India as a potential rival to China. But so far, Delhi appears unable or unwilling to take advantage of the opportunities that lie ahead, or at least not at the pace India's well-wishers around the world desire.

Indians often like the comparison that many around the world make between India and China. The two Asian powers have the world's two largest populations and have great potential as global powers. But China maintained a single-minded focus on building its economic and military capability for over two decades, before it projected itself as a world power. India, on the other hand, speaks incessantly about its potential for greatness without implementing economic reforms, which might pave the way for that greatness to materialize.

India's last major economic reforms took place in 1991 and India badly needs the next generation of economic reforms that will focus on critical areas of land, labour, and capital. Domestic policy affects foreign relations whether one likes it or not, and it is not enough to say that the currently contentious issues are India's internal matters. The lack of focus on economic growth over the last several years can be traced to an over-emphasis on socio-cultural issues and majoritarian politics.

Moreover, in the international arena, India's image has been of a status quo power, a country that sought better ties with its neighbours, and aimed to be a responsible global player. India's rivalry with China and its conflicts with Pakistan notwithstanding, the world has historically been unwilling to view India through the

Chinese or Pakistani prism. India has never been identified as having hegemonic ambitions.

In a world that looks askance at countries obtaining nuclear weapons, India is the rare exception of a state that was able to convince the international community, especially the United States, to recognize its nuclear status. The 2005 India-US civilian nuclear deal and India's acceptance in the global nuclear regimes have been possible because India is viewed as a reliable global actor. Words and actions that deviate from India's tradition of responsible behaviour, often manifested in the bombast of domestic politics, could adversely impact India's global standing. Also, India's friends and rivals would take Delhi's promise of rivalling China seriously when they see India investing more on defence and security. Instead of spending more on defence, India has been spending less and this year's defence budget (excluding pensions) stands at only 1.5 per cent of GDP.[17]

In the last few years, communal passions appear to have interrupted India's entry into the global major league. Chanakyan wisdom in the contemporary era would suggest that India's leaders should not squander their energy on trying to address real or perceived historical injustices. The focus of the Indian government should be on boosting economic growth, building human capital and strengthening military capability. These actions – not putting minorities and neighbours in their place – would help India achieve its own place in the global order, the goal that India's foreign policy thinkers have pursued from Chanakya to Modi.

Notes

INTRODUCTION

1. Kaunain Sheriff, 'Traffic Hazard: Tribunal concerned over animal-driven carts on roads', *The Indian Express*, 9 May 2015.
2. Stuart Auerbach, 'From India: A Bullock Cart That Meets the Needs of Modern Times', *The Washington Post*, 11 December 1981.
3. Text of Prime Minister Narendra Modi's speech before the UN General Assembly, New York, 27 September 2014, http://www.ndtv.com/india-news/full-text-of-pm-narendra-modis-address-at-un-general-assembly-671757 (accessed on 5 June 2016).
4. Asoke Mukerji, 'Revealed: The Diplomatic Moves that Delivered Modi His Yoga Day', The Wire, 21 June 2016.
5. Text of PM Narendra Modi's Speech to the US Congress, Washington DC, 8 June 2016, http://indianexpress.com/article/india/india-news-india/prime-minister-narendra-modi-us-congress-speech-2842046/ (accessed on 10 June 2016).
6. 'Millions stretch and bend on International Day of Yoga in India', Reuters, 22 June 2016.
7. Bharat Karnad, *Why India Is Not A Great Power? (Yet)*, New Delhi: Oxford University Press, 2015, p. 1.

CHAPTER 1: INDIA AND THE WORLD

1. Walter Russell Mead, *Special Providence: American Foreign Policy and How It Changed the World*, New York: Alfred Knopf, 2001, pp. 87–89.
2. V.S. Naipaul, *India: A Wounded Civilization*, New York: Vintage Books, 1976, p. 8.

3. Sunil Khilnani, *The Idea of India,* New York: Farrar, Straus, Giroux, 1997, pp. 5–9.
4. Stephen Cohen, *Emerging Power: India*, Washington DC: Brookings Press, 2001, pp. 37–49.
5. Sumit Ganguly, *India's Foreign Policy: Retrospect and Prospect*, New Delhi: Oxford University Press, 2010.
6. Concept of civilizational sphere of influence attributed to Ambassador Husain Haqqani.
7. Y.D. Gundevia, *Outside the Archives*, Hyderabad: Sangam Books, 1984, p. 27.
8. Syed Hossain, 'What India Wants?' *The New York Times*, 9 April 1922.
9. Jawaharlal Nehru's speech on 13 December 1946 during the Constituent Assembly Debates. Taken from *Constituent Assembly Debates of India, Official Report,* Vol. I (9 December to 23 December 1946), http://164.100.47.132/LssNew/cadebatefiles/C13121946.html (accessed on 10 June 2014).
10. An Indian Official, 'India as a World Power,' *Foreign Affairs*, Vol. 27, No. 4, July 1949, pp. 540–50.
11. Devirupa Mitra, 'How India nearly gave in to US pressure to enter the Iraq killing zone', The Wire, 8 July 2016, http://thewire.in/50028/india-nearly-gave-us-pressure-join-iraq-war/ (accessed on 8 July 2016).
12. Granville Austin, *Working a Democratic Constitution: A History of the Indian Experience*, New Delhi: Oxford University Press, 1999, p. 17.
13. Letter from Nehru to all chief ministers, 26 March 1958. Taken from Jawaharlal Nehru, *Letters to Chief Ministers, 1947-64,* Volume 5: 1958-1964, New Delhi: Oxford University Press, 1989, p. 27.
14. Letter from Nehru to all chief ministers, 20 December 1958, ibid., p. 176.
15. Letter from Nehru to all chief ministers, 16 October 1959, ibid., p. 294.
16. Letter from Nehru to all chief ministers, 12 June 1960, ibid., p. 372.
17. Nehru lost his wife in 1936 and having spent most of his youth in England he did not have many friends in India. In letters to Mahatma Gandhi he poured out his feeling of loneliness. 'I felt terribly lonely in this wide world. I have always felt a little lonely almost from

childhood up.' A letter from Nehru to Gandhi, 13 August 1934, cited in Frank Moraes, *Jawaharlal Nehru: A Biography*, New Delhi: Jaico Publishing House, 1959, p. 252.

18. 'Literacy in India', *Census 2011*, n. p., n. d., http://www.census2011.co.in/literacy.php (accessed on 1 June 2016).
19. Y.D. Gundevia, *Outside the Archives*, p. 194.
20. S.D. Muni, *India's Foreign Policy: The Democracy Dimension, with Special Reference to Neighbours*, New Delhi: Foundation Books/ Cambridge University Press, 2009, p. 29.

CHAPTER 2: A RICH HERITAGE

1. Salman Rushdie, *Midnight's Children: A Novel*, New York: Random House, 1980, p. 118.
2. Shashi Tharoor, 'Globalization and the Human Imagination', *World Policy Journal*, Vol. 21, No. 2, Summer 2004, p. 88.
3. Norman Palmer, 'Review of K. Satchidananda Murty, Indian Foreign Policy', *Journal of Asian Studies*, Vol. 25, No. 2, February 1966, p. 172.
4. Arthasastra means treatise on economics; Dharmasastra treatise on dharma or moral code of conduct; Nitisastras were treatises on morality. The most well-known of the Arthasastrins was Kautilya and similarly the most well-known Dharmasastrin was Manu.
5. K. Satchidananda Murty, *Indian Foreign Policy*, Calcutta: Scientific Book Agency, 1964, p. 4.
6. Ibid., pp. 4–10.
7. Ibid.
8. Ibid.
9. Nehru's speech, Lucknow, 13 May 1963 and Nehru's address to the 67th session of the Indian National Congress, 6 January 1962, *Jawaharlal Nehru's Speeches,* Volume 5, May 1963–May 1964, and *Jawaharlal Nehru's Speeches,* Volume 4, September 1957–April 1963, New Delhi: Publications Division, Ministry of Information & Broadcasting, 1966.
10. Introduction by Quincy Wright in K. Satchidananda Murty, *Indian Foreign Policy*, Calcutta: Scientific Book Agency, 1964, pp. ix–x.
11. Giri Deshingkar, 'Strategic Thinking of Kautilya and Sun Zi', *China Report*, 1996, Vol. 32, No. 1, p. 4.

12. Nalini Kant Jha, 'Cultural and Philosophical Roots of India's Foreign Policy', *International Studies*, Vol. 26, No. 45, 1989, pp. 45–67.
13. *Jawaharlal Nehru's Speeches,* Volume 1, September 1946–May 1949, New Delhi: Publications Division, 1949, p. 232.
14. Rashed Uz Zaman, 'Kautilya: The Indian Strategic Thinker and Indian Strategic Culture', *Comparative Strategy*, Vol. 25, No. 3, 2006, pp. 233–35.
15. Ibid.
16. Ibid., pp. 236–45.
17. Michael Liebig, 'Kautilya's Relevance for India Today', *India Quarterly*, Vol. 69, No. 2, 2013, Abstract.
18. J.N. Dixit, *Makers of India's Foreign Policy: Raja Ram Mohun Roy to Yashwant Sinha*, New Delhi: HarperCollins, 2004, p. 55.
19. Ibid., p. 38.
20. For further details, please see V.N. Khanna, *Foreign Policy of India*, New Delhi: Vikas Publishing House, 1997, p. 13.
21. For details of this view please read Nalini Kant Jha, 'Cultural and Philosophical Roots of India's Foreign Policy, at pp. 46–51.
22. Nehru's first official pronouncement on foreign policy, as interim prime minister and external affairs minister, over All India Radio on 7 September 1946. Taken from Jawaharlal Nehru, *India's Foreign Policy: Select Speeches, September 1946-April 1961*, New Delhi: Ministry of Publications, Government of India, 1961, p. 2.
23. Priya Chacko, *Indian Foreign Policy: The Politics of Postcolonial Identity from 1947 to 2004,* London: Routledge, 2012, p. 2.
24. Ibid., p. 1.
25. Sunil Khilnani, Rajiv Kumar, Pratap Bhanu Mehta, Prakash Menon, Nandan Nilekani, Srinath Raghavan, Shyam Saran and Siddhartha Varadarajan, *Non Alignment 2.0: A Foreign and Strategic Policy for Indian in the Twenty-First Century*, New Delhi: Centre for Policy Research, 2012, http://www.cprindia.org/sites/default/files/Non-alignment%202.0_1.pdf (accessed on 20 May 2016).
26. K. Satchidananda Murty, *Indian Foreign Policy*, pp. 4–10.
27. Ibid., p. 13.
28. Nalini Kant Jha, 'Cultural and Philosophical Roots of India's Foreign Policy,' at pp. 61–65.
29. Speech given by Nehru at Lucknow, 13 May 1963. Taken from K. Satchidananda Murty, *Indian Foreign Policy*, pp. 7–8.

30. For details on Chola expansion into Sri Lanka and South-East Asia please see George Spencer, *The Politics of Expansion: The Chola Conquest of Sri Lanka and Sri Vijaya*, Madras: New Era Publications, 1983, pp. 5–6. Spencer explains Chola expeditions to Sri Lanka and the Sri Vijaya Empire as 'organized plundering activity' arguing that 'military campaigns of the Cholas and their Indian rivals, especially those carried out over long distances, constituted a type of compulsive behaviour dictated by the urgent needs of statecraft, especially but not exclusively its economic needs: to reaffirm the hero-credentials of kings and princes; to provide potentially restless vassals and their troops with profitable employment in distant places; and to secure access to what S.N. Eisenstaedt has called "free flowing resources" such as jewels and other valuables which were not firmly embedded in local communities, to place at the disposal of the court. These political needs were, in turn, related to the continuing importance of redistributive processes in the peasant economy. Hence they were intended to reaffirm the ruler's identity as supreme patron and benefactor in the realm: supporter of priests and poets, builder of religious monuments, dispenser of titles and booty, and therefore – at a higher level of abstraction – upholder of society and the cosmic order.'
31. For more details on the Mughals' foreign policy decision making please see N.R. Farooqi, 'Diplomacy and Diplomatic Procedure under the Mughals', *The Medieval History Journal*, Vol. 7, No. 1, 2004, p. 73.
32. Lawrence James, *Raj: The Making and Unmaking of British India*, New York: St Martin's Press, 1997, p. 640.
33. Philip Woodruff, *The Men Who Ruled India: The Founders,* New York: St Martin's Press, 1954, pp. 15–16.
34. Rudyard Kipling, 'The White Man's Burden: The United States and the Philippine Islands', *McClure's Magazine*, February 1899.
35. Philip Woodruff, *The Men Who Ruled India: The Guardians*, New York: St Martin's Press, 1954, Epigram.
36. Speech given by Lord Curzon on 20 July 1904 on the presentation of the freedom of the city of London, at the Guildhall. Taken from John Murray, *Speeches on India: Delivered by Lord Curzon of Kedleston, Viceroy and Governor-general of India, While in*

England in July-August, 1904, London, William Clowes and Sons Ltd, 1904.

37. Captain Mahan cited in H. Caldwell Lipsett, *Lord Curzon in India: 1898-1903*, Berkeley: University of California, 1903, pp. 223–28.
38. Olaf Caroe, *Wells of Power: The Oilfields of South-Western Asia: A Regional and Global Study*, New York: Da Capo Press, 1976, p. 64.
39. K.M. Panikkar, *Asia and Western Dominance: A Survey of the Vasco da Gama Epoch of Asian History 1498-1945*, London: George Allen & Unwin Ltd, 1953, pp. 111, 122.
40. Winston Churchill, 'Dominion Status', *Daily Mail*, November 1929. Taken from Winston Churchill, *India: Defending the Jewel in the Crown*, London: Dragonwyck Publications Co., 1931, Chapter II.
41. Speech given by Winston Churchill before the Indian Empire Society on 'The Round Table Conference', Canon Street, London, 12 December 1930. Taken from Winston Churchill, *India: Defending the Jewel in the Crown,* London: Dragonwyck Publications Co., 1931, Chapter III.
42. Winston Churchill's speech before the Indian Empire Society on 'A General View', Free Trade Hall, Manchester, 30 January 1931, ibid., Chapter V.
43. Winston Churchill's speech before the Indian Empire Society on 'The Round Table Conference', Canon Street, London, 12 December 1930, ibid., Chapter III.
44. Winston Churchill's speech, 'The Landslide', House of Commons, 26 January 1931, ibid., Chapter IV.
45. Conversation over lunch between Churchill and Ghanshyam Das Birla, at Churchill residence, Chartwell, in July 1935. Taken from Arthur Herman, *Gandhi & Churchill: The Epic Rivalry that Destroyed an Empire and Forged Our Age*, New York: Bantam Books, 2008, p. 401.
46. From a discussion between Winston Churchill and General Claude Auchinleck, commander of British forces in western desert, Spring 1942, ibid., p. 482.
47. Elisabeth Mariko Leake, 'British India versus the British Empire: The Indian Army and an impasse in imperial defence, circa 1919–39', *Modern Asian Studies*, Vol. 48, No. 1, January 2014, pp. 301–329, at 319–20.

48 Ibid., at pp. 320–23.
49. Olaf Caroe, *Wells of Power*, pp. xviii–xix.
50. Lord Curzon cited in ibid., p. 64.
51. K.M. Panikkar, *The Future of South-East Asia: An Indian View*, New York: The Macmillan Company, 1943, pp. 42–43.
52. K.M. Panikkar and an Englishman, *Indian Nationalism – Its Origin, History and Ideals*, London: Faith Press, 1919, pp. 104–05.
53. K.M. Panikkar, *The Future of South-East Asia*, pp. 45–46.
54. Ibid., pp. 48–50.
55. K.M. Panikkar, 'The Defense of India and Indo-British obligations', *International Affairs*, Vol. 22, No. 1, January 1946, pp. 85–90.
56. K.M. Panikkar, *The Future of South-East Asia*, pp. 1–3.
57 Ibid., pp. 6–7.
58. Ibid., p. 25.
59. Iqbal Singh, *India's Foreign Policy*, Bombay: Hind Kitab Limited, 1946, pp. 54–55.
60. V.T. Krishnamachari, 'Regional Arrangements: The Indian Ocean Area', in K.M. Panikkar, Sir V.T. Krishnamachari, Rt Hon. H.V. Evatt, K. Santhanam, I.H. Baqai, G.A. Johnsons and Manuel Canyes (eds), *Regionalism and Security*, New Delhi: Indian Council of World Affairs, 1948, pp. 10–12.
61. K.M. Panikkar, 'Regionalism and World Security', in ibid., pp. 1–2.
62. P.N. Kirpal, 'Speculation on the International Relations of a Free and United India in the Post-war World,' *The Indian Journal of Political Science*, Vol. 7, Nos 1 and 2, July – December 1945, p. 401.
63. K.N.V. Sastri, 'International Relations with Reference to the East and India', *The Indian Journal of Political Science*, Vol. 7, Nos 1 and 2, July – December 1945, p. 385.
64. Guy Wint, *British in Asia*, pp. 21–23, cited in K.M. Panikkar, *Asia and Western Dominance: A Survey of the Vasco da Gama Epoch of Asian History 1498-1945*, London: George Allen & Unwin Ltd, 1953, pp. 126–27.
65. Olaf Caroe, *Wells of Power*, p. 159.
66. H.N. Kunzru, 'Defence of India', *Annals of the American Academy of Political & Social Science*, Vol. 233 May 1944, p. 6.
67. K.M. Panikkar, 'The Defence of India and Indo-British obligations', *International Affairs*, Vol. 22, No. 1, January 1946, pp. 85–90.
68. Olaf Caroe, *Wells of Power*, p. 33.

69. J.N. Dixit, *Makers of India's Foreign Policy*, pp. 19–23.
70. Paul F. Power, 'Indian Foreign Policy: The Age of Nehru', *The Review of Politics*, Vol. 26, No. 2, April 1964, pp. 257–59.
71. Iqbal Singh, *India's Foreign Policy*, p. 10.
72. Jayantanuja Bandyopadhyaya, *The Making of India's Foreign Policy: Determinants, Institutions, Processes and Personalities*, Bombay: Allied Publishers, 1970, pp. 115–16.
73. Iqbal Singh, *India's Foreign Policy*, pp. 15–16.
74. J.N. Dixit, 'Jawaharlal Nehru – Architect of India's Foreign Policy', in *Nehru Revisited*, Mumbai: Nehru Centre, 2003, pp. 58–61.
75. Iqbal Singh, *India's Foreign Policy*, pp. 23–25.
76. Taraknath Das, 'The War comes to India', *The Antioch Review*, Vol. 2, No. 3, Autumn 1942, p. 480.
77. Iqbal Singh, *India's Foreign Policy*, pp. 20–21.
78. Ibid.
79. Muchkund Dubey, 'Nehru's Vision of the International Order', in Nehru Centre, Mumbai, *Witness to History: Transition and Transformation of India, 1947-64*, New Delhi: Oxford University Press, 2011, p. 60.

CHAPTER 3: IDEAS AND INDIVIDUALS

1. Dean Acheson, *Present at the Creation,* New York: Norton and Co., 1969, p. 336.
2. Paul F. Power, 'Indian Foreign Policy: The Age of Nehru', *The Review of Politics*, Vol. 26, No. 2, April 1964, pp. 261–63.
3. Sankar Ghose, *Jawaharlal Nehru: A Biography*, New Delhi: Allied Publishers, 1993, pp. 8–9.
4. J.N. Dixit, 'Jawaharlal Nehru – Architect of India's Foreign Policy', in *Nehru Revisited*, Mumbai: Nehru Centre, 2003, pp. 58–61.
5. A.P. Rana, 'Nehru's Foreign Policy Design and Its Relevance to a Globalizing World', in ibid., p. 429.
6. Natwar Singh, 'A Brief Survey of Nehru's Foreign Policy,' in Nehru Centre, Mumbai, *Witness to History: Transition and Transformation of India, 1947-64*, New Delhi: Oxford University Press, 2011, p. 126.
7. Ibid., p. 128.
8. J.N. Dixit, 'Jawaharlal Nehru – Architect of India's Foreign Policy'.

9. Natwar Singh, 'A Brief Survey of Nehru's Foreign Policy,' in *Witness to History: Transition and Transformation of India, 1947-64*, New Delhi: Oxford University Press, 2011, p. 129.
10. Jawaharlal Nehru's speech on 13 December 1946 during the Constituent Assembly Debates. Taken from *Constituent Assembly Debates of India, Official Report*, Vol. I (9 December to 23 December 1946), http://164.100.47.132/LssNew/cadebatefiles/C13121946.html (accessed on 10 June 2014).
11. Jawaharlal Nehru, *India's Foreign Policy: Selected Speeches, September 1946–April 1961*, New Delhi: Publications Division, Government of India, 1961, p. 56.
12. K. Satchidananda Murty, *Indian Foreign Policy*, Calcutta: Scientific Book Agency, 1964, pp. 18–19.
13. Ibid.
14. Sarvepalli Gopal, *Jawaharlal Nehru: A Biography, Volume II: 1947–1956*, New Delhi: Oxford University Press, 1975, p. 43.
15. Jawaharlal Nehru, *India's Foreign Policy,* New Delhi: Publications Division, Government of India, 1961, p. 22.
16. Jawaharlal Nehru's speech on 8 November 1948 at the Constituent Assembly. *Constituent Assembly Debates of India, Official Report,* Vol. VII (4 November 1948–8 January 1949), http://164.100.47.132/LssNew/cadebatefiles/C08111948.html (accessed on 29 July 2014).
17. J.B. Kripalani, 'For Principled Neutrality: A New Appraisal of Indian Foreign Policy,' *Foreign Affairs*, Vol. 38, No. 1, October 1959, pp. 46–60.
18. Nehru's first broadcast to the nation, New Delhi, 7 September 1946. Jawaharlal Nehru, *India's Foreign Policy,* p. 2.
19. A.P. Rana, 'Nehru's Foreign Policy Design and Its Relevance to a Globalizing World', in *Nehru Revisited*, pp. 441–42.
20. Richard Fontera, 'Anti-colonialism as a basic Indian Foreign Policy,' *The Western Political Quarterly*, Vol. 13, No. 2, June 1960, pp. 421–32.
21. S.D. Muni, *India's Foreign Policy: The Democracy Dimension, with Special Reference to Neighbours,* New Delhi: Foundation Books/Cambridge University Press, 2009, pp. 22–26.
22. J.N. Dixit, 'Jawaharlal Nehru – Architect of India's Foreign Policy', in *Nehru Revisited,* pp. 69–76.

23. S.D. Muni, *India's Foreign Policy*, p. 29.
24. Ibid., p. 44.
25. Ibid., pp. 22–26.
26. Werner Levi, 'India Debates Foreign Policy', *Far Eastern Survey*, Vol. 20, No. 5, March 1951, pp. 39–52.
27. Michael Edwardes, 'Illusion and Reality in India's Foreign Policy', *International Affairs*, Vol. 41. No. 4, January 1965, pp. 48–58.
28. Natwar Singh, 'A Brief Survey of Nehru's Foreign Policy,' in Nehru Centre, *Witness to History*, p. 133.
29. Sarvepalli Gopal, *Jawaharlal Nehru: A Biography*, Volume II: 1947–1956, New Delhi: Oxford University Press, p. 44.
30. Escott Reid, *Envoy to Nehru*, Delhi: Oxford University Press, 1981, pp. 25–26.
31. Ibid., p. 99.
32. K. Subrahmanyam, 'Nehru and Defence Policy', in *Nehru Revisited*, Mumbai: Nehru Centre, 2003, p. 82.
33. Devdutt, 'Non-alignment and India,' *The Indian Journal of Political Science*, Vol. 23, No. 1–4, January–December 1962, pp. 380–97; J.N. Dixit, 'Jawaharlal Nehru – Architect of India's Foreign Policy,' in *Nehru Revisited*, pp. 65–68; E. Malcolm House, 'India: Non-committed and non-aligned', *The Western Political Quarterly*, Vol. 13, No. 1, March 1960, pp. 70–82.
34. Werner Levi, 'India Debates Foreign Policy,' *Far Eastern Survey*, Vol. 20, No. 5, March 1951, pp. 39–52.
35. Paul F. Power, 'Indian Foreign Policy: The Age of Nehru,' *The Review of Politics*, Vol. 26, No. 2, April 1964, pp. 263–64.
36. Ibid.
37. Jawaharlal Nehru's speech on 17 May 1949 at the Constituent Assembly. *Constituent Assembly Debates of India, Official Report*, Vol. VIII (16 May–16 June 1949), http://164.100.47.132/LssNew/cadebatefiles/C17051949.html (accessed on 29 July 2014).
38. K. Subrahmanyam in Foreword to Jaswant Singh, *Defending India*, New Delhi: Macmillan Press, 1999, pp. viii–x.
39. Inder Malhotra, 'Understanding Nehru's policies', in Nehru Centre Mumbai, *Witness to History: Transition and Transformation of India, 1947-64*, New Delhi: Oxford University Press, 2011, pp. 115–16.

40. Andrew Kennedy, 'Nehru's Foreign Policy: Realism and Idealism Conjoined' in David Malone, C. Raja Mohan and Srinath Raghavan (eds), *The Oxford Handbook of Indian Foreign Policy*, New Delhi: Oxford University Press, 2015, pp. 97–99.
41. Natwar Singh, 'A Brief Survey of Nehru's Foreign Policy,' in Nehru Centre Mumbai, *Witness to History,* pp. 123–24.
42. Adda Bozeman, 'India's Foreign Policy Today: Reflection upon its sources', *World Politics*, Vol. 10, No. 2, January 1958, pp. 256–73.
43. Paul F. Power, 'Indian Foreign Policy: The Age of Nehru', *The Review of Politics*, Vol. 26, No. 2, April 1964, pp. 265.
44. Michael Edwardes, 'Illusion and Reality in India's Foreign Policy', *International Affairs*, Vol. 41, No. 4, January 1965, pp. 48–58.
45. B.M. Jain, *Global Power: India's Foreign Policy, 1947-2006,* Lantham, Maryland: Lexington Books, 2008, pp. 21–22.
46. Letter to the editor, *The Leader,* Allahabad, 2 December 1951. Quoted in G.P. Srivastava, 'Second Thoughts on Indian Foreign Policy,' *The Indian Journal of Political Science*, Vol 21, No. 2, April–June 1960, pp. 143–53.
47. J.B. Kripalani, 'For Principled Neutrality: A New Appraisal of Indian Foreign Policy,' *Foreign Affairs*, Vol. 38, No. 1, October 1959, pp. 49–50.
48. Ibid., pp. 56–60.
49. J.N. Dixit, 'Jawaharlal Nehru – Architect of India's Foreign Policy', in *Nehru Revisited*, pp. 65–68.
50. Ibid.
51. Dennis Kux, *India and the United States: Estranged Democracies, 1941-91*, Washington DC: National Defense University Press, 1992.
52. Sarvepalli Gopal, *Jawaharlal Nehru, Volume II,* p. 106.
53. Ibid., p. 139.
54. Jawaharlal Nehru, speech on 22 July 1947 at the Constituent Assembly, *Constituent Assembly Debates of India, Official Report,* Vol. IV (14 July to 31 July 1947), http://164.100.47.132/LssNew/cadebatefiles/C22071947.html (accessed on 18 June 2014).
55. Ibid.
56. Jawaharlal Nehru, speech on 16 May1949 at the Constituent Assembly, *Constituent Assembly Debates of India, Official Report,* Vol. VIII (16 May–16 June 1949), http://164.100.47.132/LssNew/cadebatefiles/C16051949.html (accessed on 29 July 2014).

57. Nehru letter to Ernest Bevin, 20 November 1950. Cited in Sarvepalli Gopal, *Jawaharlal Nehru, Volume II*, p. 108.
58. Andrew Kennedy, 'Nehru's Foreign Policy: Realism and Idealism Conjoined', in David Malone, C. Raja Mohan and Srinath Raghavan (eds), *The Oxford Handbook of Indian Foreign Policy*, New Delhi: Oxford University Press, 2015, pp. 93–95.
59. Ibid.
60. Ibid., pp. 99–100.
61. K. Satchidananda Murty, *Indian Foreign Policy*, pp. 20–24.
62. Letter from Sardar Patel to Nehru, 6 May 1948, on 'who are the people who should be sent as Ambassadors', Durga Das (ed.), *Sardar Patel's Correspondence, 1945-50*, Vol. IV, Ahmedabad: Navjivan Publishing House, 1972, p. 370; Letter from Sardar Patel to undersecretary for India and Burma in Atlee government and British MP Arthur Henderson, 3 July 1948, ibid., p. 371.
63. Howard Erdman, 'The Foreign Policy Views of the Indian Right', *Pacific Affairs*, Vol. 39, No. 1–2, Spring–Summer 1966, pp. 5–18.
64. Ibid.
65. Ibid.
66. Ibid.
67. Ibid.
68. Ibid.
69. Text of inaugural address delivered by Mr Atal Bihari Vajpayee, Minister for External Affairs, Government of India, at the seminar held by the Foreign Service School on 'Continuity and Change in India's Foreign Policy', 13–15 May 1978, in Bimal Prasad, *India's Foreign Policy: Studies in Continuity and Change*, New Delhi: Vikas Publishing House, 1979, pp. 1–8.
70. V.P. Dutt, *India's Foreign Policy in a Changing World*, New Delhi: Vikas Publishing House, 1999, p. 1.
71. This study was conducted by Baljit Singh. Baljit Singh, 'Pundits and Panchsheela: Indian Intellectuals and Their Foreign Policy', *Background*, Vol. 9, No. 2, August 1965, pp. 127–36.
72. Andrew Kennedy 'Nehru's Foreign Policy: Realism and Idealism Conjoined', p. 101.
73. J.N. Dixit, *Makers of India's Foreign Policy: Raja Ram Mohun Roy to Yashwant Sinha*, New Delhi: Harper Collins, 2004, pp. 119–23.

74. Surjit Mansingh, *India's Search for Power: Indira Gandhi's Foreign Policy, 1966-82*, New Delhi: Sage Publications, 1984, pp. 1–2.
75. Ibid.
76. J.N. Dixit, *Makers of India's Foreign Policy*, p. 119.
77. Broadcast given by Indira Gandhi forty-eight hours after taking over as prime minister on 26 January 1966. Indira Gandhi, *Indira Gandhi: Speeches and Writings,* New York: Harper & Row, 1975, pp. 53–54.
78. Indira Gandhi, 'India and the World', *Foreign Affairs*, October 1972, pp. 68–69.
79. English translation of a speech given by Indira Gandhi in Hindi on the occasion of India's Independence Day, Delhi, 15 August 1970. Indira Gandhi, *Indira Gandhi: Selected Speeches and Writings, 1969-1972: The Years of Endeavor,* New Delhi: Publications Division, Ministry of Information and Broadcasting, Government of India, 1975, p. 60.
80. Stephen Cohen, *India: Emerging Power*, Washington DC: Brookings Institution Press, 2001, pp. 137–38.
81. J.N. Dixit, *Makers of India's Foreign Policy* pp. 145–47.
82. Address given by Indira Gandhi at a seminar organized by the Congress party on 'Some Aspects of our Foreign Policy', Mavalankar Hall, New Delhi, 31 August 1970. Indira Gandhi, *Indira Gandhi: Speeches and Writings*, pp. 131–33.
83. Surjit Mansingh, *India's Search for Power*, pp. 1–2.
84. Address given by Indira Gandhi at Madras University, 1967. Indira Gandhi, *Indira Gandhi: Speeches and Writings*, p. 60.
85. Surjit Mansingh, *India's Search for Power*, pp. 18–25.
86. Address given by Indira Gandhi before the Austrian Society for Foreign Policy and International Relations, Vienna, 28 October 1971. Indira Gandhi, *Indira Gandhi: Speeches and Writings,* p. 159.
87. Indira Gandhi, 'India and the World', *Foreign Affairs*, October 1972, pp. 68–69.
88. Indira Gandhi's address at a seminar organized by the Congress party on 'Some Aspects of our Foreign Policy,' Mavalankar Hall, New Delhi, 31 August 1970. Indira Gandhi, *Indira Gandhi: Speeches and Writings,* pp. 131–33.
89. Address by Indira Gandhi before the Commonwealth Heads of Government Conference, Kingston, Jamaica, 30 April 1975. Indira

Gandhi, *Selected Speeches and Writings: 1972-1977,* New Delhi: Publications Division, Ministry of Information and Broadcasting, Government of India, 1984, pp. 711–16.

90. Inaugural address by Indira Gandhi at the New Delhi Consultations among Developing Countries, New Delhi, 22 February 1982. Indira Gandhi, *Selected Speeches and Writings: 1982-1984,* New Delhi: Publications Division, Ministry of Information and Broadcasting, Government of India,1986, p. 343.
91. Address by Indira Gandhi at a seminar organized by the Congress party on 'Some Aspects of our Foreign Policy', Mavalankar Hall, New Delhi, 31 August 1970. Indira Gandhi, *Indira Gandhi: Speeches and Writings,* pp. 131–33.
92. Indira Gandhi, 'India and the World,' *Foreign Affairs*, October 1972, pp. 68–69.
93. Ibid.
94. Surjit Mansingh, *India's Search for Power*, pp. 32–37.
95. J.N. Dixit, *Makers of India's Foreign Policy*, pp. 187–89.
96. Kathleen Healy, *Rajiv Gandhi: The Years of Power,* New Delhi: Vikas Publishing House, 1989, p. 58.
97. Srinath Raghavan, 'At the Cusp of Transformation: The Rajiv Gandhi Years, 1984-89', in David Malone, C. Raja Mohan and Srinath Raghavan (eds), *The Oxford Handbook of Indian Foreign Policy*, pp. 117–29.
98. Ibid.
99. Broadcast to the nation, 12 November 1984. Rajiv Gandhi, *Rajiv Gandhi: Selected Speeches and Writings,* Vol. I, 1984-85, New Delhi: Publications Division, Ministry of Information and Broadcasting, Government of India, 1990, p. 9.
100. Rajiv Gandhi's broadcast to the nation, 12 November 1984. Kathleen Healy, *Rajiv Gandhi: The Years of Power*, p. 60.
101. Rajiv Gandhi's interview with Judy Woodruff, for the PBS show, MacNeil–Lehrer News Hour, PBS, New York, 14 June 1984. Kathleen Healy, *Rajiv Gandhi: The Years of Power*, p. 60.
102. Ibid., p. 6.
103. Speech by Rajiv Gandhi on Doordarshan Television, 12 November 1984. Kathleen Healy, *Rajiv Gandhi: The Years of Power,* p. 27.
104. Rajiv Gandhi's Inaugural address at the SAARC Summit, Bangalore,

16 November 1986. Rajiv Gandhi, *Rajiv Gandhi: Selected Speeches and Writings: January 1-December 31, 1986,* New Delhi: Publications Division, Ministry of Information and Broadcasting, Government of India, 1986, p. 318.

105. J.N. Dixit, *Makers of India's Foreign Policy,* pp. 205–06.
106. Rajiv Gandhi's speech at the Council on Foreign Relations, New York, 23 October 1985. Kathleen Healy, *Rajiv Gandhi: The Years of Power,* p. 42.
107. Rajiv Gandhi's speech at a banquet hosted in his honour by the Australian prime minister, Mr Robert Hawke, Canberra, 14 October 1986. Rajiv Gandhi, *Rajiv Gandhi: Selected Speeches and Writings: 1 January 1-December 31, 1986,* New Delhi: Publications Division, Ministry of Information and Broadcasting, Government of India, 1986, p. 305.
108. Rajiv Gandhi's speech at a luncheon hosted by the Auckland Chamber of Commerce, New Zealand, 17 October 1986. Rajiv Gandhi, *Rajiv Gandhi: Selected Speeches and Writings: January 1-December 31, 1986,* New Delhi: Publications Division, Ministry of Information and Broadcasting, Government of India, 1986, pp. 310–11.
109. Rajiv Gandhi's speech at the twenty-fifth anniversary of the NAM, Harare, Zimbabwe, 1 September 1986. Rajiv Gandhi, *Rajiv Gandhi: Selected Speeches and Writings: January 1-December 31, 1986,* New Delhi: Publications Division, Ministry of Information and Broadcasting, Government of India, 1986, pp. 289–90.
110. Rajiv Gandhi's banquet speech, Port Louis, Mauritius, 4 July 1986. Rajiv Gandhi, *Rajiv Gandhi: Selected Speeches and Writings: January 1-December 31, 1986,* New Delhi: Publications Division, Ministry of Information and Broadcasting, Government of India, 1986, p. 265.
111. Rajiv Gandhi's speech at the twenty-fifth anniversary of the NAM, Harare, Zimbabwe, 1 September 1, 1986. *Rajiv Gandhi: Selected Speeches and Writings,* January 1–December 31, 1986, New Delhi: Publications Division, Ministry of Information and Broadcasting, 1986, pp. 289–90.
112. Kathleen Healy, *Rajiv Gandhi: The Years of Power,* p. 57.
113. Rajiv Gandhi's speech at the Ninth Non-aligned Summit, Belgrade, 5 September 1989. Rajiv Gandhi. *Rajiv Gandhi: Selected Speeches and*

Writings: January 1–December 31, 1989, New Delhi: Publications Division, Ministry of Information and Broadcasting, Government of India, 1991, pp. 271–72.

114. Kathleen Healy, *Rajiv Gandhi: The Years of Power*, p. 7.
115. Rajiv Gandhi's speech at a state dinner, Luanda, Angola, 16 May 1986. Rajiv Gandhi, *Rajiv Gandhi: Selected Speeches and Writings: January 1-December 31, 1986*, New Delhi: Publications Division, Ministry of Information and Broadcasting, Government of India, 1986, p. 253.
116. Rajiv Gandhi's speech on Africa Day, New Delhi, 25 May 1986. Rajiv Gandhi, *Rajiv Gandhi: Selected Speeches and Writings: January 1-December 31, 1986*, New Delhi: Publications Division, Ministry of Information and Broadcasting, Government of India, 1986, p. 259.
117. Srinath Raghavan, 'At the Cusp of Transformation: The Rajiv Gandhi Years, 1984-89' in David Malone, C. Raja Mohan and Srinath Raghavan (eds), *The Oxford Handbook of Indian Foreign Policy*, pp. 117–29.
118. Rajiv Gandhi's speech at the Council on Foreign Relations, New York, 23 October 1985. Kathleen Healy, *Rajiv Gandhi: The Years of Power*, pp. 60–61.
119. Rajiv Gandhi's speech at the NAM Summit, Harare, Zimbabwe, 2 September 1986. Kathleen Healy, *Rajiv Gandhi: The Years of Power*, p. 107.
120. Rajiv Gandhi's speech on the occasion of Africa Day, New Delhi, 25 May 1986. Rajiv Gandhi, *Rajiv Gandhi: Selected Speeches and Writings: January 1-December 31, 1986*, New Delhi, Publications Division, Ministry of Information and Broadcasting, Government of India, 1986, pp. 263–64.
121. Rajiv Gandhi's speech as chairman of the NAM, Harare Summit, Zimbabwe, 2 September 1986. Rajiv Gandhi, *Rajiv Gandhi: Selected Speeches and Writings: January 1-December 31, 1986*, New Delhi, Publications Division, Ministry of Information and Broadcasting, Government of India, 1986, pp. 292–94.
122. Rajiv Gandhi's address to the National Press Club, Canberra, Australia, 15 October 1986. Rajiv Gandhi, *Rajiv Gandhi: Selected Speeches and Writings: January 1-December 31, 1986*, New Delhi,

Publications Division, Ministry of Information and Broadcasting, Government of India, 1986, p. 359.

123. English translation of Rajiv Gandhi's speech on the occasion of Independence Day, New Delhi, 15 August 1988. Rajiv Gandhi, *Rajiv Gandhi, Selected Speeches and Writings: January 1-December 31, 1988,* New Delhi, Publications Division, Ministry of Information and Broadcasting, Government of India, 1989, pp. 64–65.
124. Rajiv Gandhi's speech at a special session hosted by the Federation of German Industries, German Association of Industry and German Foreign Policy Association, Bonn, 7 June 1988. Rajiv Gandhi, *Rajiv Gandhi: Selected Speeches and Writings: January 1-December 31, 1988,* New Delhi: Publications Division, Ministry of Information and Broadcasting, Government of India, 1989, pp. 324–25.
125. The Declaration for a Nuclear-Weapon-Free and Non-Violent World signed by Rajiv Gandhi and the general secretary of CPSU, Mikhail Gorbachev, New Delhi, 27 November 1986. Rajiv Gandhi, *Rajiv Gandhi: Selected Speeches and Writings: January 1-December 31, 1986,* New Delhi: Publications Division, Ministry of Information and Broadcasting, Government of India, 1986, pp. 333–34.
126. Rajiv Gandhi's address to the Third Special Session on Disarmament, United Nations General Assembly, New York, 9 June1988. Rajiv Gandhi, *Rajiv Gandhi: Selected Speeches and Writings: January 1-December 31, 1988,* New Delhi: Publications Division, Ministry of Information and Broadcasting, Government of India, 1989, p. 334.
127. Harish Kapur, *India's Foreign Policy, 1947–92: Shadows and Substance,* New Delhi: Sage Publications, 1994, pp. 193–97.
128. J.N. Dixit, *Makers of India's Foreign Policy*, pp. 205–06.
129. Speech by I.K. Gujral at the Bombay Centre, 3 January 1997. I.K. Gujral, *A Foreign Policy for India,* New Delhi: External Publicity Division, Ministry of External Affairs, 1998, p. 7.
130. Author's interview with a former adviser to Chandra Shekhar, Delhi, October 2013.
131. J.N. Dixit, *Makers of India's Foreign Policy*, p. 225.
132. Ibid., pp. 245–46.
133. For more details, please see Jaswant Singh, *Defending India,* Bangalore: Macmillan Press, 1999.

134. Sanjaya Baru. *The Accidental Prime Minister: The Making and Unmaking of Manmohan Singh*, New Delhi: Penguin, 2014, pp. 165–66; Sanjaya Baru, 'The Singh Doctrine', *The Indian Express*, 6 November 2013, http://archive.indianexpress.com/news/the-singh-doctrine/1191321/0 (accessed on 2 June 2015); C. Raja Mohan 'Rethinking Indian Grand Strategy', in N.S. Sisodia and C. Uday Bhaskar (eds), *Emerging India: Security and Foreign Policy Perspectives*, New Delhi, Institute of Defence and Strategic Analyses, 2005, pp. 38–42.
135. Shubhajit Roy, 'Secularism guides our foreign policy: PM', *The Indian Express*, New Delhi, 5 November 2013.
136. 'India's Foreign Policy under Modi: One Year In', Asia Society, http://asiasociety.org/video/indias-foreign-policy-under-modi-one-year-complete (accessed on 18 June 2015).
137. Kishore Mahbubani, 'One year of Narendra Modi: Bold moves on World stage', *The Indian Express*, 29 May 2015.
138. Ibid.
139. Christophe Jaffrelot, 'A Modi doctrine?' *The Indian Express*, 20 November 2014.
140. Harsh Pant, 'Out with Non-Alignment, In with a Modi doctrine?' *The Diplomat*, 13 November 2014.
141. Indrani Bagchi, 'New Developments in MEA under Modi: Indian envoys get a strategic overview of Modi government's world vision', *The Times of India*, 23 February 2015.
142. Jawaharlal Nehru's speech in the Constituent Assembly, 22 January 1947, *Constituent Assembly Debates of India, Official Report,* Vol. II (20 January to 25 January 1947), http://164.100.47.132/LssNew/cadebatefiles/C20011947.html (accessed on 10 June 2014).
143. Vijaya Lakshmi Pandit's speech in the Constituent Assembly, 20 January 1947, ibid.
144. V.N. Khanna, *Foreign Policy of India,* New Delhi: Vikas Publishing House, 1997, p. 24.

CHAPTER 4: PRINCIPLES AND INTERESTS

1. Speech of Rajendra Prasad as president of the Constituent Assembly, 14 August 1947, the website of the Indian parliament, http://parliamentofindia.nic.in/ls/debates/vol5p1.htm (accessed on 9 July 2014).

2. Ibid.
3. For details please look at various presidential speeches. Here are a few: Giani Zail Singh, address to parliament, New Delhi, 20 February 1986, *Speeches of President Giani Zail Singh*, Vol II, New Delhi: Publications Division, Ministry of Information and Broadcasting, Government of India, 1992, pp. 14–23; Giani Zail Singh, address to parliament, New Delhi, 23 February 1987, ibid., pp. 139–51; A.P.J. Abdul Kalam, address to joint session of parliament, 24 March 2003, from http://www.indianembassy.ru/index.php/en/component/content/article/113-media/statements-speeches-interviews-archives/258-24032003-the-president-of-india-dr-apj-abdul-kalam (accessed on 31 December 2014); A.P.J. Abdul Kalam's address to joint session of parliament, 7 June 2004, from http://architexturez.net/doc/az-cf-21867#off-canvas (accessed on 31 December 2014).
4. Jawaharlal Nehru's speech to the Constituent Assembly, 8 March 1949, Jawaharlal Nehru, *Independence and After* (*Speeches*), New Delhi: Publications Division, Ministry of Information and Broadcasting, Government of India, 1949, p. 237.
5. Itty Abraham, 'From Bandung to NAM: Non-alignment and Indian Foreign Policy, 1947–65', *Commonwealth & Comparative Politics*, Vol. 46, No. 2, 2008, pp. 195–96.
6. Ibid., p. 198.
7. Werner Levi, 'Indian Neutralism Reconsidered', *Pacific Affairs*, Vol. 37, No. 2, Summer 1964, pp. 137–47.
8. Surjit Mansingh, *India's Search for Power: Indira Gandhi's Foreign Policy, 1966-82*, New Delhi: Sage Publications, 1984, pp. 14–18.
9. Sumit Ganguly and Manjeet Pardesi, 'Explaining Sixty Years of India's Foreign Policy', *India Review*, Vol. 8, No. 1, January–March 2009, pp. 12–16.
10. For details please see: Purushottam Das Tandon's speech on 13 December 1946 in the Constituent Assembly, *Constituent Assembly Debates of India, Official Report*, Vol. I (9 December to 23 December 1946), http://164.100.47.132/LssNew/cadebatefiles/C13121946.html (accessed on 10 June 2014); Sri Krishna Sinha's speech on 16 December 1946 in the Constituent Assembly, ibid., Vijaylakshmi Pandit's speech on 20 January 1947 in the Constituent Assembly, *Constituent Assembly Debates of India, Official Report*,

Vol. II (20th January to 25th January 1947) http://164.100.47.132/LssNew/cadebatefiles/C20011947.html (accessed on 10 June 2014); Algurai Shastri's speech on 20 January 1947 in the Constituent Assembly, ibid.

11. Jawaharlal Nehru's speech on 22 January 1947 in the Constituent Assembly, ibid.
12. Sisir K. Bose and Sugata Bose (eds), *The Essential Writings of Netaji Subhas Chandra Bose,* New Delhi: Oxford University Press, 2004, pp. 105, 205, 216–18.
13. Rajagopalachari's speech at the annual convocation of the Madras University on 24 August 1948, *Speeches of C. Rajagopalachari: Only Indian Governor General of India: June 1948–January 1950,* Coimbatore: Bharatiya Vidya Bhawan, 1950, p. 64.
14. President K.R. Narayanan's address to parliament, New Delhi, 25 October 1999, http://www.krnarayanan.in/html/speeches/others/oct25_1998.htm (accessed on 31 December 2014).
15. Giani Zail Singh, 'Address to the Parliament', New Delhi, 20 February 1986, *Speeches of President Giani Zail Singh,* Vol II, New Delhi: Publications Division, Ministry of Information and Broadcasting, Government of India, 1992, pp. 14–23.
16. Pranab Mukherjee's speech to the joint session of parliament, 21 February 2013, http://pib.nic.in/newsite/PrintRelease.aspx?relid=92351 (accessed on 31 December 2014).
17. Ibid.
18. S.D. Muni, 'India and Regionalism in South Asia: A Political Perspective', in Bimal Prasad (ed.), *India's Foreign Policy: Studies in Continuity and Change*, New Delhi: Vikas Publishing House, 1979, pp. 107–08.
19. 'Nehru vows to bar invasion of Nepal', *The New York Times*, 17 March 1950; Robert Trumbull, 'India, Bhutan Sign Perpetual Pact, Himalayan Kingdom Gets Subsidy', *The New York Times*, 8 August 1949; Robert Trumbull, 'India Assumes Defense of Sikkim, Strategic Principality in Himalayas', *The New York Times*, 5 December 1950.
20. Ashok Kapur, 'Strategic choices in Indian foreign policy', *International Journal,* Vol. 27, No. 3, Summer 1972, pp. 448–50.
21. For details, please read Aparna Pande, *Explaining Pakistan's Foreign Policy: Escaping India,* London: Routledge, 2011.

22. Jayantanuja Bandyopadhyaya, *The Making of India's Foreign Policy: Determinants, Institutions, Processes and Personalities*, Bombay: Allied Publishers, 1970, p. 173.
23. Surjit Mansingh, *India's Search for Power*, pp. 317–25.
24. Sumit Ganguly and Manjeet Pardesi, 'Explaining Sixty Years of India's Foreign Policy', *India Review*, Vol. 8, No. 1, January–March, 2009, pp. 9–11.
25. Anjli Raval, 'India eyes oil demand growth top spot', *Financial Times*, 22 July 2016.
26. Sushant Singh, 'SIPRI data shows India world's biggest arms importer at three times of China', *The Indian Express*, 16 March 2015.
27. Donald G. Mcneil Jr, 'India Alters Law on Drug Patents', *The New York Times*, 24 March 2005.
28. 'India and United Nations: Peacekeeping and Peacebuilding', Permanent Mission of India to the UN, New York, https://www.pminewyork.org/pages.php?id=1985 (accessed on 11 June 2016).
29. 'Country Summary: India', World Bank Group Finances, Washington DC: World Bank, https://finances.worldbank.org/countries/India (accessed on 12 June 2016).
30. 'At a Glance: India and the IMF', International Monetary Fund, Washington DC: International Monetary Fund, https://www.imf.org/external/country/IND/rr/glance.htm (accessed on 12 June 2016).
31. 'Agreement on the New Development Bank', New Development Bank (NDB) BRICS website, http://ndbbrics.org/agreement.html (accessed on 13 June 2016).
32. 'What is Asian Infrastructure Investment Bank?', Asian Infrastructure Investment Bank (AIIB) website, https://www.aiib.org/en/about-aiib/index.html (accessed on 30 June 2016).
33. Jayantanuja Bandyopadhyaya, *The Making of India's Foreign Policy*, pp. 115–16.
34. Y.D. Gundevia, *Outside the Archives*, Hyderabad: Sangam Books, 1984, p. 46.
35. Ibid.
36. For more, please see Ramachandra Guha, *Gandhi before India*, New York: Knopf, 2014.
37. Nehru's speech titled 'The Romance of Migration', Constituent Assembly, 4 December 1947, Jawaharlal Nehru, *India's Foreign*

Policy: Selected Speeches, September 1946–April 1961, New Delhi: Publications Division, Ministry of Information and Broadcasting, Government of India, 1961, p. 127.

38. Ibid.
39. Ibid.
40. Nehru's speech on the 'Issue of citizenship', Constituent Assembly, 8 March 1948, Jawaharlal Nehru, *India's Foreign Policy: Selected Speeches, September 1946-April 1961*, New Delhi: Publications Division, Ministry of 'Information and Broadcasting, Government of India, 1961, p. 128.
41. A.P.J. Abdul Kalam's address to joint session of parliament 2003, 24 March 2003. Taken from http://www.indianembassy.ru/index.php/en/component/content/article/113-media/statements-speeches-interviews-archives/258-24032003-the-president-of-india-dr-apj-abdul-kalam (accessed on 31 December 2014).
42. Nehru's speech on the 'Right policy for the settlers', reply to debate on foreign affairs, Lok Sabha, 17 December 1957. From Jawaharlal Nehru, *India's Foreign Policy: Selected Speeches, September 1946-April 1961*, New Delhi: Publications Division, Ministry of Information and Broadcasting, Government of India, 1961, pp. 129–30.
43. Figures have been taken from Y.D. Gundevia, *Outside the Archives*, pp. 48–49.
44. 'The worldwide web: India should make more of a valuable asset abroad', *The Economist*, 23 May 2015.
45. 'India-Bahrain sign deal to protect workers', Press Trust of India, 20 June 2009.
46. Nehru's speech on the 'Issue of citizenship', Jawaharlal Nehru, *India's Foreign Policy: Selected Speeches, September 1946-April 1961*, New Delhi: Publications Division, Ministry of Information and Broadcasting, Government of India, 1961, pp. 129–30.
47. 'Modi talks to Obama over H1B, L1 visa concerns', Press Trust of India, 17 December 2015; Mica Rosenberg, Stephen Nellis and Emily Stephenson, 'Trump, tech tycoons talk overhaul of H1B', Reuters, 12 January 2017.

CHAPTER 5: INSTITUTIONS AND STRATEGIC CULTURE

1. K. Subrahmanyam, 'Nehru and Defence Policy,' in *Nehru Revisited,* Mumbai: Nehru Centre, 2003, pp. 93–95.
2. Author's interview with former foreign minister Jaswant Singh, October 2012, Delhi.
3. K. Subrahmanyam in Foreword to Jaswant Singh, *Defending India,* Bangalore: Macmillan Press, 1999, pp. x–xiv.
4. Ibid., p. 20.
5. Author's interview with a former senior government official, Delhi, October 2012.
6. K. Subrahmanyam, 'Nehru and Defence Policy', in *Nehru Revisited,* pp. 89–90.
7. Jaswant Singh, *Defending India,* p. 34.
8. K. Subrahmanyam, 'Nehru and Defence Policy', in *Nehru Revisited,* pp. 89–90.
9. R. Venkataraman, 'Address to the Parliament', 22 February 1988, *Speeches of President R. Venkataraman,* New Delhi: Publications Division, Ministry of Information and Broadcasting, Government of India, 1995, pp. 27–38.
10. Pratibha Patil's address to the joint session of parliament, 2009, http://pib.nic.in/newsite/erelease.aspx?relid=49043 (accessed on 31 December 2014).
11. Mohannan B. Pillai and L. Premashekhara (eds), *Foreign Policy of India: Continuity & Change,* New Delhi: New Century Publications, 2010, pp. 20–23.
12. Author's interview with a former senior government official, Delhi, October 2012.
13. Author's interview with a retired diplomat and former ambassador, Delhi, October 2012.
14. Author's interviews with three former foreign ministers, October 2012.
15. Jayantanuja Bandyopadhyaya, *The Making of India's Foreign Policy: Determinants, Institutions, Processes and Personalities,* Bombay: Allied Publishers, 1970, pp. 169–70.
16. Y.D. Gundevia, *Outside the Archives,* Hyderabad: Sangam Books. 1984, pp. 191–92.

17. Jayantanuja Bandyopadhyaya, *The Making of India's Foreign Policy*, p. 147.
18. Ibid.
19. Surjit Mansingh, *India's Search for Power: Indira Gandhi's Foreign Policy, 1966-82*, New Delhi: Sage Publications, 1984, pp. 41–44.
20. The mission to airdrop supplies was referred to as Operation Poomalai (literal translation from Tamil 'Flower Garland',) and took place on 4 June 1987. Rajiv and Sri Lankan President R. Jayewardene signed the Indo–Sri Lanka Accord on 29 July 1987. For further details, please see Kunwar Natwar Singh, *One Life is not Enough: An Autobiography*, New Delhi: Rupa Publications, 2014.
21. Jayantanuja Bandyopadhyaya, *The Making of India's Foreign Policy*, pp. 217–20.
22. Author's interview with a former foreign secretary, March 2013.
23. Author's interview with a veteran Indian journalist, March 2013.
24. Kanchan Gupta, 'The truth behind Kandahar', *The Pioneer*, 24 December 2008.
25. A.S. Dulat, *Kashmir: The Vajpayee Years*, New Delhi: HarperCollins, 2015, pp. 38–39.
26. Javed Ansari, ' IC 814 hijacking still haunts Jaswant Singh', *India Today*, 31 October 2013; Jaswant Singh, *India at Risk: Mistakes, Misconceptions and Misadventures of Security Policy*, New Delhi: Rupa Publications, 2013, pp. 205–18.
27. Sanjaya Baru, *The Accidental Prime Minister: The Making and Unmaking of Manmohan Singh*, New Delhi: Penguin, 2014, p. 74.
28. H.V. Kamath, speech on 10 August 1949 at the Constituent Assembly, *Constituent Assembly Debates of India, Official Report*, Vol. IX (30th July to 18th September 1949), http://164.100.47.132/LssNew/cadebatefiles/vol9.html (accessed on 19 August 2014).
29. Krishan Mathur and P.M. Kamath, *Conduct of India's Foreign Policy*, New Delhi: South Asian Publishers, 1996, pp. 71–81.
30. For details about the Consultative Committee on External Affairs, http://www.mpa.nic.in/MPA/ccms_rpt.aspx (accessed on 10 February 2017).
31. For details about the Standing Committee on External Affairs, http://www.prsindia.org/uploads/media/Constitution%20119/SCR-%20119th%20(A)%20Bill.pdf (accessed on 31 January 2015).

32. Letter from Sardar Patel to Nehru, 27 April 1948, on the issue of the recruitment of services, Durga Das (ed.), *Sardar Patel's Correspondence, 1945–50,* Vol. IV, Ahmedabad: Navjivan Publishing House, 1972, pp. 324–25.
33. Ibid.
34. Y.D. Gundevia, *Outside the Archives,* pp. 23, 188.
35. Ibid., pp. 23–24.
36. Figures were taken from Annual Report 2014-2015 of the Ministry of External Affairs, p. 209, http://mea.gov.in/Uploads/PublicationDocs/25009_External_Affairs_2014-2015__English_.pdf (accessed on 15 June 2016).
37. Sudha Ramachandran, 'India's surging aid to Maldvies points to its strategic location', *Asia Times*, April 2015, http://www. atimes.com/article/indias-surging-aid-to-maldives–points-to-its-strategic-location/ (accessed on 20 December 2015).
38. Indrani Bagchi, 'New Developments in MEA under Modi: Indian envoys get a strategic overview of Modi government's world vision', *The Times of India*, 23 February 2015.
39. Jayantanuja Bandyopadhyaya, *The Making of India's Foreign Policy,* pp. 211–12.
40. 'Indian Foreign Service', Ministry of External Affairs Website, http://www.mea.gov.in/indian-foreign-service.htm (accessed on 30 March 2015).
41. Elizabeth Roche, 'Ministry of External Affairs to hire from private sector,' *The Mint*, 18 June 2015.
42. Indrani Bagchi, 'Crisis point: Not enough diplomats in India', *The Times of India,* 30 April 2007, http://articles.timesofindia.indiatimes.com/2007-04-30/india/27878506_1_indian-diplomat-mea-foreign-policy (accessed on 28 February 2015).
43. Y.D. Gundevia, *Outside the Archives,* pp. 189–90.
44. Ibid.
45. Elizabeth Roche, 'Ministry of External Affairs to hire from private sector', *The Mint*, 18 June 2015.
46. Ibid.
47. Author's interview with former foreign secretary K.S. Bajpai, March 2013.
48. Shivshankar Menon, *Choices: Inside the Making of India's Foreign Policy*, Washington DC: The Brookings Institution, 2016.

49. Sanjaya Baru, *The Accidental Prime Minister: The Making and Unmaking of Manmohan Singh*, New Delhi: Penguin, 2014, p. 39.
50. Author's interview with a former foreign minister, October 2013.
51. Author's interview with a senior retired civil servant, Delhi, October 2012.
52. Jayantanuja Bandyopadhyaya, *The Making of India's Foreign Policy*, p. 177–80.
53. Text and Recommendations of the Naresh Chandra Committee, http://www.gktoday.in/naresh-chandra-committee-recommendations/ (accessed on 30 June 2015).
54. Indrani Bagchi, 'India, Bangladesh sign historic land boundary agreement, end 41-year-long misery of 50,000 stateless people', *The Times of India*, 7 June 2015.
55. Colin Cram, 'Why Singapore is building a new Indian city 10 times its own size?', *The Guardian*, 7 January 2015.
56. G.S. Bhargava, 'The Ills of the Indian Foreign Service', *Economic and Political Weekly,* Vol. 10, No. 10, October 1966, pp. 407–10.
57. Author's interview with former foreign minister Jaswant Singh.
58. Author's interview with former ambassador K.S. Bajpai.

6: OUTLOOK FOR A FUTURE POWER

1. 'India, Sri Lanka sign 4 pacts during Modi visit', *The Times of India*, 13 March 2015.
2. 'Narendra Modi wins hearts by speaking in Nepali', Press Trust of India, 3 August 2014.
3. 'PM Narendra Modi signs 10 agreements with Nepal, inaugurates bus service', *The Times of India*, 26 November 2014.
4. Keshav Pradhan, 'Nepal's big 3 parties unite against India', *The Times of India*, 4 October 2015.
5. Bhekh Bahadur Thapa, 'Nepal-India relations won't improve unless they're redefined in new terms', *Kathmandu Post*, 11 July 2016
6. 'Disappointment at SAARC as Pakistan blocks 3 key connectivity agreements,' Press Trust of India, 26 November 2014.
7. 'SAARC Connectivity: India inks landmark motor pact with Bhutan, Bangladesh and Nepal', *The Economic Times*, 16 June 2015.
8. 'Modi announces $2 bn credit to Bangladesh', Press Trust of India, 6 June 2015.

9. 'Excerpts from PM Modi's address to the Afghan parliament', Press Trust of India, 26 December 2015.
10. Policy Planning and Research Division, Ministry of External Affairs, 'Annual Report, 2014-15', New Delhi: Government of India, p. 209, http://mea.gov.in/Uploads/PublicationDocs/25009_External_Affairs_2014-2015__English_.pdf (accessed on 30 January 2016).
11. 'PM Modi speaks at Madison Square Garden: Highlights', Press Trust of India, 29 September 2015.
12. 'Full text of Narendra Modi's speech at San Jose', *The Hindu*, 27 September 2015.
13. Manoj C.G., 'PM Modi's UAE visit: In Dubai heat, packed stadium on its feet', *The Indian Express*, 18 August 2015.
14. G. Sudhakar Nair, 'Modi announces visa on arrival for Pacific island nations', Press Trust of India, 19 November 2014.
15. Elizabeth Roche, 'Narendra Modi pitches for stronger ties with Pacific Island nations', *The Mint*, 22 August 2015.
16. 'India's Narendra Modi Gives Speech in China', *Wall Street Journal*, 15 May 2015.
17. 'Full Text of Prime Minister Narendra Modi's Speech at the India-China Business Forum in Shanghai', Press Trust of India, 16 May 2015.
18. 'PM Narendra Modi's Japan visit: 10 key takeaways', *The Economic Times*, 2 September 2014.
19. Author's interview with a retired foreign secretary, Delhi, October 2012.
20. K. Subrahmanyam, 'Nehru and Defense Policy', *Nehru Revisited*, p. 96.
21. Author's interview with former foreign secretary and ambassador K.S. Bajpai.

7: AFTERWORD

1 'Details of Foreign/Domestic Visits', Prime Minister of India, 26 May 2014, www.pmindia.gov.in/en/details-of-foreigndomestic-visits/ (accessed on 20 February 2020).

2 'Prime Minister's Keynote Address at Shangri-La Dialogue (1 June 2018),' https://www.mea.gov.in/Speeches-Statements.

htm?dtl/29943/Prime+Ministers+Keynote+Address+at+Shangri+La+Dialogue+June+01+2018, (accessed on 20 February 2020).

3 External affairs minister in conversation at Raisina Dialogue 2020: 'The India Way,' https://mea.gov.in/interviews.htm?dtl/32305/External_Affairs_Minister_in_Conversation_at_Raisina_Dialogue_2020__The_India_Way, (accessed on 20 February 2020).

4 'Modi government to restructure Ministry of External Affairs,' *The New Indian Express*, 1 February 2020 https://www.newindianexpress.com/nation/2020/feb/01/modi-government-to-restructure-ministry-of-external-affairs-2097285.html (accessed on 20 February 2020).

5 Pranab Dal Samanta, 'NSA gets teeth, Secretariat put in government business rules,' *The Economic Times*, 3 October 2019 https://economictimes.indiatimes.com/news/politics-and-nation/nsa-gets-teeth-secretariat-put-in-government-business-rules/articleshow/71416098.cms?from=mdr, (accessed on 20 February 2020).

6 India, Ministry of External Affairs, 'Annual Report, 2016–17', Policy Planning and Research Division, Ministry of External Affairs, New Delhi. Available from: http://www.mea.gov.in/Uploads/PublicationDocs/29521_MEA_ANNUAL_REPORT_2016_17_new.pdf (2017), p. 328, (accessed on 20 February 2020).

7 India, M.E.A., 'Annual Report, 2018–19', Policy Planning and Research Division, Ministry of External Affairs, New Delhi. Available from: http://www.mea.gov.in/Uploads/PublicationDocs/31719_MEA_AR18_19.pdf, (2019), p. 377, (accessed on 20 February 2020).

8 Ibid.

9 Samir Yasir and Maria Abi-Habib, 'Kashmir Suffers From the Worst Attack There in 30 Years,' *The New York Times*, 14 February 2019, https://www.nytimes.com/2019/02/14/world/asia/pulwama-attack-kashmir.html, (accessed on 20 February 2020).

10 Simon Scarr, Chris Inton and Han Huang, 'An air strike and its aftermath,' Reuters, 6 March 2019, https://graphics.reuters.com/INDIA-KASHMIR/010090XM162/index.html, (accessed on 24 February 2020).

11 India, M.E.A. 'India-Saudi Arabia Bilateral Relations', Policy Planning and Research Division, Ministry of External Affairs, New Delhi. Available from: https://mea.gov.in/Portal/ForeignRelation/India-Saudi_Arabia_Bilateral_Relations_2019.pdf (2019), p. 1, (accessed on 20 February 2020).

12 'Record High Remittances Sent Globally in 2018', the World Bank, 8 April 2019, www.worldbank.org/en/news/press-release/2019/04/08/record-high-remittances-sent-globally-in-2018, (accessed on 20 February 2020).

13 Elizabeth Roche, 'India invited as "guest of honour" to OIC meet, Sushma Swaraj to attend,' Livemint, 24 February 2019, https://www.livemint.com/politics/news/india-invited-as-guest-of-honour-to-oic-meet-sushma-swaraj-to-attend-1550913750935.html, (accessed on 24 February 2020).

14 Brad Brooks and Steve Holland, 'Howdy, Modi!': Thousands, plus Trump, rally in Texas for India's leader,' Reuters, 22 September 2019 https://www.reuters.com/article/us-usa-india/howdy-modi-thousands-plus-trump-rally-in-texas-for-indias-leader-idUSKBN1W70B2, (accessed on 24 February 2020). Michael Crowley, 'America Loves India,' Trump Declares at Rally With Modi,' *The New York Times*, 24 February 2020, https://www.nytimes.com/2020/02/24/world/asia/trump-india.html, (accessed on 24 February 2020).

15 India, M.E.A. 'India-U.S. Bilateral Relations', Policy Planning and Research Division, Ministry of External Affairs, New Delhi. Available from: https://mea.gov.in/Portal/ForeignRelation/India_U_S_Bilateral.pdf (2020), p. 5, (accessed on 24 February 2020).

16 'GDP Growth Slows down to 4.5 per cent in Q2, Hits More than 6-Year Low', *Business Today*, 29 November 2019, www.businesstoday.in/current/economy-politics/q2-gdp-growth-rate-data-india-slows-down-to4-7-percent-lowest-in-6-years/story/391255.html, (accessed on 24 February 2020).

17 Rahul Bedi, 'India's low defence budget for FY 2020/21 to hit military modernization,' *Janes Defence Weekly*, 3 February 2020, https://www.janes.com/article/94060/india-s-low-defence-budget-for-fy-2020-21-to-hit-military-modernisation, (accessed on 24 February 2020).

Index

Acknowledgements

THIS BOOK WOULD not have been possible without the guidance and support of my colleagues at Hudson Institute, especially Mr Eric Brown, Dr Hillel Fradkin, Mr John Walters, Dr Kenneth Weinstein and Chairperson Sarah Stern.

I would like to thank friends who have over the years provided guidance and advice, especially Mr Bruce Riedel, Dr C. Christine Fair, Ms Lisa Curtis, Dr Marvin Weinbaum and Dr Stephen P. Cohen. In the course of researching this book there were countless diplomats, officials and academics I interviewed in India and who provided advice. It will not be possible to name all of them but I would like to extend my immense gratitude.

I would like to thank close friends like Angelica Zolnierowicz, Joya Laha, Seema Sirohi and my sister Swati Pande for their support and friendship. A special thanks to Farahnaz Ispahani for always being there for me.

A number of research interns helped with my book over the years including Devin Chavira, Hari Krishna Prasad, Kabir Sandrolini, Sanjana Hariprasad and Siddhanta Mehta.

I would also like to thank HarperCollins for publishing this book. They have done so in a remarkably short period of time. My particular thanks to Antony Thomas, Shantanu Ray Chaudhuri, Udayan Mitra and Ananth Padmanabhan.

My deepest debt of gratitude goes to my mentor and senior colleague at the Hudson Institute, Ambassador Husain Haqqani, who has always inspired me never to compromise on quality. I trust this work meets with his approval on all counts.

All I am I owe to my parents, Vinita and Kamal Pande, whose love, guidance and encouragement gave me the courage to even think about a career in research.

About the Author

DR APARNA PANDE is director of the Initiative on the Future of India and South Asia at the Hudson Institute, Washington D.C.

Born in India, Pande received her bachelor's and master's degrees in History from St. Stephen's College, University of Delhi, before receiving an M. Phil in International Relations from Jawaharlal Nehru University. She completed her Ph.D. in Political Science at Boston University in the United States.

She is the author of *Making India Great: The Promise of a Reluctant Global Power* (2020), *Explaining Pakistan's Foreign Policy: Escaping India* (Routledge, 2010) and is the editor of *Contemporary Handbook on Pakistan* (Routledge, 2017).

ALSO BY
APARNA PANDE

In *Making India Great*, Aparna Pande examines the challenges we face in the areas of social, economic, military and foreign policy and strategy. She brings to light the dichotomy that lies at the heart of the nation: our belief in becoming a global power and the reluctance to consistently implement policies and take actions that would help us achieve that goal.

'Essential reading at a time when India debates fundamental issues, not just about the kind of power she wishes to be, but also about the very nature of the India that is emerging. A sane, skilful and knowledgeable analysis of India's potential as a great power and what is holding her back, weaving together the domestic, external and ideational considerations that will determine India's course.'

– Shishankar Menon, former Foreign Secretary and National Security Advisor